Master and Disciple

The Birth of a Warrior

Written by
Bernard Grégoire

Translated by
Alex Paillé

© 2016
ISBN 978-2-9815240-2-7

Table of Contents

Introduction 9
Chapter 1   Acceptance 10
Chapter 2   Bad energy 14
Chapter 3   Judgment 18
Chapter 4   Strange powers 22
Chapter 5   Too fast 25
Chapter 6   Becoming old 29
Chapter 7   Managing our personality 33
Chapter 8   Why 37
Chapter 9   The serenity of the earth 41
Chapter 10   The Warrior 45
Chapter 11   Question of reflex 48
Chapter 12   *Henka* 52
Chapter 13   Upstream 54
Chapter 14   The wrong angle 58
Chapter 15   Relevant arguments 62
Chapter 16   Time 66
Chapter 17   The killer instinct 71
Chapter 18   *Giri* 76
Chapter 19   A brief moment 80
Chapter 20   The beginner 83
Chapter 21   Master in the making 86
Chapter 22   Reading between the lines 91
Chapter 23   No sense 95
Chapter 24   The art of moving 100
Chapter 25   The power of water 104
Chapter 26   Kiaijutsu 107
Chapter 27   The Basics 110
Chapter 28   Bread and games 114
Chapter 29   Rhythm 117

Chapter 30	Lack of balance	121
Chapter 31	Bugei	125
Chapter 32	Hat	130
Chapter 33	Mystique	134
Chapter 34	The spirit of the blade	138
Chapter 35	Who am I?	141
Chapter 36	A matter of choice	144
Chapter 37	The music of *budo*	146
Chapter 38	Out of our shell	149
Chapter 39	Tyrants	152
Chapter 40	Submission	155
Chapter 41	Living in fear	158
Chapter 42	Overflow	161
Chapter 43	Kamae	164
Chapter 44	Predictable	168
Chapter 45	*Shizen*	172
Chapter 46	State of mind	175
Chapter 47	The art of words	178
Chapter 48	Larger than life	182
Chapter 49	Endurance	185
Chapter 50	Anger	189
Chapter 51	Kukan	193
Chapter 52	The best	197
Chapter 53	Contact	201
Chapter 54	The aggressive energy	205
Chapter 55	Budo finesse	208
Chapter 56	The soul of the *katana*	211
Chapter 57	Playing Instructor	215
Chapter 58	Rewarding meetings	219
Chapter 59	Hitting harder	222

Chapter 60	*Kage no me*	226
Chapter 61	**Aging**	229
Chapter 62	**Extreme fatigue**	232
Chapter 63	**Learning curves**	235
Chapter 64	**A Pure Heart**	239
Chapter 65	**Unpretentious**	243
Chapter 66	**The other's stare**	247
Chapter 67	**Kihon to the rescue**	250
Lexicon		253
Special Thanks		257

Introduction

A master-disciple relationship is never easy. Especially when it is tied in Japanese culture. One should not confuse the master of a sect that seeks to gather as many followers as possible with a master who has taken on the task of helping someone in his evolution. A real master does not aim to get the admiration of others. He aims to bring his disciple to understand their surroundings and develop the ability to see the laws that govern the universe. His mission is to share his wisdom and pass on his knowledge. To achieve this, a master can only train a few disciples at a time.

The best way to understand the unique relationship a master and his disciple have, is to attend their private discussions, to share these key moments that can raise questions and reflections, and to feel the emotions that the disciple can experience during his apprenticeship. We will quickly see that being an apprentice is not always easy. The master's teachings sometimes prove to be complex, even confusing. Understanding such a master is not always easy. His role is not to explain everything in detail, but to stimulate reflection.

The chapters in this novel are very short. In popular Japanese manga, each chapter is designed so it can be read between two train stations. This concept allows readers to read each part separately without losing track of the story.

This work, which is used as a backdrop in the world of martial arts, can be transposed to our acts in daily life. Even if it may be inspired by some real events, the basic story is purely fictional.

Chapter 1

Acceptance

"I'm not like the majority of people who are already dead and do not know it yet."

I think these are the words that convinced the old master to accept me as his disciple. For many years, he dispensed his wisdom and teachings to various groups, but he refused to take on new disciples. He had seen those he had trained so hard disappear one by one. Age is relentless, he had lived longer than most of his students who were younger than him. He was saying that he was now too old to accept such responsibility. Of course, many students came from all corners of the earth to train in his *dojo*, but it was not the same. There is a huge difference between becoming a disciple, and being a student. I did not want to be just a student.

Who I am is not important. I could be you, your neighbor, I could be any martial art practitioner. The messenger does not change the content of the message. What counts is sharing the knowledge that I gained from this extraordinary man. I had been doing martial arts for several years, but the more I learned, the more I realized I stagnated at the same level. Admittedly, I had high skills and held several black belts with many degrees in each style. As is often inevitable in such circumstances, the ego came as a bonus with all those hard-earned degrees. Fortunately for me, this spark we call consciousness one day lit up inside me, that little something that makes us realize our triviality, that little something that leads us to ask questions. In short, it makes us realize that in our every day life, we have reached our threshold of incompetence and that if we attempt to mount a new level, our mediocrity will be revealed in the face of people who have the chance of being aware.

Too many people are just surviving, waiting for retirement, and then death. It is perhaps this brutal awakening that allowed me to be accepted by the old master. I say accepted, but in reality, I was being tested. I had the privilege of trying to prove to him that I could change. I had already attended many classes he taught so generously. Despite that, I remained hungry. Of course, I learned techniques that were unknown to me, I acquired new principles, but it was not enough, I wanted more, I had to dig deeper. I was unable to break through the barrier that made me feel stagnant for so long. Most of my partners were pleased to acquire these different ways to fight, but not me.

Perhaps it has already happened for you to perform a job or task and to feel that there must be something more to it, that your life can not be reduced to what you are right now. You feel trapped in a matrix that reproduces and repeats your daily routine. At that time, I thought the way of true martial arts was a unique path which we had to find the entrance to. In reality, there is a multitude of intricate paths available to us. Everything lies in our ability to see, to realize that we can change the course of our lives whenever we want. It is just a matter of choosing the way that is destined for us, or in the worst case, dare come out of our comfort zone.

I am now an elderly man and the chronological order of events is blurred in my memory, but I believe that the following conversation took place in the first year of my training. I do not remember what we were doing, but I can still see my master squeezing my hand very hard. The pain was horrible. I had already had kidney stones and that pain was mild compared to the infernal noose that had closed over my knuckles. It was between two spasms that this strange question came to my mind. When he delivered me from this suffering, the old master looked at me and smiled. His eyelids opened on dark slanted eyes who had the power to pierce my soul.

"Master, why don't men seek the way? Why do they accept to remain as they are?" I asked.

Anyone would probably have thought it strange to ask such a question, rather than to talk about what he had put me through, but my teacher did not seem at all surprised.

"What has prevented you from changing?"

Although I was accustomed to him answering a question with another question, this time I did not know what to say.

"I do not know, I was not ready."

"Wrong answer," he said, nodding.

I remember his stare. He did not speak, he was content to wait in silence. The more he looked at me, the more I felt that my thoughts were intertwined. He came to my aid.

"Is it possible that you needed so much time because you thought you were on top of the pyramid?"

I took a moment to reflect. He was right, for years, I was among the best. I thought I knew everything, or at least knew the essential. The rest being only different arrangements of the same moves.

"It is true that as long as we do not realize that there is something else, we do nothing to reach it," he went on, "but nowadays, there are so many books and films that talk about spirituality we can not ignore that there is something else out there."

I thought about all those movies where the hero, nearly annihilated, rose from the ashes to defeat evil after an almost magical illumination. Once again, I had the impression that the old master had read in me.

"Most people expect the change to take place miraculously. They believe that it will come by itself with the years. When you told me that you were not like the majority of people who had died, but did not know it yet, you had taken an important step. If you look around you and think back about your old friends, from school or work, most of them after five, ten, twenty or even fifty years, remain unchanged. They made new acquisitions, they have improved their living conditions in significant ways. They drive around with more expensive cars, but despite all that, they are the same. Their concerns have not changed, everything is centered around their little lives, they have the same character, the same way of thinking, they have not evolved. When you meet these people after several years, you realize that they are still the same good old friends you knew a long time ago."

I thought of some old friends that I had recently seen. Indeed, their lives were all quite similar. Poor sleep quality due to everyday stress, a diet based on foods rich in cholesterol and sugar, jobs based on image and big pay checks . Once the holidays are over, this unhealthy haste to reach the next year's vacation is back. The same priorities that I once had.

"Most people do not want change, they want to improve their living conditions," said the master. "This usually means more money. Everything revolves around that. If the economic situation deteriorates, couples do not usually recover from it. The stress created will lower the tolerance levels which will lead to arguments and fights."

"I do not understand the relation with martial arts."

The old master looked at me and smiled.

"Because *budo*, the way, is life. When we learn to deepen our understanding of martial arts, it is the way of life that we choose."

My limited understanding at the time did not allow me to grasp the hidden meaning of these words.

"Okay, but if we have no money, we can not do martial arts."

I was happy with my answer and was certain that the old master could not argue with something that obvious.

"That is quite true, if you buy techniques, but if you're a true practitioner at heart, you will continue to train alone, at home, in a park, in the forest. If you can not pay for a class, maybe it is just because you've reached the point of making life choices."

The memory of an old student of mine came to mind. He seemed motivated and loved taking my classes. One day, he told me he had no money to continue training. I then offered to let him take the classes for free, until I learned that he had bought new, expensive ski equipment. It was his choice, skiing down on snow was more important to him than martial arts. My teacher pulled me from my thoughts.

"For many practitioners, martial arts are a social activity, and that's good. They need to have contact with other people. The purpose of the warrior is to help people live peacefully. The purpose of man is to improve and to find happiness. If happiness is simple, there is nothing wrong with that. For most people, it all comes down to a series of small desires they satisfy whenever they can. However there may come a time when we realize that there is a void in our lives, then it is probably the right time to move, to take another path. If we do not seize this opportunity, it's safe to say that we will remain at the same point for the rest of our lives. There will always be this feeling that we have missed something."

He let me meditate on these words for a few moments, then continued.

"Whether it is in martial arts or for the creation of a nation, the motivations are the same. The founding fathers of a nation usually have a vision. Unfortunately, those who take over only have desires. It's one of the differences between the divine, and mere physical possessions, between understanding and collecting."

"I do not understand the connection between my question on the way of martial arts, and the founding fathers."

"Vision. Everything is a matter of vision. In martial arts and politics, most thoughts translate into 'I know', rather than 'it should be'. Be careful not to confuse it with "I want it to be". There is a difference between the I and the divine, the natural that should guide us."

I was more lost than ever.

"In martial arts, people want to be effective, to know a particular secret technique, to be able to beat a multitude of fighters with just the strength of their fists. The path they take is that of collecting. It is the way of the mind and not the heart. The successors of the founding fathers do the same. When they forget the heart, they turn their backs on the basics, they only work on their desires, not on what they should become."

It took me several years to be able to read between the lines of the old master's teachings. Even today, I'm not sure I can understand in full the depth of his teachings.

The old master looked at me and smiled, taking my hand again. It is with all my heart that I wanted the pain to stop.

Chapter 2
Bad energy

The old master had managed to destabilize me from the first moment he took me in his charge. I had never expected to train this way. I thought he would invite me to his *dojo* for my first day of training. Instead, he told me to come to his home around 3 am. I was leaning on the low wall that protected the privacy of the house across from his. A light rain had just settled into fine droplets on the umbrella I was holding. Not wanting to risk being late, I arrived fifteen minutes early. I did not dare ring the bell at this door. I knew I was expected, but I thought I was too early and it would be impolite to insist. The sand in the hourglass must have been wet that morning, because I felt that time stood still. Finally, my watch read 3 o'clock. Nothing happened. No light was on at the old master's house. I decided to wait five minutes before pressing the button. In the end, I kept pushing back ringing the bell by 5 minutes. What if he had forgotten about me, or had fallen asleep? At his age, he would need a lot of sleep.

The big hand on my watch had just reached the half-hour mark when I was about to leave. Upon reaching the corner, I saw a shadow coming towards me. Two representatives of the canine race accompanied the silhouette. The moment he came under the dim light of a lamppost, I recognized the old master. He was walking his dogs. He had not even bothered to bring an umbrella.

"Where are you going like that?" He asked. "Don't tell me you are impatient."

"I was afraid to disturb you, I thought you were asleep. It is almost 3:30 am."

"What don't you understand by the word wait?" Asked the old master, raising his eyebrows ornate with watery pearls.

I did not know what to answer, or rather, I did not dare argue the subject.

"Here, take this," he said, handing me a leash.

Without worrying about me, he went on walking again. The dog he had handed me kept a constant stress on the rope. From time to time he stopped sniffing random oddities camouflaged by the darkness of the night. Suddenly, he stopped in the middle of the sidewalk to relieve himself. The old master looked at me angrily.

"Don't you have a plastic bag with you? We can not leave that there."

"No, I do not have a bag, I did not expect to go walk your dogs at 3 in the morning."

"It does not matter, when we return home, I'll give you one and you can come back here to pick it up."

What? He was walking his dogs without carrying any bags and wanted me to return to clean their excrement. If this was a test for my ego, he had chosen it well. The tenser I got, the more the dog pulled on the leash to go smell the middle of the street.

"What are you doing?" Asked the man I wanted as my mentor.

"He's the one who keeps stopping."

"I thought you were good at martial arts," said the old man.

"At martial arts, yes, but I'm not going to beat him up."

"So, to you, *budo* means hitting?"

That was it, I was losing control of the situation, and my first training with the old master...If we could even call it training. He motioned me to give him the leash. The moment he took it in his hand, the dog became calm, and relaxed the tension in the rope. The mutt ceased pulling. She walked obediently beside him.

"Strikes are only a manifestation of the energy that a practitioner may use. The power of a martial artist must be spread well before action is taken. Martial skill should be judged by the fights a person has not fought, rather than the fights he has won."

Suddenly, the old master handed me the leash again. At the same instant, without the dog even looking at me, he began to sniff left and right.

"I do not understand, how is this possible?"

"It's just a matter of energy."

"But I have energy, I'm in great shape."

"What a shame that energy and intelligence do not go together!" The old man said with a sigh.

I could not believe I was being insulted on our first meeting as master and student. No, as master and disciple. He had never been so hard on any of his students. I began to understand that the road would be long. My teacher looked at me and smiled. I came to understand the lesson.

"Please teach me. What do you mean by a simple question of energy?"

"Ki, or energy, if you prefer, can manifest itself in different ways. The dog does not respect you because your energy level is lower than his."

I hesitated to determine if he was insulting me or teaching me. Then I had what I think was a slight enlightenment.

"You're saying I do not impose sufficient fear?"

"There you go again, you think with your muscles instead of your head. No, it is not a question of fear, but respect, self-confidence. If an animal does not feel that that state of mind which leads to obedience, how can an opponent take you seriously?"

The old master had seen right. I was not comfortable at all pulling this little fur ball around who could not have weighed more than fifteen kilos. It was the dog who walked me and not vice versa.

"How can I do that?"

"Budo is primarily a state of mind. If it is only worked with the body, it brings its practitioner to become a tool void of any reflection, just able to hit."

I wanted to be elsewhere. I felt that all my years of training had suddenly become useless.

"Through the leash, you transmit energy or should I say, your lack of energy. The dog can feel the assurance that you release. Take a deep breath and imagine yourself walking in a forest or doing your shopping. You have to think of a scenario where you are sure of yourself. Then it becomes simple, you just have to move forward keeping this state of mind."

I took a few deep breaths, and then I pulled one or two times on the leash. The message seemed to go through. The dog approached me and began to walk beside me. It was not totally obedient, but the improvement was obvious. The Master smiled at my progress. The rain had stopped and the darkness was retreating slowly. Between the buildings, we could see the efforts the sun was making to win over the clouds. The master headed back in the direction of his house.

"You said that energy can manifest itself in many ways. What did you imply by that?"

"Everything is energy. The intention you put in when punching is a different kind of force from the one your muscles use. Yet they complement each other. The energy you need to accomplish your daily tasks is different from that which is necessary to make a speech in public. Nevertheless, in both cases it is energy, or a manifestation of energy. Most practitioners combine physical ardor and energy. A colossus with extraordinary biceps may seem impressive, but without the power of energy, he can be easily defeated."

"A tough guy's punching power will be greater if he controls that energy you speak of."

"Yes, but those who have strength usually tend to be content with it. Their large muscles become an obstacle to true power."

"You mean we should not try to develop our body?"

"It is not bad in itself. It is even a good thing, but muscle size should not be the goal to aim for."

The old master folded his arms and felt his biceps.

"His hit may be more powerful, but without good control of energy, it will never reach its full potential. Energy is acquired with great effort. The time you use to make your muscles grow, you are not using to develop that energy. Also, if you stop training, your large muscles will quickly turn into shapeless mass worthy of your Western culture."

I did not know how to take this affront to my culture. Then I thought about the wrongdoings of the Western diet. The master did not give me time to cogitate a way to defend myself.

"Energy is the cement that is used to link two opponents."

"I do not understand what you mean by linking two opponents."

"We do not fight against someone, we fight with someone," the old man explained.

"Why be united? We use our eyes to counter his technique. A fight is won with the speed of our reflexes, right?"

"I agree with you. That is the right way to do it... for beginners. But we must mature. Eyes are slow, they see the fist coming, they transmit the information to the brain, who realizes what is happening. The latter must then develops a defensive strategy, and after all that, it sends the data to the muscles through the nerves. Only thereafter, the arm will block the attack if it is not already too late.

"So energy does not need eyes?" I asked in a tone that might have seemed sarcastic.

"Yes, you can use them to assess the situation, but the energy can do the same job. It connects you with your opponent and with everything around you."

"Everything around me! I think I'd rather trust my eyes rather than this connection of energy."

"Too bad for you, that connection could have avoided you this problem."

"What problem?" I asked, as I felt my foot come in contact with a soft substance. I had placed my foot in the droppings my little friend had left before.

Chapter 3

Judgment

By becoming his disciple, I had the chance to share more intimate moments with my teacher. In a relationship between student and teacher, the latter exchange techniques for monetary sums. This approach is quite normal. Most of those who manage martial arts schools have to deal with numerous fees that make teaching martial arts, in most cases, become a vocation. For those who are doing well in this business, the love of the art is often replaced by the marketing aspect.

I often accompanied my mentor in all kinds of places, be it for shopping, simple walks, or for going out to eat. That day, we were sitting in one of the many restaurants he had in his address book. The place was more chic than where I used to go with him. A lady in a traditional *kimono* brought us different dishes he had ordered for us. I admired the elegance with which she was kneeling to serve us. Despite the wide sleeves of her dress, she laid the plates on the table with no part of the beautiful fabric touching anything. When she stretched her arms, a light, spicy fragrance succeed in my nostrils. I could not tell if the effluvium emanated from her or the tray she had laid before me. Then, meticulously, she slightly rotated the plate on itself. I admired the beauty of the gesture. Driven as if a light breeze was controlling her body, she bowed before leaving. I lowered my gaze on the table and some discomfort seized me.

"That's the problem?" Asked the old master.

"What? How? I didn't say anything."

"You did not need to say a word, the look on your face says more than enough."

I knew that I had expressed no emotion watching the woman walk away, but I could not say the same about the moment I looked down to see the food.

"What do you mean exactly?" I asked, feigning surprise.

"You have not even tasted the food yet you are judging it."

In one of the plates, a strange fish laid and did not seem very appetizing. Lying in the middle of a white rectangular plate, the animal kept fixing me with his beady eye. If he had wanted to taunt me, he would not have looked at me differently. Light reflections on his slimy body gave the impression that he had just swam in a sea of oil. The whole was accompanied by a bowl of rice and, as is common in Japan, many small dishes of vegetables and condiments completed the outfit.

"It's him, he doesn't inspire anything good. Are you sure this is not disguised fugu, the poisonous fish that kills people every year?"

"No, you would not have the means to pay for such delicious food. If there are some who die every year, it is only because the cook did not have the competence to prepare this meal too refined for the likes of you."

Not only had I just learned that I was a barbarian, but it was I who had to pay the bill.

"I'm not judging, it's just that…"

"It's just that you judge based on appearances. Like I said, that's your problem."

Several months had already passed since I had the chance to revolve around the old master. I understood that he held nothing against me, that he was teaching me a lesson. Although he appeared hard on me, I knew that everything he was saying was to help me. I was silent to allow him to continue.

"This way of thinking is what keeps a lot of martial artists to go up in level. With some luck, some may reach a slightly more advanced stage, but they will have to settle for that, a mediocre level."

At that time, the concept of levels was still a vague one in my mind. Apart from the order of belts, I separated martial artists into two categories. The gifted group, which I considered myself belonging to, and ordinary practitioners, who would never reach the highest levels of *budo*. Without knowing it, like many teachers who were similar to me, I thought I was superior to most. I was looking for a way to counter what my mentor had said.

"On the contrary, being able to quickly analyze a situation should be a strategic advantage, not a handicap," I said.

"Most people look but see nothing. Our brain works by sealing the gaps it does not see. There is a small area of the eye that can not see. We do not realize it because our brain compensates for this space where there is nothing. If there is something that is unclear, our brain will manage to fill the information gap."

"What is the connection with the monstrous creature on my plate and this way of thinking?"

"To compensate for what it does not understand, the pea that acts as your brain bases itself on your past experiences. It creates a scenario drawing its data in the baggage it has accumulated over the years."

The old master smiled, turned his gaze away on my pittance then slowly turned his head towards me by speaking in a Japanese dialect difficult to understand. I think he said something about the West and the Cro-Magnon. After a short pause, he continued.

"You have the same problem when I teach. Rather than being receptive to what I show you, you repeatedly refer to the martial baggage you have acquired. You can not see new things, you're just comparing what I teach with the meager knowledge you possess. You look, but you can not see. Your brain projects images referring to what you already know. It's not bad, it's just that you limit yourself."

"I do not agree with you, I have a trained eye that can see every detail."

"Well then, look into my eyes and do not look away."

The old master thrust his head towards mine, blocking most of my field of vision.

"There is a man behind me..."

I was quite proud to be able to describe this man.

"Yes, the one who has a scar under his left eye," I replied.

"It's him I want to talk to you about. Can you describe what he's wearing?"

"I think he has a dark jacket with a striped tie."

"You are saying that because most people here are dressed that way, but you're wrong. You're way off the mark."

The old master moved so I could see the man wearing a black shirt. How could I forget his clothing? His scar had obstructed my vision.

"At least I was right about the scar."

"That is what I'm saying, you notice what binds you to your past or fears. For many people, ending up with such a mark on their face is to end their existence as they know it."

By the time my teacher was about to point his chopsticks at his plate, he stopped and looked at me.

"Our brains lead us to see what we want. We are led by our desire or dominant emotions. You would not like to have such a scar, so it's the first thing you noticed. If you didn't care, you probably would have noticed his clothes," the master smiled and went on. "If it was a beautiful tall blonde with dominant cleavage, you would not even have noticed her scar."

The master's fish was similar to mine. He removed the skin and planted his chopsticks into the monstrous aquatic specimen's flesh. He closed his eyes as though taking time to enjoy his mouthful before swallowing. He seemed to find it delicious.

"Have you ever seen those phrases where only the first letter and last letters of each word are in the right position? Most people are able to read the sentences because our brain manages to compensate for what is inconsistent."

"This is an advantage in a fight," I said, thinking I would impress the old master.

"Perhaps in some cases, but if you have an opponent who is a little smarter than you, he will use this flaw to manipulate your mind.

He will adapt his body language in order to make you see the sequence he wishes you to see."

All the times I was sure to reach him with a punch during intensive training came to mind. Each time, I found myself hitting nothing. The old master looked at me and smiled.

"Well, perhaps there is some hope after all. I see that a few of your neurons are trying to be useful."

The old master plunged his chopsticks into his fish. I took my chopsticks, but there seemed to be an invisible force field that pushed my hands away from my plate. A few deep breaths finally allowed me to conquer this dark force. After savoring a bite from his dish, he resumed the conversation.

"Every time you attack me, my brain can analyze the possible actions your body can make and I can position myself where you do not expect. Naturally, in order to do that, I do not say things like I will advance my right foot and he will punch. No, it's simpler than that. There is no need to analyze it gesture by gesture, we develop an overview. With experience, the attacker becomes predictable. When one is accustomed to seeing it, it becomes easy to give false information."

"Lucky for me it's so easy," I replied sarcastically. "How can I achieve such results?"

"The first step is to eat your fish."

After some hesitation, I released the tension in my jaws. The tiny bite that I had torn placed itself on my tongue. I almost instantly felt the flesh melt in my mouth. An exquisite taste invaded the roof of my mouth and was asking for more. The master smiled at me.

"It's a bit like *budo*. We see with our eyes, we taste with our body, and our heart asks for more."

Chapter 4
Strange powers

Whenever I think of this story, countless questions pop into my mind. I was attending a class my teacher was giving to a group of young Westerners. A Japanese man came into the *dojo* to meet the old master. Apparently they knew each other well. The two men were talking and laughing. The visitor, though younger than the master, had exceeded the 70 year-old mark.

On the *tatami*, everybody was training with the *bo*, a stick of about two meters long. As it often happens in a crowded *dojo*, some students dominated by the excitement of the moment did not always manage to control their actions. At one point, one of them lost control of his weapon. The stick flew off at full speed and was about to crash into the back of the master's head. I watched the scene helplessly. Completely absorbed in his conversation, he could not see what was coming. When the inevitable impact was about to happen, he leaned his head forward in order to dodge the blow. The stick missed its target and hit nothing but air. The old man glanced toward the student at fault and continued his discussion as if nothing had happened.

The next day, while we were walking back home, I told him that I had seen him avoid the collision.

"I admire the way you dodged the *bo*, I'd love to have such powers too."

The old master paused, stared into my eyes and then continued walking.

"A power... What are you talking about?"

"About this ability you have to know what's happening in the back of your head."

"Flying over a building is to have power. Moving objects with my mind, shooting lightning, talking with spirits, those are powers. Unfortunately, I have no such abilities."

"Do not try to make me believe that what you did is natural. You dodged the impact at the last moment. That's no coincidence."

"In a moment, a red truck will come around the corner without making its stop."

I stopped moving completely. I stuck out my ear trying to detect a suspicious noise. I did not dare blink in fear of missing the moment when the vehicle would pass. After a while, I turned my head towards the master. He showed a big smile. He examined me as he would watch a young child unwrap a gift.

"What? Like I said, I have no special powers."

"So how can you explain avoiding the stick flying at you at the *dojo*?"

"Oh, that has nothing to do with powers, that was, let's say, instinct."

"Instinct! I wish I had as much instinct as you."

"You have instinct. It's just that you stopped listening to it long ago."

"I do not think that I have ever ducked a stick coming at me from behind."

"When you were a child, has it never happened to you to have the impression that one of your friends was hidden, waiting to surprise you, and you knew where he was without having seen him?"

Some images appeared in my mind. Confused, jerky scenes, unrelated to each other. Then suddenly I saw a kid from my neighborhood lurking on the other side of a fence with a water bucket in hand. The master did not give me time to remember completely.

"Has it never happened to you to think of someone you had not seen for a long time, and to suddenly run into them on the street?"

My response was instantaneous.

"Yes, I've lived this. Several times even."

"Well, it's the same thing, that is instinct," he said.

"I'm ready to believe that there may be some connection between people, but the stick from yesterday wasn't alive."

"The stick maybe, but the person who handled it was."

I had not thought of that. A weapon is nothing without the hand controlling it.

"But for me it's just luck. For you, it seems to be as natural as walking," I replied.

"You can not imagine how I appreciate the simple act of walking in the street. I find myself extremely privileged to move. There are so many people who have all kinds of problems. Think of those who are in wheelchairs."

"What is the connection between this perception and the act of walking?"

"Really, you do not understand what life is."

"Yes, I know what life is. The chance to walk, to move, to have a roof over my head, eating well and having a good job."

"Sorry, that's not what life is. What you're talking about is more like survival."

"Survival? What do you mean?"

"Um, I do not know where to start. I guess you're usually not very busy..."

"On the contrary, I never have any free time. I often do ten-hour work days. I have to prepare my meals, study, and the rest of the time, I dedicate it to *budo* and..."

"That's what I said, you are just surviving. With the exception of our conversations, when was your last time you had a real conversation with another person?"

"I regularly converse with my friends when we see each other."

"What are the usual subjects you talk about?"

"It varies, we talk about all kinds of things. Technology, cinema, martial arts, all the important stuff, I guess."

"I'll ask the question again, when was the last real conversation you had, not your discussions about the banalities of life."

I began to see where he was going with this. Of course, there were the robotic responses, such as "hello, how are you?" Thinking about it, our exchanges were more entertaining than profound. This often meant we imposed our ideas rather than just accepted those of others.

"I understand what you're trying to say. You are talking about empathy, right?"

The master looked at me pointing his thumb to his nose.

"I have a good nose, I knew that we would eventually light up this glimmer of hope that shines inside of you."

"Do you think I lack empathy?"

"No, you are just not aware of it."

"Is empathy a good tool to detect an attack from behind like you did?"

"Putting yourself in the shoes of a beggar, a merchant, a thug, or a mother, can develop this connection which is essential to martial arts. As long as a practitioner projects an image of what something is, rather than seeing what it really is, it is impossible to access those old primitive instincts. The connection will be difficult."

That's what we were talking about. Connection, one of the strangest concepts of the higher levels of *budo*.

"Is this an exercise I should often do?"

"This is not an exercise, it is a state of mind. It has to become second nature to have empathy for the people you meet. Initially, it will be emotional, then one day, you'll probably discover a dimension that most people have no idea exists."

"So it's not magic."

"Do I look like a wizard?" Asked the old master before putting his hand on my chest to keep me from stepping down the sidewalk the moment a red truck came around the corner at full speed without making its stop.

Chapter 5
Too fast

By the time I met the old master, I was already teaching many different groups. At that time, when my students were participating in a competition, we always came back with a variety of awards and medals. I was certain that with so many good results from my students, I had to be an excellent teacher. At this time in my life, I was not aware that I didn't know much.

One day, my teacher made me do a rather unusual training exercise. We were in one of the *dojo*, a small clearing with enough space to allow any type of martial training. I was waiting in the center of this empty area. I thought he would join me, but instead, he remained in the forest, one hundred meters away. He amused himself moving slowly around a tree and then moved to another. It took him about fifteen minutes to circle one of these formidable opponents. I could not help but smile, seeing him do these movements that seemed completely useless. Tiptoeing, I quietly approached, expecting him to try to hit me at any time, but it never happened. He just kept on moving, I would like to say he was taking a walk, but that wasn't it. His movements were strange. Not really *tai chi*, and not really walking, he seemed to move like a ghost floating in the air. Even though his feet touched the ground, they practically left no footprints among the dead leaves. No sound betrayed his presence either.

"*Sensei*, what are you doing?" I finally asked.

Not bothering to look at me, he replied.

"Can't you see? I'm practicing my speed."

The only response that came to mind seemed like a sarcastic one.

"It sure is working, the trees can't keep up with you."

The old master turned his head in my direction for a moment, then continued his exercise without minding me. He had been doing this for well over one hour, going through the forest, circling trees and ferns. A certain embarrassment came over me. Remaining there doing nothing suddenly made me feel awkward. I began to imitate his movements, frequently losing my stability on some malicious roots that were only waiting for the right moment to ridicule me. I almost got my eye into a branch as I tilted my body to move on to another tree. The monster had defended itself by attacking me to the cornea with one of its tentacles. A little blood trickled from my lower eyelid. While I raised my arm to wipe the warm drop that fell on my cheek, my teacher spoke.

"Too fast..."

"How was that too fast?" I asked in a tone that bordered impatience.

"Too fast, you're going too fast. That's why you're not connected to the forest. That's why it defended itself."

"A forest can not defend itself," I replied.

"So you did this to yourself. Therefore you are stupid, you have to be stupid to deliberately injure yourself."

"It was not on purpose, it was an accident."

"That's what I said, you're not connected."

I did not want to have this kind of discussion with the old master, so I kept silent, but he had not said his last word.

"What is speed for you?" He asked, without looking up.

"Speed is when you go fast," I said without realizing how redundant I was.

"Bravo, beautiful answer. I wonder why I agreed to spend time with you."

That sentence was like a cold shower. It was I who had approached him, begged him to take me as his disciple. Damn my pride.

"I apologize for this silly answer. Speed is to be able to move well enough to avoid any aggression. It is to be able to strike more quickly than our opponent. It is..."

He did not give me time to continue.

"If I understand correctly, you are fast when you manage to dodge attacks. That's easy. We are fast when we are able to avoid the blade of a sword swinging down at us."

"Yes, that's it. Being able to escape the attack of a *katana*."

I felt the excitement in my voice. I saw myself jumping aside to avoid getting sliced in half by a mysterious assassin wearing a dark hood.

"Do you think you possess this extraordinary talent to avoid such aggression?" Asked the old master who looked into my eyes for the first time.

"I think so," I replied happy to have his full attention.

"So the tree that attacked you is probably faster than a good swordsman," said the master squinting.

I felt his gaze engulf my soul.

"Speed is an illusion, we must get to know our opponent. How can you hope to defend yourself against a *katana* if you're not even able to avoid a twig?"

"But then *sensei*, what is speed if it's just an illusion?"

The master walked towards me. I knew training would become a little more physical.

"Hit me," he said.

"Don't worry about actually hitting me, it is I who commands you to do so. Hit me if you want me to keep you as my disciple."

Naturally, my attempts to reach the old man ended in failure. A feigned right hook followed by a roundhouse kick gave me hope for a split second. I do not understand how, but my foot only hit air.

"You act too quickly, you do not think. It's fine for playing with children, but in a real fight, you're a poor opponent. You rely on the speed of your muscles, and that's an illusion. I wonder why I'm wasting my time here," he said with a sigh.

"You are here because you know that I can achieve something, but I can't do it without you. I need you, do not give up on me, please... Master."

The old teacher smiled.

"You are on the right track. Let's do it again, try to hit me, but this time I'm going to fight back."

I came to realize that I was fighting against a shadow, a ghost, an entity that merely avoided my attacks. I gave my first punch with violence fueled by fear. Fear of him giving up on me, fear of the pain that was to follow. As soon as my arm tried to regain its position after missing its target, I felt a burning pain in my right pectoral. I felt like the muscle fibers were tearing apart, like I could never raise my arm again. When he released me, my legs soften, but I still found the energy to counter-attack with a left punch. The old man redirected my arm down, and placed his other hand on top of my head. Without realizing what had happened, I found myself thrown into a fern bouquet. My buttocks banged against a sharp stone that stuck up. My pride forbade me to feel sorry for myself. After several unsuccessful attempts, the master forced me to go back to practice around the trees. I was glad to stop trying to hit him. My body, but especially my ego, surely would need several days to recover from this training.

"Too fast."

I must have heard those words dozens of times. Each time, I slowed down, but soon after, without realizing it, I accelerated the pace again.

"Master, I do not understand how this exercise will help my speed. Can such training actually make me go faster?"

"Did you have the impression that I was moving quickly when I fought you just now?"

"No, at times I even had the feeling you were standing still."

"I was almost motionless, that's all you need when the opponent is not very efficient. We do not need to move a lot. This is what you have to learn here, not to move, but to connect."

Without saying a word, I returned to my routine around a tree that seemed to be at least 100 years old. I looked at the old oak, calling it *sensei*. In Japanese the word *sensei* translates to teacher. The kanji, sen can mean forward, previously, prior; while the second kanji, sei, can mean life, birth. We can then translate this word by "one born before us". I do not know why or how, but I was being taught by a tree.

"Too fast! Concentrate, otherwise you will never succeed."

I took a deep breath and continued the exercise by focusing on what stood before me. Then I slowed my movements. I was trying to feel everything around me, with every cell of my body.

"Well, you're beginning to understand. There is perhaps some hope after all."

Somehow the old master could feel what I was feeling, but for the first time, I realized the importance of this connection. The more I felt all that was around me, the more a feeling of power came over me.

"Be careful," said the master.

I was so excited that I had lost my connection with everything around me. I wanted to reassure my master about my ability to reconnect.

"Do not worry, Master, I will fix this. It'll be easy to reconnect with the forest."

"That's not what I'm talking about," he replied.

"Everything is under control, do not worry, leave it to me. I am no longer a child."

"Okay, but I just wanted to tell you not to..."

Hot, sharp pain suddenly shot down my leg. I lost the rhythm necessary for the exercise. The old master called out to me.

"The nest! You stepped on a wasp nest!" The old master yelled, watching me escape at full speed. Running as fast as possible, I had the time to hear his last words.

"Too slow."

Chapter 6
Becoming old

This conversation took place at the beginning of my relationship with the old master. I was in the *dojo* with some friends, watching a video of a martial artist showing off his physical ability. The man in his fifties was in a form that my training companions all envied. I had not noticed that the old master was watching over my shoulder.

"Some people sure are desperate to stay on top of their game," he said.

"You mean his physical form makes him a great martial artist?"

"No, I'm saying he is trying to hold on to the past."

"You can not deny the fact that this man demonstrates incredible will,"

I was confused and skeptical. I did not understand how one could denigrate someone who showed as much ardor.

"I do not know how strong-willed he is, but it is certainly very nice to watch," said the old man.

"Nice? I find it spectacular."

"I respect the tenacity, perseverance and will of this individual in his attempt to stay young, but in martial arts you do not really need to do gymnastics."

"In any case, it can not hurt," I snapped back almost desperately.

I really admired the work this fellow did. He had to make so much effort to remain as athletic as he was.

"It does not cause any harm if he does not use up his martial arts training time."

"You do not seem to appreciate what this man is doing," I said.

"No, I really admire what he does, believe me, but do not confuse martial arts and gymnastics."

"*Ninja* were great athletes," I threw with confidence.

"Some of the younger ones probably were, but the more mature certainly did not rely on their acrobatics to survive."

"It may be that they were not as fit as this man."

The wise old man looked at me, smiling. He seemed to pity me. He went on about the same subject.

"When you reach a certain age, you have to accept getting old. Sure, we must try to maintain our body in optimal condition. However, we should not neglect training. If you do it for yourself because you enjoy doing acrobatics at sixty then I have nothing against that, but if you do it to impress others and you associate it with martial arts, I'm gonna have to disagree with that."

I did not give up on my point of view.

"Yes, but if you are fitter, you become faster, stronger. This is the secret of performing well in fights."

"How much downtime does it take an Olympic champion to lose a good percentage of his physical condition?"

He asked, but did not give me time to answer.

"In two months, he will probably have lost a large percentage of his ability. However, if you train martially and take two months off, your skill will not decrease. Even after ten years, something will remain,"

I began to understand what he was trying to say. He then raised another point which I had not thought of.

"Can we do those movements on the spot without warming up our muscles?"

"Of course not, we need to stretch and warm up if we are to avoid injury," I replied.

"I imagine that in a fight if you ask an opponent to wait to give you enough time to get ready, he will acquiesce to your request?"

I had trouble seeing myself doing stretching exercises in front of an attacker waiting for me patiently.

"Okay, you have a point. I had not thought of that."

"Many people fear growing old. Many martial arts instructors are afraid to lose the admiration of their students. They often lose a little confidence when they find that they their reflexes and movements slow down. They try to compensate with more physical effort rather than by acquiring more accuracy."

"Did you feel the same?" I asked. Several other students seemed uncomfortable with me asking such a question to the master.

"Of course. We practice a technique we have not done for some time and we realize when stepping forward that the ground is a little less steady than it used to be. We say that it is temporary, that it is due to fatigue or something else, but no, it's age settling in."

"What did you do? Did it discourage you?"

"I was sad. I realized that all my abilities were diminishing. For a short period, I thought about stopping everything. Then I thought about my teacher, an elderly man who could play with me with one hand. I thought that if he could be as effective at his age, so could I. So I started thinking about his way of moving."

The first time I had seen my teacher move, I noticed that he moved like no other I had seen before. At that time I did not understand what made his movements so special. He continued.

"I have reviewed and changed my way of training. I analyzed and focused on the small points that make up each technique I know. Why is such a gesture so effective? How can I improve this with less effort? Will I be faster than a younger assailant in top shape? The answer was yes. All I had to do was save reaction time by exploiting the proper angles. It is also during this reflection that I understood the importance of capturing the mind of an opponent."

I literally drank the words of my teacher. These words still remain engraved in my memory. I did not know at the time how to use them, but I knew that one day I too would have to go through this.

"One morning we realize that our strikes are less powerful. How can we offset the damaging effects of age? Bone alignment, good use of energy with efficient body movements, and all of a sudden not only do I hit faster, but I also gained power."

Saying this, the old man punched the inside of his hand tremendously hard. I would not want to receive this attack.

"When the time to grab an opponent comes, our fingers no longer have the same gripping ease as before. That's not a problem, the knowledge of *kyusho* will compensate for this lack of power. For years, I did martial arts like everyone else, ignoring why the movements are executed in a certain way. Comprehension of the techniques led me to where I am today."

"Do you regret getting older?" I asked.

"I accept with serenity the fact that I am aging. I'm just disappointed of not having understood earlier what I now know. This is why I teach the way I do. I wish for you to learn the important things *budo* have to offer as early as possible."

One of the points that had fascinated me about him was his generosity. He distributed his knowledge without any restrictions. That was a big change from the professors I had had in the past, which gave out only tiny drops of the knowledge they possessed. Naturally, I could not resist asking him more questions on the subject.

"If you had to change something in your life, what would it be?"

"I would not change anything in my life. I had a fulfilling, happy life. I had the privilege of having the best martial art teachers one can dream of having. I consider myself lucky and especially fortunate to be able to continue teaching at my age. I do not think that if I had invested so much time at the gym that I would be where I am today."

"What is the most important thing for us to do in our training?"

I had no idea what I was expecting asking that. Maybe subconsciously I wanted to know one of the secrets that old masters possess.

"The most crucial thing in your training? Hmm... that's a good question."

The old man rubbed his chin, looked at the floor and then turned to me, raising his eyebrows as if surprised by his own answer.

"*Ishiki*," he said, "without a doubt, it is *ishiki*. To be aware, aware of what you do, how you do it, and why you do it. Being aware of your weaknesses and your strengths, aware of what's around you."

The old master was silent for a moment, then looked up and smiled.

"Most people regret the fact of getting older. They are sad, thinking of all the things they have not done, and anything they could have accomplished in their lives. We must be aware that we are living, that we can do all sorts of things. Man is made to create, to do great things. Too many people have already died, but don't know it yet."

Before even knowing my master, I had read an article where were written similar words. This was the trigger that had brought me to want to follow his teachings. I did not want to be like all those people who barely live, in a constant lethargic state all throughout their lives, mere shadows that live by proxy. People that exist, but do not act.

Chapter 7
Managing our personality

"It's like I'm fighting an empty shell," said the old man.

There we go, he is in a bad mood, I thought. He just asked me to hit him and then scolded me for some reason I didn't know. My punch was powerful and fast after all.

"You do not project enough intention, you have to attack me on all levels, not just physically."

This training took place a few weeks before I dared ask him to take me as his disciple. I was a student among all those who would visit regularly. My martial understanding was far more limited than I thought. It was with obvious frustration that I replied:

"I'm not sure we can do much damage by engaging battle with our thoughts."

Little did I know my sarcasm would set the tone for the training that day.

"Okay, if that's what we have to do to make you learn, I'm game. It is I who will hit you."

I expected to be able to avoid his attacks easily. His age should have given me the advantage of speed. Unfortunately, it was not that simple. When his fist was halfway on its course to hit me, I felt a wave of emotion sweep through my mind. For a moment, I felt panic, fear. I was afraid of him. How was that possible? Then a sudden sensation of pain in my stomach made me realize that his knuckles had crashed into me and that I couldn't even react. He waited patiently until I regained my breath.

"So, now you see the difference between an empty shell and one which is filled with intent."

I could not explain what had happened, but it was obvious that it was something beyond a simple physical attack.

"You should not underestimate the power of the mind. Our mind is something malleable. It can be used to project emotions or to go unnoticed. Does anyone know what *henso jutsu* is?"

"It is the art of disguise," said one of the students.

"Yes, but it's much more than that. *Ninja* used these principles to blend into crowds and influence those around them. Putting on beautiful clothes to camouflage oneself is easy, but to succeed in convincing people you meet that you really are the person you are dressing as is another story. At that level, we enter depersonalization."

"What connection is there between the punch you just delivered and these techniques?" I asked

"It is the difference between will and knowledge. You wanted to hit hard, and I knew I could hit hard,"

I absolutely did not see how this response could help me understand.

"The exploitation of the mind is used by the great men who rule this world," continued the master, "these people have unwavering charisma, those men for whom some would even risk their lives. They learned how to project energy. Imagine two people who have the same general education, the same physical abilities and the same financial resources. These two individuals present themselves for election to any office, but one of them doesn't have self-confidence, fails to impose himself while his counterpart looks you straight in the eye, and use all the space he can. For whom will you vote? Probably the one that has more personality. It is a sign of strength, confidence and self-control."

I remembered a scene where politicians in the Philippines had come to hit each other with heavy blows at the parliament. Although I guess the master was not referring to that.

"You must learn to connect to the emotion you want to display. For example, if you go to an interview for a young dynamic company that has the wind in its sails, you should not present yourself as someone stable, traditionalist. You have to project an image of someone full of energy, the image of someone just waiting to be challenged. If you are applying for a more conservative company, you should hide your innovative, or challenging side. You must project the image that suits the culture of the company."

"You said a few weeks ago, that we have to be natural. Isn't taking another personality contrary to that?" I asked.

"Taking different attitudes must become natural to you. You do not deny who you are, you're just projecting a new image, an energy. What disturbed you most just now? The punch you received or what I projected?"

"I was destabilized even before you reached me. I do not know what you did, but I felt like a wave pushed me."

"Before you can even analyze anything, your brain immediately perceived the confidence I was emitting. It was enough to cast doubt in your subconscious and create confusion which prevented you to react. I projected a winning image and not that of a fighter. Unconsciously, you felt the agony of defeat. You believed it."

A student raised his hand.

"I have already taken a sales course. A requirement for success was to believe in our product. If you doubt what you sell, the customer will perceive it and it will be harder to convince him if he does not need what we are trying to sell."

"That is an excellent example. Whether it be for a verbal exchange or one with our fists, it is our ideas that we are trying to get the other person to accept. We can talk or fight without knowing where we are going, but as soon as you put in intention with great determination, you have a better chance to succeed. We also must learn to project our energy forward. If I punch and my body seems to want to retreat, to hide, the impact of my attack will be only physical. We must impress the opponent by showing no fear."

Something about this strategy bothered me.

"Is there no danger of getting hit if we expose ourselves this way?"

"Yes, but, as we know, we offer certain targets, it becomes easy to predict the possible responses of the assailant. By blocking his attacks we reinforce the winner image that we project."

The wise old man paused for a moment, took a few steps. No one dared break the silence. He turned and his eyes met mine.

"Sometimes we have to do the opposite and appear weak and vulnerable. This may be advantageous to project the idea that we are afraid and trying to hide it. It is necessary that the person in front of us has the feeling that we want to impress without having the strength of character to back it up.'

"'This will give him a confidence boost that will turn against him," I hastened to say.

"That's right. Manipulating the image we give out can offer many benefits."

"How can we get to properly control this?'" Asked one of the students.

"The first step is simple, *ishiki*, consciousness. We must be aware of the image that we present. If you have been filmed without knowing it, take the time to observe what you have projected. Otherwise, look in a mirror and try to emulate certain emotions. Compassion and empathy, anger, fear and all those who pass through your head. Learn to compartmentalize these various expressions. Your emotions and your body must be synchronized to project the same thing."

The old master started walking around the *dojo*. In three or four steps, his way of walking transformed.

"Maybe a simple walking exercise can help. Get up, everybody. Walk around the *dojo*, walk and be aware of the image you display."

Everyone stood up and walked. After a few minutes, the entire group turned in the same direction. It reminded me of the Jack Nicholson movie, One Flew Over the Cuckoo's Nest. I decided to go in the opposite direction. The master smiled at me before we stopped.

"Good. Now you will walk while showing anxiety as if you were afraid. Observe how your body will adapt to that emotion."

Curiously, I felt my shoulders lower, my eyes stared down at the floor. I avoided the others with a greater distance.

"Have you noticed how this attitude is easy to take? We all have unconscious fears that are pervasive, just waiting to speak out. You will now find a way to turn this around, a way that will give you a feeling of power. Invent a powerful walk, something that will project a strong image."

The first steps were ordinary. Then at some point, my chin rose. Next it was my shoulders' turn to take a little more space. Without exactly spreading my legs, I felt like my hips widened further which propelled me forward by occupying more space than usual. Sometimes my arms swung around, sometimes I placed my hands on my hips. I did not understand why, but this walk gave me a sense of power. I could focus a greater amount of energy more easily. A strange feeling of freedom took the place of the skepticism that I had during my first steps.

"Quite an interesting way of walking, is not it?" Commented the master.

We all agree that it powered us up.

"Why does it do that?" Asked a student.

"Because this is probably the best way for you to walk. Your body knows what it needs. To move this way in a crowd may seem a bit odd. Most people hesitate to indulge in such behavior."

The time was flying away at full speed. Just before the end of the class, I made a comment on what we had just studied.

"If I understand correctly, we will have to get used to project, to hide, or change our emotions and energy."

"In a way yes," replied the master.

"Must we learn to tap into our energy and even to project it?"

"Basically, something like that."

"It is the same thing as when Obi-Wan Kenobi told Luke to use force in the Star Wars film," I said.

"Not quite. In the Japanese version they do not say to use force, instead, they say to believe in the force. That makes the whole difference," replied the master.

Chapter 8

Why

The word that was said most often that morning was undoubtedly *doshite*. A student was attacking by placing his fists against his hips in the karate fashion. Master had asked him why he was acting this way.

"I do not know. In the other martial arts I practiced, we had to hit like that. When questioning one of my instructors about this stance, he told me that I should not call into question his teaching. I did not dare go further into my quest for knowledge."

"You should have!" Master said in a tone that showed revolt. "We must always know why the things we are learning are done in a certain way. In *budo*, real *budo*, there are reasons for each gesture, nothing is left to chance. You can not entrust your reactions to luck when your security and life depends on it. You must know how the tools you use work."

Master's eyes never left the poor student's gaze, who must have been quite uncomfortable. Master waited for the student to nod before going on. Finally, he stopped staring at the young man to speak to us all.

"If you ask a doctor why he is prescribing you medicine and he replies that he does not know, that would be a problem. If he tells you that one of his professors just told him to prescribe this medicine in university, would you trust him? If so, you may be in trouble. Certain drugs have been banned for years and all of a sudden reappear on the market. It is the duty of your doctor to be updated, to give you what is most appropriate for you. Above all, he should understand the reasons for his decision."

I suddenly remembered that one of my dogs after having received a vaccine had had a terrible reaction to the drug. The vet seemed completely distraught about the state of my pooch. The master went on with another example.

"Would you feel safe if, passing over a bridge with the engineer who built it, you discovered he had no idea why he chose this type of structure over another? "I felt like trying this one, I saw it in a magazine, I found it pretty," he answers you. I think it would not be very reassuring. Not knowing why you are doing the techniques I teach you is not the best way to reach a higher level. We must try to understand, to ask the right questions. We must learn the purpose behind everything we do."

The master was always available to answer our questions. He never showed signs of annoyance or of being disturbed when someone asked to teach him the mechanics of a technique. His patience was infinite for those who made an effort. A question crossed my mind.

"Master, do the people who teach martial arts without explaining why they do a technique a certain way actually know the reason themselves?"

After asking this, I was afraid to put him in an embarrassing situation because he was friends with many teachers of different styles, but as always, he said what he had in mind, he was not afraid of words.

"Unfortunately, the reality is that too many of them merely retransmit their knowledge without really understanding the mechanics behind it. If they tell you that you are not ready to understand without giving you any explanation, they probably just do not know the answer. In many cases, these teachers will render themselves inaccessible to their students. They will surround themselves with an aura that will ensure that no one will dare to ask them anything."

"How is it that in most cases, they have so many students? They are often popular and highly sought," I said.

I thought of some teachers who were more than incompetent and still managed to find enough students and have well-established businesses.

"Studies have shown that in society, people who are most successful are those who talk the most and who are good liars. You meet a lot of people with this type of personality in martial arts. We are far from the days when transmitting traditions inherited was a vocation rather than a business."

"But then why do federations tolerate such teachers?" Asked a woman in her forties.

"Usually those who are the heads of well-structured international organizations, or federations, are too remote to be able to see what is really happening. In reality, it is up to the student to ask the right questions. Why did I choose this school or this teacher over another? Is he is competent or not? Do I rely more on the spectacular aspect rather than true effectiveness? We all have the instructor we deserve."

I thought about the first time I had set foot in a karate class. The simple fact of seeing people wearing a black belt was enough to impress me. How could I, at the time, have dared to doubt anyone with this rank? I decided to share my thoughts with my master.

"When we start off in martial arts, it is unclear whether someone is competent or not. We do not have enough experience to judge," I said.

"This is why we must ask many questions. We do not select a master on his ability to make demonstrations, but the relevance of the things he says. We should never blindly trust a teacher, we must judge, evaluate and see if what he is transmitting makes sense. We must not be blinded by the cinematic look of movements. We must try to see the realism in the techniques. If I block a knife attack, but the attacker can easily hit me on the temple with his other hand, then I should ask myself some serious questions. We don't need to be a master to find such weaknesses, it is only a matter of common sense."

"It might also be a good thing if the instructors asked themselves these questions too," I added.

"Unfortunately, not everyone is ready to make the necessary efforts to improve. In many cases, the act of a good self-examination involves rejecting the martial art style in which we have invested a considerable amount of time. To question ourselves requires a lot of courage."

"You told us just now not to believe our teachers, does that apply to you too?" Asked the same woman.

"That goes for all teachers, including me. When I demonstrate a technique, I do it with a partner that has parameters that are personal to him. I act taking into account his size, strength, flexibility, the overall body he has. What works with him will not necessarily work with someone of a different stature. We must learn to adapt our response according to each opponent. What is true for one is not necessarily true for another."

The master had just raised a good point. The same technique can not be used on all opponents. A person under the influence of drugs will not offer the same resistance as someone sober. We must consider these factors in martial arts. In most cases, a woman does not have the power of a man and the latter is disadvantaged by a higher center of gravity. There are so many parameters involved that makes each confrontation unique. The master resumed his explanation.

"Not believing your teacher forces you to understand the mechanics of a gesture or strike. This way of thinking forces you to see the before, during, and after the move. A fight is a game of chess where you must learn to place your pieces in order to trap the opponent. Only fanatics have absolute faith," said the old man.

"At what point should we use the word why?" Asked another student.

"At any time," replied the old master, "every movement, every angle, every look, you have to ask the question."

He asked the student to hit him. When the fist came, he moved to the side, resting his left hand under the right elbow of the attacker.

"Why did I place myself here?" The old man asked the group.

"To avoid getting hit," someone called out.

"I could position myself anywhere outside the path of the fist and I would not have been affected. The question is why am I here rather than somewhere else?"

"Because you control the balance of your opponent if he tries to attack you a second time," I said.

"That's right," he said.

He asked the student to hit with his other fist. When he tried to reach him, the master pushed on the elbow which brought his attacker to lose stability. The master then pressed the corner of the student's eye with his right index, forcing him to fall on the floor. The battle had been won with his fingertips.

"Now you understand why it's so important to ask questions."

Chapter 9
The serenity of the earth

The small *dojo* was crowded. People generally behaved in a civilized manner even in these circumstances. Of course there are always exceptions. That day, the exception took the form of a tall blond man who did not hesitate to occupy more space than was actually available. He threw his training companion as if they had the *dojo* to themselves. The moment a foot grazed my head, I asked the two men to be careful, to slow the pace. The calm did not last more than ten minutes. Another student got violently hit in the back. The blond man was visibly the guilty one, his partner merely suffered his assaults. He was a danger to all who stood around him.

"Hey! Try to mind your surroundings," I did not feel like getting kicked in the face.

The troublemaker turned his head towards me with raised eyebrows. He looked at me with contempt. My partner asked if it was his first visit to Japan. He retorted with an insulted air that no, it was not his first time. His arrogance made me angry. I could not contain myself.

"Do you act like that because you're stupid or you're just you're not intelligent?" I asked him.

"I'm not stupid," he replied in a tone which denoted frustration.

Then suddenly, he realized the trap of my question. His face turned red, he shrugged advancing towards me, and then he turned back. He went and stood in a corner of the room and remained quiet until the end of the class. Before leaving, his partner came to me to apologize. He did not know this man, but he was the only person that was available to train.

On the way back, the master mentioned what had happened.

"I saw that you put another student in his place, you did well. It was not proper martial training, he was simply trying to prove how good he was. However, I'm a little disappointed in you."

I expected anything but to hear that.

"What did I do? You just said I had done well."

"For that, yes, you made the right decision, but I'm talking about your state of mind at the time. I thought I felt anger emanating from you. If he had continued to advance, I feel you would have jumped on him."

"I admit that he enraged me a little. I was ready to defend myself, that's all."

"Defending yourself is one thing, being angry is another. I think it's time we talked about how to manage emotions related to the earth element."

Of course, I knew that in traditional martial arts, elements were often used to demonstrate various ways to move. It was sort of an instruction manual to determine the type of energy to apply. Although in this context, I did not see the connection with my altercation. We had just arrived at his house, and he invited me in. Usually, when he was home, he left the door unlocked, open to all. This time he turned the lock, thus ensuring absolute tranquility. We sat on the floor in the tiny cluttered room that served as his living room. I sat near the old TV that was from the pre-digital era.

"Look at my fingers and place them in the same way," he instructed.

In each hand, I pressed my little finger against the tip of my thumb, forming what he called an earth ring. I knew that for meditation we created a similar shape with the thumb and index. Subsequently, I learned that it represented the air element. In this configuration, the little finger represents earth. Each finger has an element assigned to it, and the thumb completes the lot by representing void. The master made me close my eyes, and after bringing me to take a few deep breaths to relax, he continued with a visualization exercise.

"Concentrate and imagine a tiny pebble in your belly, a few centimeters below your navel. With each breath, look at the small pebble and notice how it gets bigger and bigger. The more it grows, the more your thoughts become stable, immutable. You feel good, completely relaxed."

For several long minutes, he kept repeating the same words, but adding the fact that the rock was growing out of my stomach, I now found myself in the middle of this rock which took the form of a small mountain. He made me aware of the stability of my body. I had the feeling of being more connected to my body as I had ever been. I felt more physically and emotionally stable. My lower stomach gave me the impression of being immutable, and my faith in my abilities brought me a sense of confidence that I had never had before. I could not tell if it was the visualization or if it was he who transmitted me an invisible energy, but something was happening inside me. His voice seemed to be more and more distant. Despite the sense of distance, every word was clear and distinct without giving the impression they were passing by my ear canal.

"Now feel anger, connect yourself to it when it comes to you. Then watch how it plays on your glands, on your emotions."

I thought back about the blond guy shoving everyone around, and I felt my breathing quicken. I realized that my teeth clenched, and my fists wanted to tighten themselves close. I did not let them though, I kept the earth ring that my fingers formed.

"Take that anger and project it through the mountain surrounding you. Let it become the cement that will strengthen the whole structure. Use this emotion in a positive way to reinforce yourself and not to cause harm."

I visualized my anger as a veil which amalgamated the whole structure around me. The veil decomposed into a grey mist that came flowing through the smallest crevices of the rock. I instantly felt a sense of calm and serenity come over me. My own anger brought me peace.

"Now every time you feel anger, you will only have to recreate the earth ring with one of your hands and imagine this mountain for a split second and immediately you will feel in control. Your anger will not control you anymore, it is you who will reign over it."

The master made me visualize the mountain who became smaller and smaller to the point of reverting back to the stone it was at the beginning of the meditation. Then he told me to open my eyes and suggested that I would be completely relaxed, fresh and rested, which was indeed the case. I had the impression of having taken a long nap. Now I understand why he had locked the door. He did not want to be disturbed in the middle of this exercise. Without minding me, he went into the kitchen to boil water for tea.

"You think this will work, I'll be able to control my anger?" I asked, raising my voice to be sure he would hear me despite the noise from the tap.

"Absolutely not."

I thought he hadn't heard me well. I got up to repeat the question. The answer was the same

"But then, why did we do that? We both wasted our time, If I understand correctly."

"Absolutely not. I do not do magic. Such meditation is only an instruction manual. For this to be effective, you must repeat the exercise on your own for three weeks without missing a single day."

"And it will work?"

"That's the time it takes to... um, how shall I put it, reprogram yourself."

I knew that the *ninja* used hypnosis techniques. This art was called *saiminjutsu*. Legend has it that these fierce warriors possessed powers that made them superhuman.

"What we did was an old *ninja* technique, wasn't it?"

"Yes, a warrior can not be effective if he does not have the serenity of the earth. It is this mindset that can allow you to make the right decision when all seems confused. Earth provides confidence and most importantly, it increases our emotional and physical stability."

"I'm not sure I understand what you mean."

"Imagine that you are being pursued by a group of people. It's been a while that they've been after you. You're tired, your energy is at its lowest. You find a hiding place, but you know it will protect you only for a certain time. You feel yourself panicked, you're not thinking clearly. In your shelter you position your hands to form the earth ring. Right away, you find yourself a little quieter. Your breathing slows down and you realize that you no longer perceive the situation the same way, from the same angle. You discover possibilities of escape and even counterattacks you did not see a minute ago. Once you have acquired the ability to reach this mental state quickly, you can use it in such contexts. It helps clear your mind when all is chaos and confusion."

"Maybe it can help in many situations, but if there is nothing we can do, if there exists no solution to bail us out, I do not think it can be of any use to us."

"Think again. It will make you face death with greater serenity."

Chapter 10
The Warrior

This class took place a few months before I dared ask the master to become his disciple. That day, there were a lot of us training in the *dojo*. During the break, Master seemed to talk about everything and nothing. The conversation turned to what martial arts could bring.

"They do not only serve as a way to defend ourselves," said the old man, "they teach us how to live, a way to manage our emotions, especially when they are at their lowest and at their highest."

"The way of the just middle," the immature *budoka* I was at the time shyly said. The master looked at me, approving with a shaking of the head and continued.

"We are a whole. It is important to be able to defend our physical shell, but we must also know how to preserve our spirit from decay, despair, and vanity. The practitioner of martial arts must learn to know his own strengths and weaknesses."

A new student raised his hand.

"What do you mean by protecting own mind from all of that?"

"When our living conditions change, it can affect our temperament in various ways. Sometimes for the better and occasionally for the worse, it depends. Regardless of these changes, you should remain aware. If you become more stable monetarily, you probably will not look at poor people in the same way. Priorities will change, they will follow your new lifestyle. You will do everything possible not to lose that hard-earned comfort. You will probably try to stay away from these underprivileged people you used to frequently come across. The opposite is true if you become poor, it may be that you will blame society, that you will see wealthy people as your enemy. The martial way should help you overcome these obstacles that lead to enlightenment."

Before moving on, the master paused as if to make sure we understood what he meant.

"Budo is beyond the world of men. Its mission is to seek the divine that is in each of us."

At that time, I was not ready for that kind of talk. The old man must have noticed my little sarcastic smile. He did not seem preoccupied with it, at least that's what I thought. He continued.

"For the simple-minded, the concept of the divine can be difficult to accept. But do not worry, the more you sink into the path of *budo*, the more you will discover what the divine is. Of course, this can only be done with real traditional martial arts, it is a different story from modern combat sports."

The master seemed like he was reflecting on something, then went on.

"Although, it may happen that some athletes become aware of the divine inside of them," the old man gave the impression of examining us with his eyes.

Then, realizing he had forgotten to say something, he jumped to the next point.

"Be careful not to mix a Judaeo-Christian God with the concept of the divine in the orient. It is not at all the same thing."

He did not go on further into the subject.

"Without this level of spirituality, it is difficult to fight a multitude of people simultaneously. This aspect of God gives us the ability to read in the heart of the enemy. It allows us to know ourselves better and to seek the necessary energy to fight."

"Are there different kinds of warriors?" Asked the same student.

Fortunately for me, I did not open my mouth. At that time, the image I had was based on Rambo and Chuck Norris. For this reason, I found the question simplistic. After listening to the master, it is I who felt stupid.

"That is a very pertinent question," replied the master, looking at me as if he could read my mind. "Indeed, there are several kinds. The question we must ask is: What is a warrior?"

This time, I could not help but give my opinion.

"Soldiers, men in the special forces, guys like Rambo are good examples of warriors."

"You're quite right," said the old man.

I was particularly proud of my answer. I thought I was well placed to know what a warrior was. It must be said that at that time I was convinced I was one myself.

"Sure, they could represent that, but that is not the only category. The warrior is not one who fights. It is someone that protects. It is someone who gave himself the task to protect his family, his village, his country. It is someone who is ready to sacrifice his life for others. In addition, a warrior can use anything other than a gun or a knife as a weapon. The pen is a formidable tool in the hands of someone clever. The journalist or blogger who denounces injustice knowing that he will probably end up in jail is a warrior. He knows that every word he writes on paper is likely to be condemned. Despite these risks, he goes to the end of his convictions."

I had never thought of it that way, it takes a lot of courage to face a government or large companies. Several people have had their lives destroyed fighting uneven forces. The old master did not give me time to meditate on the subject.

"A mother who fights for the welfare of her children is a warrior. She will sacrifice herself without hesitation so that her offspring can thrive, and even in some cases fight for them to simply survive. Simply acting becomes the tool she uses. She works without complaining, sometimes confronting obstacles that many men would not be able to overcome. Discouragement is often part of her daily cycle. But there is something divine in her that makes it so she is ready to fight to the end."

During these early years with the master, I would never have thought to put a mother in the category of warrior. It is true that life itself is a long struggle. The master went on with his reflections.

"How many people have joined forces to preserve the survival of various charities? Others met to ensure the maintenance of sports teams for young people or for the rehabilitation of a certain historical monument. All these people are fighting for a cause, they have a purpose. The warrior is someone who gives himself a goal. Their weapon is effort. They solicit, account for, educate in difficult conditions."

Hearing this, I thought I personally would not give them the title of warrior. It took me a long time to accept that fact. The master continued his talk.

"The greatest warriors are not always those who fight on the battlefield. They are often found among the most peaceful people. Who can claim to be more of a warrior than a man like the Dalai Lama? I think it is the best example we can give when we speak of the divine itself. The weapon he uses is peace. It is such an effective weapon that he managed to inconvenience and embarrass a country as powerful as China."

"How do we know if we are a warrior?" Asked a student.

"It is not necessarily fighting that makes us a warrior. Many soldiers do it for the salary or because they do not have a choice. How many of them joined the army because they had found no better job elsewhere? Not all soldiers are warriors. We can effectively fight and not be tied to the divine. You know that you are a warrior when you have a purpose, a job to do and that the divine comes to you. When all the conditions are there, we no longer have doubts, we know why we are there. We do not just think we are there for the safety of our fellow human beings, we know it. Never forget, a warrior is a protector. He devotes his energy into protecting. When you know you are helping the welfare of someone else, only then you start walking in the path of the warrior."

Chapter 11
Question of reflex

I have always regretted not having properly taken any notes when these lessons were given. If I remember correctly, at that time, Master had just passed the seventy year-old mark. His martial ability was increasing. One would think that with age, his reflexes would decline, but that day he proved me wrong in a beautiful way. We were on a break. The master stood up and took his last sip of tea. We were in the *dojo* for a group training.

"What you see here is more than just a cup of tea. It is a formidable weapon in the hands of someone who knows how to use it," he said.

I could not tell if he was joking or if he was serious. Looking at him like that in the middle of the room, holding a small cup of fine English porcelain between his fingers, there was nothing terrifying about that.

"Attack me," I was ordered.

Without hesitation, I rushed over to him, trying to reach him with my right fist. He then placed the empty cup before my fist and redirected it to the side. Instead of following his face, my knuckles stupidly pointed to the object he was holding. With his other hand, he pressed his fingers into my eyes and led me to the ground with one hand.

"What happened to you? Why have you tried to assault this poor cup?" He asked.

"I have no idea what happened. When you put the cup in front of me, it became my target even though I was asking myself what I was doing."

"That's right and quite normal. There was a substitution. Old and experienced martial artists are familiar with this phenomenon. If you change a target at the right time in the right space, the attacker will look for a new target. Hit me again," he ordered.

This time, he just put his hand over his face as a diversion. Once again my fist followed his hand rather than his face. This hesitation lasted only a split second, but it was enough for me to lose the fight.

"What I just did may seem easy, but it requires a lot of precision. Naturally, as a tea cup is quite an unusual object in a confrontation, your subconscious is even more disrupted."

"How does it work?" Asked a friend, "I think it should be easy for the one striking not to be distracted from his target."

"Everything happens in the subconscious. Once it has, how should I say, locked its trajectory onto its target, it no longer makes a difference if we change the objective. It will follow anything that is on the path it has predetermined. It does not notice that the route has changed since a target is always offered. Naturally, it is necessary that the aggressor be in a spirit of real combat. If he gives a punch with no intention, it will be easy for him to make adjustments."

He repeated the demonstration with several people and the result was invariably the same. A stupid idea came to mind. I took an empty cup of tea and when he asked me to attack I threw it at him, thinking that he would catch it. The porcelain object rolled on the mat without breaking.

The master looked at me with raised eyebrows.

"I thought you were going to catch it and forget my fist was coming."

"Ah! I had not noticed you had thrown the cup. What can I say, at my age reflexes are not what they used to be."

I was certain that he possessed superior reflexes and agility when necessary. I do not know why, but I was a little disappointed. Perhaps I had set the bar too high. The master turned away from me and continued his explanations.

"The subconscious enables us to perform actions that can sometimes feel like they are straight out of a science fiction story. For example, the speed with which we perceive movements may differ significantly according to our mood at that moment."

He asked one of my friends to hit me as fast as he could. I had to move forward on the attack by avoiding it at the last second, by gently pulling on his arm to control him. My assailant was standing a little over an arm's length in front of me. Under such conditions, it became almost impossible to avoid his fist. All my attempts resulted in impacts to my stomach. I must say in my defense that Master had chosen someone who was particularly fast.

"That way, you never will avoid it. Hit me," he told my friend.

He stepped forward slightly pushing the opposing arm. How could he achieve this when I couldn't? I conclude that it was a matter of speed and not reflexes. Other students claimed that the attack had taken place with the same velocity.

"Wow! I'm always surprised at how fast you are."

"I'm not fast. I simply have a better view of things, the correct way to perceive what is happening. You see the attack like an obstacle to overcome. I just wait for him, I look forward to it as if I was expecting an old girlfriend to come visit me. Do the same thing, but tell yourself that you are happy about the attack, you're ready and it'll be nice to welcome it. Do not see it as an enemy but as a friend."

I tried somehow not to put myself in the shoes of someone who was about to take another shot in the belly, but someone who was receiving a gift. I took a deep breath, and then I noticed that my shoulders slightly lowered. I repeated words like, "bring on the punch, I'm ready, I'm waiting for it." My friend jumped at me, I suddenly had the feeling he advanced much more slowly. I put my left hand on his elbow and gently pulled it away from his body. I had passed the test.

"You hit me more slowly, didn't you? I had the impression that your attack was almost lazy."

Everyone assured me that it had not been the case. The assault had been faster than before. I looked at the old master, hoping for some explanation.

"Professional drivers and goalkeepers are familiar with this phenomenon of slow motion vision."

The phrase was well chosen, I really felt that the seconds had stretched. The master went on.

"In martial arts, after a number of years if training was done in the right way, it is quite normal to develop this slowing-up mechanism. If we fear the attack, our muscles are tense. At the time of reacting, you have to release them and then perform the motor action. This process is long and harmful. If you are not afraid of the assault, wait for it with confidence, your muscles will be ready to respond. Your subconscious is already prepared to move. There is no longer the surprise effect that we have when we are tense and fear the fist will come at any moment. The mind must be calm."

The master made us practice this exercise for a long time. Then he continued his explanation.

"Whether it be for a fight or a stressful situation in everyday life, we must learn to face the problem head on. Trying to escape it only increases stress and makes us less effective. It is here that the *bushido* code is important. We must be prepared to face an assailant without fear of the consequences or death. We must look reality in the face and accept it. Escape is unworthy. However, be careful not to mix strategic retreat with disarray," added the old man, laughing.

He then had us do another exercise where we did not look at the opponent directly. We had to look at a point on the ground to the right of the attacker's feet. The result was even more amazing. We had the impression the action was taking place very slowly. The more I repeated the phrases to myself, the more I felt calm, in control of the situation. I never would have thought of fighting without looking at the opponent's chest or eyes. And even then, it was only when we were sure of ourselves that looking into the eyes did not intimidate us. To be sure I understood well, the master had me stand at a distance where he could hit me on the head. Whenever I met his eyes, he easily managed to come hit me on top of the skull, whereas when my gaze pointed to his chest, I managed to block his hit. He explained that a brief glance between two people was a form of psychological battle and by the time our eyes detached themselves, it was too late to react.

"If you have studied hypnosis, or if you have a relationship that puts you at a psychological advantage over your opponent, the latter will be unable to react quickly enough to avoid your attack when looking into your eyes."

He concluded his lesson after showing us how we must look an opponent in the eye if we want to turn that to our advantage. It was simple, and terribly effective.

The class had ended for some time and no one seemed to want to leave the *dojo*. A student holding a tray of teacups approached us. When he came up to the master, one of the practitioners I did not know made a sudden movement and bumped into the student as he presented a cup to the old man. I saw the cup slip from his hands and fall over, the liquid heading straight to the ground. What happened thereafter will always remain etched in my memory. The master grabbed the teacup in flight and descended rapidly to recover the hot tea before it hit the ground. Then he bowed his head in token of thanks and sipped slowly on the amber liquid.

Chapter 12
Henka

A martial art that does not use *henka* is not alive. Variations are part of life. We must learn to react to changes. For many people, a simple change of habits is a source of fear and uncertainty. This can be daunting, sad, or sometimes scary. Budo is life. Adjustments are inevitable. When we accept to face these changes, they can become exciting, joyful and pleasant.

The master was answering a question asked by a student about *henka*, these technical changes he liked so much.

"Like life, an attack rarely happens like you expect it to. If we resist change, it will take a different path to bypass us. To adapt and understand how to use what is present is by far the best option we have to survive without really sustaining any damage."

I did not know whether he was referring to martial arts or life in general.

"Denying adapting is to impose rigidity, intransigence. We have learned from the past and on this basis we are building for the future. We accommodate ourselves to change, ensuring we evolve healthily. The past gives us the foundation to create our future. Contrary to being rigid, we must be flexible. We must not hesitate to transform our assets based on current needs. Everything happens in cycles in life. We are born, become ill, we heal, we grow old and die. The climate varies, the seasons pass. Everything is changing. We have to live with these changes. Agreeing to change our views and our philosophy is not a sign of weakness but of strength. We must consent to detach ourselves from our ego to not have to prove anything to anyone."

The original question was simple. Can we adapt a defensive technique if necessary? In most schools, practitioners are taught to use the techniques taught in an integral manner. The technique is done one way and we should not question it. The master did not hesitate to change the structure of the defense. I decided to try to stir the topic back to variations in martial arts.

"Of course, we must not neglect the basics. I think they are necessary in order to understand what we do."

"You're absolutely right. The basics are the way we play musical notes. If a note is off, the whole work will be tainted. Far too many people make changes because they are unable to execute the basics correctly. They flee their incompetence by making others believe they are creative. Do not confuse change and escape. Many people will run rather than try to adapt to a difficult situation."

Again he was drifting between martial arts and everyday life. The thought I had in mind at that time was simple. As he had said, *budo* is life. The master continued on the topic.

"Too often do we want to show how strong and powerful we are. There are situations where gentleness is preferable to brute force. We must learn to see what needs to be done in the present moment and not go after what we want to do."

"How do we know when the technique must be modified in a fight? What that tells us that this change will be good?" Asked a Brazilian friend.

"All this comes with experience, gradually over the years. We do not change things for fun, we do it when necessary. We must keep a common thread with the past which is the guarantor of our future. If the enemy attacks us in a way we have never seen before, we should not resist this change, we must adapt. We must start from what is already known and has proven itself and acclimate to our needs of the moment. Acceptance is the key to success. If you hesitate, if you feel sorry about what happens, you will lose. You must abandon the idea of wanting to control everything immediately. We must take a step back to avoid being hit, then apply a technique or its variation which will lead to victory."

Looking at the other students, I saw that I was not the only one who was confused. The master seemed to notice that we were all a bit lost.

"For years, you were trained to punch hard. You have hardened your knuckles to the point where you can break bricks. But your attacker under the influence of drugs, does not feel anything. You feel like you're hitting a punching bag. If you have never been trained in the idea to adapt yourself, you will probably continue to try to hit your opponent until one of you wins the fight. But if your sense of adaptation is present, you will simply put a finger in his eye. If it does not work, then you will go to the other eye, then you will turn your back and leave the premises. Your survival will be ensured and he will no longer attack. Whether it be in a fight or in life, one must learn to adjust, to make concessions."

"I do not see what concession was made here. Poking the eyes out of someone, that gives me chills," said another student.

"If it is a matter of survival, we must do what is necessary. You do not want to mutilate your attacker, you simply want to live without being disabled or having permanent damage. We must learn to be able to turn in all directions to get to this goal. You will have to concede everything your moral principles prevented you use before. You always have a choice: die or adapt."

Chapter 13

Upstream

At the time, my personality and way of thinking were quite different from what they are now. I was young and imbued with my person. I thought I deserved the best education and to achieve this I had made many sacrifices. I had finally found the ideal teacher. I did not, however, imagine that the person who agreed to take me as a disciple would teach me other things than martial arts. He had repeatedly attacked my personality. I understood much later that psychology and *budo* are intertwined.

That day, the master had returned empty-handed from a visit to a well-known antiques dealer. We were walking in Yoyogi Park where some discordant music reached our ears.

"Let's go take a look," he said.

"At what?"

"At the Rockabilly dancers."

I had heard of them, but I had never seen them in person. A group of people dressed in leather jackets sporting retro haircuts from the sixties and seventies waddled to the sound of old American songs, each one catchier than each other. The spring sun did not manage to evaporate the drops of sweat that their contortions engendered. Many tourists took the opportunity to join them and take pictures.

"Wow! What a strange way to have fun!"

"You think it's probably a waste of time, right?"

I dared not confess what was going on in my mind.

"Well, to be honest, I guess there are better things to do. Showing off is not my forte. I think it looks..."

"What makes you think they don't think the same way about martial arts? Have you never done any public demonstrations?" He asked me.

"Yes, of course, but it's different. Martial arts are way smarter than that dancing is. It is not by fluttering this way they will know how to defend themselves."

"So, you train martial arts only for your safety?"

"No, I also do it because I like it. It's fascinating to practice a discipline which I can learn my whole life," I was sure I had won here.

"They are doing this because they get pleasure from it. Look how they seem to feel good about themselves. They are happy to wear these clothes, they become those people from another era. You condemn them without even knowing their motivations. You judge them on their appearance, their hairstyles, and dance they perform. You have the same problem when you train."

"What problem? I don't have a problem!"

"Yes, you judge quickly without understanding. You do not take the time to analyze. You want results immediately, but you do not see the big picture. You criticize without compassion and your lack of empathy prevents you from being effective."

Crushing me didn't bother the old man. At that time, I must admit that I was frustrated. I dared not reply, because I wanted to continue to train and access his knowledge. I took a deep breath before opening my mouth. Turning my head in his direction, I met his eyes that stared at me without blinking, eyes filled with a burning fire.

"Perhaps you're right. I am occasionally too quick to respond and judge."

"Occasionally?" He said with a smile.

Watching him smile, I felt some of my stress leave me. I finally left the slippery slope I had made without realizing it. The master was amused to see these young people dancing to a tune catchier than the previous one.

"I agree with you, martial arts are, say, more beneficial in the long term. But not everyone loves *budo*. Look at the situation from a different perspective. Those people could, like a big part of the planet does, sit at a computer and play video games all day. But instead of that, they move, they get exercise. You think they would be less weird if they kicked a ball around, for example? It is sometimes difficult to find vacant land to practice these sports. Many sports require a lot of money if you wish to advance to the next level. While waddling, as you say so well, requires little space. And between you and me, the cardio work they do is very demanding. As a bonus, music purifies the soul and they are pleasant to look at."

I thought he was talking more about stress relief than about esoteric things. With him, you never knew which way to turn. Thinking about it, I felt less ridiculous seeing these people dancing to an Elvis song. A question suddenly came to me.

"You said that I had the same problem with martial arts. What did you mean by that?"

"You're still in an action-reaction mode. You never see the big picture. We give you a punch and you block without taking into account what came before and what will come after. In a confrontation, there is always an upstream, the chain of events that led to the fight. Here with these young people, the upstream I am referring to is their past, what brought them where they are today; Rockabilly dancers, and not martial artists. You have judged them on what they are doing, ignoring what led them there. Tell me, in your opinion, when does a fight start?"

I was about to respond quickly because I was convinced that the answer was simple, but with him, nothing was ever as clear as it seemed.

"A fight starts when the enemy attacks us. If he punches, we must defend ourselves."

"What seems obvious to most people is not for a warrior. A confrontation begins well before that. If it is someone he meets on a regular basis, the warrior will probably notice the change in the state of mind of that person. He will attempt to coax the situation even before it begins. Once again we come back to *ishiki*, awareness, the recognition of the reality of all that surrounds us."

"Yes, but if it's someone we do not know, as is often the case in bars, it will be difficult to predict what will happen."

"There still is an upstream before a fight. In a bar, a good doorman knows instinctively who will cause trouble that evening. He will keep an eye on these people; he has experienced facing these types of people before. He must anticipate when the provoking will start or the small gesture that will trigger hostility. If he can not avoid the escalation of the conflict, he will position himself quickly in a way to control the customers without maiming anyone in the process. But before having to be physical, he will try to defuse the situation through words. There is always a before, a during, and an after."

At this time in my life, I knew that each fight was a game of chess, but I was far from suspecting that we could predict almost the entire game. Unfortunately, at that time, what I thought was a solid base of martial arts, was actually a frail scaffolding. Being in contact with the old master, I realized the extent of my ignorance, and knew it was partly a matter of poor judgment. An image came to mind.

"Yes, but if you walk into an alley and someone attacks you from behind, there is no more upstream."

"There is always an upstream. There is more risk at night than during the day. Isolated areas are more dangerous than crowded ones. There are areas filled with tourists and others that have nothing inviting. All this information is part of the upstream. If you are walking in an alley, you should be aware of everything that moves around you."

"Isn't that paranoia?"

"Yes, if you only focus on the danger. It isn't if inspecting the area becomes a second nature that is done without harming a conversation. I bet you did not notice that one of your comrades has been watching you for several minutes now?"

Looking behind me, I saw a blond man who smiled when our eyes met.

"What does he want? I don't like men."

"You're judging without thinking again," said the master.

The young man came in our direction. He was accompanied by a young Japanese woman. He handed me a leaflet. He was preaching the word of God. I quickly put an end to this situation that I did not particularly like.

"I have never appreciated being approached by anyone."

I turned to the old master, he was gone. My eyes had left him only for a second. I looked towards the crowd but failed to find him. Then, returning to the group of dancers, I saw him holding the hand of a beautiful young rocker who was twisting in the style of the 60's.

Chapter 14
The wrong angle

Years before I even became *deshi*, my teacher's disciple, did his teachings put my training into question. I was in one of the classes he gave to many students, mostly foreigners, and we had to perform an easy technique. Our partner gripped us by the collar with both hands and we simply had to move in a way to keep our partner off balance. I was certain that it would be a breeze. When my partner's hands grabbed me, I took a step back, pulling him forward. I knew that my timing was impeccable. The old master had seen my performance. I watched him with pride, awaiting congratulations, given the precision of my technique.

"Not good," it was the only thing he said. He turned his back and walked over to other students.

"What do you mean, not good? My opponent was destabilized, is not that the goal?"

"You pulled him, but he did not lose his balance. You did not use the right angle."

"I pulled him to tip of the triangle. This is what we need to do, I'm pretty sure of that."

I had known the principle of the triangle for a long time. We only have two support points on the ground. By bringing the body of a person forward or backward in his center, we get a triangle. In this axis, we can force an opponent to redistribute the weight of his body. During this time, a variety of techniques can be performed. The teacher went on.

"First, you used too much force, and secondly, you did not go in the right direction."

"Okay, I admit that I may have used some force. But the direction was perfect. I brought him forward, he had no choice but to take a step to regain his stability. I took him to the tip of his triangle."

"Ah, okay, I understand."

These words did not reassure me.

"So you're still just at that level." He said quietly.

At that time, I still possessed the characteristic arrogance of those who held black belts for many years.

"What do you mean? I did my homework, I couldn't have performed this technique any more precisely."

The old man did not seem taken back by what I said.

"Really, then let's do a little experiment."

He asked my friend to take a strong stance. The latter moved his left leg forward, bent his knees to lower his center of gravity and be more stable.

"Can you pull or bring him to the ground by breaking his stability?"

It is with confidence that I walked up to him and grab his dogi with both hands. I felt the fabric of the garment distend from his body, and my partner's strength forced me to work a little harder with both hands. Finally, he had no choice but to move his front leg to compensate. I clung to him even stronger and turning my body, I finally managed to take him down to one knee. I was proud of my success.

"You see, I did not use too much force," I said looking at the teacher in the eyes.

"You said too much force. The word too is connected to the misuse of the angle of his legs."

"My direction was correct, I pulled him towards the tip of his triangle, I'm sure."

"This is what was your mistake was. You paid too much attention to his feet, you did not notice that his knee was not aligned with his foot."

I did not dare reply to that.

"I'll repeat the experiment with your friend. Look carefully."

My partner positioned himself in the same way. Instead of grabbing with both hands, the teacher grabbed his dogi slightly between his thumb and right index. He gently pulled him to a slightly offset angle of the tip of the triangle. Immediately, the shoulders of his guinea pig rose, his pelvis slightly changed direction making him lean closer to the ground, my friend quickly fell forward, without having the time to be able to regain his balance as he had done with me. All this had been achieved with the teacher's fingertips.

"What you did was good, but you should be able to do better. A human body is a structure of high-precision. You see his legs like two straight segments which link the trunk to the floor. The angle of the knees and the direction in which they are bent must be taken into account. One must also take into account the angle of the pelvis. And if we go a little further, we must learn to see the angle of the shoulders. The shoulders and neck are excellent indicators of the positioning of an opponent in combat. Neglecting it is a mistake that every beginner makes."

During my meetings with him, I was often pulled back to the beginner level. Although I did not like this tactic, it was necessary to deflate my massive ego. He asked my friend to explain how he felt during this technique.

"It was strange. I felt like I was falling on my own. I did not feel like I was pulled at all. I fell, quite simply, without knowing why."

The teacher resumed his lesson.

"Angles are everywhere in martial arts. Whether it is to help us take the balance of a bigger opponent, or to simply take a safe distance from the attacker faster."

He asked a student to take a training sword and attack him. When the blade came down on his head, the old man moved to his left, stepping back slightly. He asked his attacker to see if the blade could reach him. There was less than one centimeter separating the tip of the sword and the master's body. Far enough not to be touched, had he explained.

"In the body structure itself, there are a multitude of angles. These angles can be used to weaken the whole framework of an opponent. Furthermore, as you probably just saw, you can offset the need for speed through proper management of movements."

At the time, I had not paid attention, but indeed, he had moved slowly without rushing. He asked me to hit him. I took an aggressive posture and I advanced my right leg throwing my fist at his face. He pulled back leaving my line of attack, and then he put his hand over my fist, barely touching it.

"Try another attack," he requested.

I attacked again with a straight punch from my other fist, but instead of pursuing its path, my body was deported to my left, I could not do anything about it. It was impossible for me to reach my master.

"How... how did you do that?"

I did not understand why my attack could not reach him.

"It's simple, I changed the angle of rotation of your fist, which affected your whole structure."

"But I did not feel anything."

"The change was too subtle for you to notice."

He made me repeat the same exercise, but this time, he showed me how he slightly rotated my wrist with his fingertips. When I gave the second punch, he only had to pull my arm to his right to twist my body in another direction.

"It's like magic," I said enthusiastically.

"No, it is mechanical, or rather biomechanical. When we know the human body, we understand how malleable it is and how we can modify sections to get to manipulate it easily."

These few hours of training had been decisive for me. I came to realize that my knowledge was extremely far from his. Towards the end of the class, when I tried to hit him, he made sure that I found myself kneeling on the ground, hands resting on the mat. Whenever I tried to regain my position, he applied pressure with his fingertips on different parts of my body. Each of these contacts broke my balance dramatically. I was unable to get up. He was just changing the angle of one of my hips or forearm to create a new loss of balance. Whenever I compensated to regain control of the situation, pressure on another part of my body brought me back to a state of imbalance. Finally, he stopped playing with me. When I was getting up, a friend came up to me.

"It's obvious that with such light contact you were faking not being able to get up."

I was aware that if we had filmed the class and someone had watched the video in a different context, I would have looked like someone who was in league with the teacher, but it was not so, I was simply unable to get up, deprived of solid ground to grab on to. The master spoke again.

"In martial arts, as in the problems one can encounter in everyday life, we tend to seek more obvious solutions, bigger ones, neglecting paying attention to detail. One should not use a plane when a fine sandpaper can do the job with a better finish. Learning to see the angles is a must when you want to reach a higher level of *budo*."

Chapter 15
Relevant arguments

The world of martial arts is fascinating. There are few disciplines that allow us to evolve throughout our lives. In most sports, we reach our level of competence fairly quickly, or should I say incompetence. The following discussion took place during my second year of training with the old master. Autumn had cast its colors for a few weeks already. At that time, I considered myself a good "breaker". I had broken many boards, concrete slabs and even blocks used for construction. When I talked of my exploits to my teacher, he laughed.

"I'm sure you're a formidable fighter," he said, "all wooden objects must tremble in fear when you're around."

"What, you don't believe me? I really broke all of those things."

"I don't doubt it," he said, displaying a smile that held more compassion than mockery.

Nothing in the world could shake the confidence I had on my ability to give a powerful punch.

"I know it sounds pretentious, but it's true. I managed to break these bricks and these boards. Most people can not do that."

We were walking on a country road. The autumn sun beat on our heads.

"I believe you, it's just that I wonder what relationship there is between your exploits and martial arts. I really can not see it."

"You... you do not understand? Really, you're kidding."

"No, it's just that I do not understand the connection between that and *budo*."

"If you can break concrete easily, you can neutralize an aggressor with much more efficiency."

"Ah! That's what it is about," said the old master, nodding, "I see where you're going with this. You're confusing two things that are completely different."

"I am not mixing anything up, if we can blow up a concrete block, what do you think would happen to an opponent if we hit him with the same force?"

"Not much, in my opinion."

I stared at my teacher blankly. How could he deny something so obvious? For a moment, I began to think that the effects of time were affecting his brain. It could only be that. I remained silent without noticing that he had shifted to a private residence. A beautiful apple tree stood in front of the house. An elderly couple was busy working in the large garden on the side of the tidy house. He went towards the people and bowed. He addressed them in a more formal Japanese which I could not translate completely. Then returned to me.

"These charming people accepted that I use their tree to show you something. Follow me."

The apple tree seemed as old as its owners. Its solid trunk ascended straight up to the first branches that were at the height of my head. Old unhealed wounds showed that it had been regularly carved in order to draw its maximum fruit potential.

"Well, try to break this tree with a punch," He said.

"What? This is a joke, right? Look at the diameter of the trunk, I'll never be able to do that."

"Didn't you tell me you had already managed to break more bricks? It should exceed the diameter of this tree."

I felt driven to a wall. Yet he was right, I had already hit several targets much thicker than that. At that time, my pride often still controlled my logic.

"Well, okay, I'll try. After all, it can not be harder than what I've broken before."

I placed myself in fighting position, I aligned my fist where the tree was less rough. I took several deep breaths and slowly, as if to record the right trajectory in my subconscious, I tapped on the surface of the tree with my fist. Then, releasing a powerful cry, I knocked against the bark with all my strength. The leaves shivered a little to the shock of my knuckles. Two or three apples fell to the ground. Severe pain took hold of my hand. At a moment, one of my joints began to swell, compressing the neighboring knuckles. Looking behind, I saw the elderly couple who sneered at me with my teacher. I had succeeded at understanding a few words.

"He is very young, but I believe with time, he will eventually learn."

"I knew it was impossible," I said, holding my hand.

My jaw was clenched. I watched my master with an insistence that bordered rudeness.

"Then why did you do it?"

"I imagined, well, I was hoping that it could be done. I thought back about the stacks of bricks that I broke during competitions."

"Yes, but your bricks were dry, dry and dead like the boards you broke. This apple tree is alive. This makes a huge difference. The same techniques used to hit bricks, the human body, or a tree like this can not be used."

He walked up to the apple tree, and without taking time to adjust himself, without seeming to make any effort, he smashed into the giant that seemed to shake down to its deepest roots. Most of the fruit fell off and rolled on the ground.

"I did that because this elderly couple told me they wanted to pick the ripest apples. This way, they will not need to climb a ladder to do the picking."

He bowed, saluting the people who thanked him. They bowed repeatedly until we left their property.

"How did you do that? You did not use any force, it's amazing!"

"It's simple, I used a striking technique applicable to the human body and not to concrete."

"I do not understand, why are they so different?"

"What is the percentage of water in a brick?" He asked me.

"I do not know, three or four percent humidity. When breaking them, they must not be wet, otherwise it becomes difficult to break."

"And what is the percentage of water in the human body?" He asked.

"I think I've read that it was around sixty percent, or more."

"So now you see that we can not use the same type of strikes for such different materials."

I had never thought of that. He did not give me time to ponder over this revelation.

"Your strikes can not penetrate good abdominals. Yes, they can cause bruises, succeed in breaking some ribs, but the damage remains fairly superficial. With the technique I used on the tree, we create fluid shock wave."

"What do you mean by that?"

"Imagine throwing a pebble into a pond. At the moment of impact, it will create a small wave that will move water to reach the ledge. Now imagine a big wave, a *tsunami*. The force created can go beyond what lies over the limit of the water. The liquid is not altered in any way. These percussion techniques do the same work on a human body. They pass through the muscles without damaging them directly, and affect the organs inside."

I visualized a tidal wave that smashed houses as if they were children's toys. The old master went on.

"Another important factor to consider is stability. The moment you demolished a brick, it is stable, it will not retreat one millimeter. But if you attack someone, his body will move at the time of impact. Much of the energy of your punch is lost when the body reacts to the movement. The type of percussion that I used can not be applied on an opponent in motion."

From that moment on, under his tutelage, I have completely revised my way of hitting. I worked a long time trying to understand and properly use these techniques. I have not dismissed what I had already acquired with the bricks, I just added one more string to my bow. Several years later, I met a guy who had fun making bets receiving punches to the stomach. His abdominals looked like a concrete wall.

The game was childish. He laid a hundred dollars on the table, you also placed one on the table, and you had the right to punch him in the stomach. If he stepped back from the impact, it was you who pocketed two hundred dollars. People around him told me that he had never lost this challenge.

"I'm taking the bet," I said after he explained the rules of the challenged.

"I am even willing to put a thousand dollars at stake, but I demand one condition before we go on."

Speaking of such a high amount, the man's eyes shone. He must have thought it was his lucky day.

"I wish that before we make the bet, that I do a test with this. I do not want to send you to the hospital."

He looked at me with a confident smirk. His military-style haircut gave him a stern look.

"I want you to press this phone book on your belly to protect yourself from my hit."

He did not take me seriously. He must have found me pretentious and childish, but as the amount was tempting, he accepted the test. The book I had with me was about six to seven centimeters thick. He placed the mass of paper against his stomach. I aligned myself like the old master had taught me and without seeming to make any effort I unfolded my arm by transferring all the weight of my body to the center of the book that folded under the impact.

The man took several steps back and arched his body forward, holding his stomach. His expression had changed. He looked at me like I was the devil himself.

"So, do you still agree to do this little bet with me?" I asked without expressing my joy of having succeeded my demonstration.

"No way I'm trying this without the phone book. I don't know what kind of hit that was, but I want to learn it."

I knew that these techniques were effective, but with this giant, I had found the ideal candidate to validate what my teacher had taught me. There was now no doubt in my mind that there was no connection between breaking a board and hitting a human body.

Chapter 16
Time

The memories are intertwined in my mind, there are so many. The following story took place during the second year the old master accepted me as a disciple. We were training in one of the exterior *dojo* in a secluded location at the foot of a small mountain. I tried to hit him, but as always, my fists were unable to reach their target.

"I admit defeat, you're much too fast for me," I said, lowering my hands.

In a split second, his arm stretched out, hitting the side of my jaw.

"It's not about speed, but time."

The moment I was about to reply, I could not pronounce any words. The blow he had given me had dislocated my jaw. Distraught, I was trying to explain the problem to my teacher who did not seem concerned about me. He continued to speak to me as if nothing had happened.

"Most people are dominated by time. We must learn to use it to our advantage."

The more I tried to speak, the more I panicked. My teacher did not seem worried to see me mouth wide open, inviting all the insects to visit the orifice. In desperation, I grabbed the sleeve of his cardigan and pulled several times to get his attention. He looked at me, laughing.

"What's wrong? Feeling a little uncomfortable? Come here, I'll put that back in place."

A sharp pain pierced my jaw as it was snapped back into its original position.

"Ouch! Why did you do this to me?"

"Do what?" He asked, staring at me as if he did not understand my question. "Oh that! You're talking about your jaw? It was just so that I could speak uninterrupted for while."

I knew his sense of humor was sometimes a bit odd, but he had gone too far. I stroke my face to make sure everything was in order. His remarks on time came to my mind.

"You were talking about time, how can we use it to our advantage? Time is time. We can not control it, its flow is out of our hands."

"Time takes place at the pace you feel it. What goes the fastest? Spending two hours in good company with your friends or attending a boring lecture that lasts the same amount of time?"

"Two hours I'm with my friends. But this is only a perception, time is the same in both cases."

"This is what I'm saying, time does not change. Simply put, your idea of time changes everything."

"So how can it be useful in martial arts?" I asked.

"If several opponents attack you, they will not strike at the same time. The control of time will allow you to see in what order the shots will be coming, and how to avoid them. It is often said that we should not think during a fight. I say otherwise. If you are a good martial artist, you can examine the scene. The time it takes between the first contractions of the muscles and the instant the fist reaches its target is very long."

"This goes against everything I learned. I was always told not to think during a fight."

The old master looked at me and sighed.

"What can I say, some people will never understand *budo*."

"How can we achieve this?"

"Would you like to try an initiatory exercise reserved for the privileged few?"

The word privileged was enough to get me to accept anything.

"Okay, come with me, let's look at what we can do for you."

Without saying a word, the teacher turned onto a footpath towards the foot of the mountain. He progressed at a rapid pace, without answering any of my questions. He left the easy path to sneak into one of the gaps between the wall of trees. Despite his advanced age, I had to run to keep up with him. We walked along a small stream that had crossed our path. I watched the shimmering sun reflects on the surface of the stream. This day could only get better for me. Between two large rocks, I could see water spring from an opening at the foot of the rock wall. The master had to kneel in the water to enter the gap. I hesitated a moment, then also got on all fours to follow him. Inside was a cavity barely a meter high and two meters long. At the bottom of this gallery, the water surged from a sort of funnel that seemed to sink deep within the mountain.

"Go down this hole over a distance of about ten meters. You can not get lost, at some point after the curve, you will not be able to go further. Unless an earthquake has widened the breach," the old master seemed to say to himself.

"Why? What do you want me to do there?"

"It's part of the lesson, you have to stay there at least 24 hours. Give me your watch and your phone."

"I... I do not have them."

The little light that came from the mouth of the cave gave his eyes the air of a demon. His gaze seemed so severe that I had no intention of arguing his command. I had to undergo this initiation.

"When you know that 24 hours have passed, come join me, I will be waiting for you."

"I have to spend all that time in the water? I'll catch my death."

"The worst you'll catch is a child's cold," he said, leaving the scene.

Reluctantly, I began to crawl into the water. The more I sank, the more I scratched my arms along the walls. The road veered to the left cutting the last glimmer of daylight I had left. I never knew that covering a distance of ten meters could seem so long. Bumping my head on the wall told me that I could not go any further. Fortunately for me, the water was not cold. A hot spring somewhere in the mountains controlled the temperature of the water. The warmth soothed my many scratches.

"Well," I told myself, "It'll be easy, I just have to take this opportunity to do some meditation in this darkness." My eyes were unable to distinguish anything. I breathed out slowly and began to relax every part of my body. My legs were doing rather well until I felt a little animal running across my stomach. Surprised, I tried to drive it away with my hand. Unfortunately, I failed to move my arm. I shouted at the rodent that made off at once. My second attempt at meditation was disturbed by something crawling on my face. I began to realize that it might be the longest 24 hours of my life.

The sound of water I had always found soothing was taunting me. It showed me that time, like this source, continued to flow inexorably. I had the impression that the cave was completely overrun with strange sounds, a multitude of living beings that I could not see. At times, I panicked and wanted to back out of there. A low rumble came into my ear. A slight tremor vibrated the walls between which I was stuck. A weak earthquake so common in this country made me question the need for this test. If everything fell down, no one would ever find me. For hours, I imagined a range of catastrophic scenarios where, inevitably, I could not save myself.

From where I was standing, several hours had passed since the earthquake. I felt strange, like I was in clothing too loose for me. I realized that this impression was not from my clothes, but my skin. I had forgotten the very reason that led me to be in a situation as unreal as this one. Despite my uncomfortable position, I felt an urge to sleep that came over me more and more. It was getting late. I had been there since nine or ten o'clock in the morning. Curiously, I was not hungry. It was more and more difficult to keep my eyelids raised. Was it sleep or loss of consciousness? The water was nearly the same temperature as my body. At times, I felt like an integral part of the cave. Confused images appeared in my mind intermittently.

I do not know how long I slept, but as I opened my eyes, I felt energized like I hadn't been in a long time. Maybe it was the energy of the water, I do not know. I had the impression of having slept for hours. Outside, morning should have come a while ago already. The idea of leaving this place delighted me. Before falling asleep, I had recognized the sound of the bats flapping their wings. I was hoping not to come into contact with their highly toxic excrement.

My assessment of the time was telling me it would soon be time for me to exit this trap. It's crazy everything we can think about in one day's time. We never take enough time to be alone with ourselves. I loved the experience of being thus isolated, with nothing from the outside that can disturb me. My mind was strangely clear. I had the sensation of being able to see behind the images that appeared in my mind, as if they were three-dimensional, as if hiding something else. The sounds came to my ears vividly. I seemed to hear them before they even occurred.

Leaving the narrow place was more difficult than I had anticipated. My body seemed to have increased in size. With painful effort I managed to move back to the main cave. The small entrance cast a blinding light. I remained there a few minutes to let my eyes get used to it. Then I crawled out to join the outside world.

"There you are," said a familiar voice.

"You came to make sure I was okay. That's nice of you."

"I never left," said the old master.

"What? You spent the night here?" I was moved thinking he had remained with me all this time, he watched over my safety.

"How long do you think you were here?" He asked me.

"Just over 24 hours. I must have broken some kind of record," I said proudly.

"Your number is almost good. You only have to remove the two and you have the time you stayed underground."

I was not sure I understood.

"You mean I stayed there 22 hours?"

"No, only four hours. Do you think I would have stayed here waiting for you if I thought you'd remained there all day?"

"I-I got the impression it was longer than that."

"Now perhaps you will understand how time works a little better." The more he spoke, the more I felt lost.

"Why did you make me undergo this test?"

"This experience has many levels. This is a step a true disciple must go through. It tests the trust that unites a master and his disciple, and brings down the barriers that prevent certain kinds of reflections."

I thought back at the memories and images I had seen, and had the feeling I could dig further into these visions.

"I thought you had me go through that in relation to the perception of time."

"That's right, but before you see its benefits, it will take more time. Let's just say for now that we have planted a seed that will grow. Come, let's head back."

"So, you won't tell me more?"
"I'm sorry, I'm hungry. We don't have time for that."

Chapter 17
The killer instinct

Everyone has heard the expression "to have skeletons in his closet." I could not tell if the old master did, but if it was necessary, he probably would not have hesitated to execute anyone. Why am I so convinced? Because it was part of the art he was teaching. One day he told me that if I was not ready to kill, it was useless to continue my training under his supervision. I will never forget how he taught me this lesson.

As we frequently did, we found ourselves in one of the outside *dojo*. That morning, he handed me an eye mask often used on airplanes to help passengers sleep. I took the object and spun it around my index finger with the elastic.

"Oh no, thank you, I got enough rest that night," I said, finding myself funny.

The old master looked at me with a straight face.

"Put it on right now," he replied in a tone that did not allow a single objection.

The moment my sight was blocked, I imagined having to parry his blows without seeing anything. I took a defensive fighting stance, ready to fall at the slightest noise, the smallest air movement. I think I watched too many martial arts films. I remained motionless for what seemed like an eternity, turning my head towards every creak of trees. I think I even tried to dodge a crow screaming in the distance.

"What do I do now?" I asked when I realized that no attack came.

"Come find me here. I will not move as long as you don't come to me," said a voice in the distance.

"How much time do I have to do that?"

No reply came. The old master did not answer my calls.

I began to move slowly. As he had taught me, one hand raised in front of my head protected me from obstacles that could have reached my face and eyes. My other hand, held at the same distance from my body, protected my groin. Both palms were facing me. The first time he had taught me this way of moving, I found this way of placing my hands strange. He explained to me that if my hand touched an electric wire, the shock would push me away, but if my palms were facing forward, my reflex would be to close my hands. Long before this exercise, he had me get used to feeling the attacks of an aggressor with the back of the hands rather than the palms. He told me that every contact with the body of an opponent is an opportunity to collect information. By proceeding in this way, one could feel more intent and the biomechanics of the opponent's body.

I progressed towards the place I thought his voice came from. On a few occasions, branches flayed me. From time to time, I was making unnecessary stops that brought me nothing from a strategic point of view.

"So are you coming or must I go look for you?"

Now I knew exactly the direction to take. I progressed with difficulty. I assumed that he had purposely chosen a tortuous path, in which at every step branches would assault me in attempt to curb my lead. I began to find this little game particularly unpleasant. Playing hide and seek was not the way I imagined my training. I do not know how it happened, but I hit my shin against a stone. Blood was running down my leg, but no way I would stop, he would certainly not allow me.

Naturally, I progressed slowly. I had lost all sense of time. Though I tried to concentrate and use various meditation techniques, nothing worked. It seems that the old master was reading me like an open book.

"You're stopping? That's all it takes for you to give up? Bravo, what a fearsome warrior."

I dared not move or respond. I was content to suffer his provocations. The more he talked, the more I found it difficult to contain my anger. The fact of having no vision exacerbated the effect of his words.

"You are starting to have adequate emotions. Now, channel them into positive energy."

I did not understand what he meant. He had identified my anger, but what did he mean by transforming it into positive energy? His voice was getting closer to me. He was not more than a meter away from me. I expected to be hit at any moment. As I was about to remove my eye mask, he ordered me to keep it on.

"Do you know what the killer instinct is?" He asked me.

"That's what a psychopath feels when he kills someone," I risked an answer.

"No, a psychopath feels nothing. The killer instinct is when the circumstances leave you no choice, you have the courage to eliminate your enemy. But to make the most of it, you have to be able to justify reaching that point."

The fact that I could not see anything made the voice of my teacher resound more than usually. These disturbing words fanned the idea that I could soon get hit.

"You can be the best martial artist in the world with all the knowledge to get out of any attack, but without this instinct, there is a good chance you will lose the fight if the opponent's level is close to yours."

"It is determination," I said.

"It's more than that. Taking someone's life is something sacred, an act that most people are not willing to do. A hard limit to cross. It is not without reason that many soldiers return from war with post-traumatic symptoms."

Protected from any visual distraction, I felt that my mind was clear, but even in this state, I could not understand where he was going with all of this. Did he mean that I had to defend myself as if my last breath depended on it?

"Imagine you are in a fight where the outcome could be fatal. The confrontation started because you tried to seduce the girlfriend of another guy in a bar. You knew very well that by doing so the situation would escalate. The fight took a dramatic turn. Three of his friends joined the attacker. A crowd of people gathered around and you understand that you're going to have to hit in order to injure or even kill. How would you feel in this situation?"

"I... I do not know. All this would have happened because of me. I'm not sure how I would react. But I think fear would give me the energy need to get through."

"It is indeed the case, but try to imagine the emotions you would experience. Fear creates stress and loss of control. That is not the goal of the warrior. Now let's look at another scenario. Three or four adults are beating a girl of twelve years old in an alley. You arrive there and the abusers turn against you. Do you have the same emotions? Will you have the same energy, the same fears?"

I began to see where the old man was going.

"I think I would fight in a more... released state. I would be afraid, but I would be in the right, unlike the other situation."

He did not speak, but I knew he liked my answer.

"This is what separates the warrior from the thugs and lunatics. This energy is one facet of the killer instinct. When the warrior is in the right, that emotion can give him great power. If he fights believing he is in disgrace, in error or in undignified circumstances, this mindset will not come through. Fear will settle in, and in combat, doubt and shame will render him ineffective."

"I know I would react differently in both cases. In the first scenario I would defend myself, and in the second situation I would rescue someone."

"Right. The killer instinct will enable you to use the techniques required to reach victory," said the old master.

I knew he meant something like "even if you are forced to poke out an eye to survive".

"Now you are beginning to understand some of the essence of *budo*."

Closing my eyes helped me better feel my emotions. I could easily distinguish the two emotions generated by these scenarios. The justification was the key to this teaching. Having to fight is sometimes unavoidable, so if a similar situation comes about, I'd rather do it for a noble cause rather than to prove something. My mind was working at high speed to analyze this new information. I do not know how long I remained standing there, lost in thought, at one point the master's voice took me out of this state.

"Come join me and use this killer instinct," a distant voice called to me.

I took several quick breaths. I imagined the scenario with the thugs attacking a young girl. After a few tries, I managed to feel the emotions that I would have in such a situation. I had the feeling that my body was bigger, taller, that my spine stretched higher.

"I think I understand," I cried out unnecessarily.

Instead of progressing slowly step by step as I had done previously, it is with large steps that I plunged into the forest. I had the impression that my hands and my body had become more receptive. At the slightest touch, I knew instinctively how to get around obstacles. I kept walking no matter what. I turned on myself a few times as to dance with obstacles. My feet adapted themselves as soon as a root tried to hinder my mission. I managed to perceive the direction to take to find my master. I was fully determined to complete this quest. I managed to recreate the same energy as when I saw myself defending the girl in the second scenario. An incredible force led me not to give up, to go further. Then I felt I was approaching something alive. It was at that moment the old master spoke to me.

"Well done, you managed to awaken that instinct that all warriors know well. You can now remove your blindfold," said the voice to my left.

I turned towards the master before removing the mask. When the fabric slid across my eyebrows, darkness gave way to a bright light. My mentor had the sun in his back. What I saw was a shadow in front of a fireball, but something stood out of that dark spot. Two small eyes and a forked tongue stood a few centimeters from my nose. My reflex was to take a step back. When I backed up, I felt emptiness under my shoe. The void pulled my body from behind. There was a brief falling sensation accompanied by a "splash". I plunged underwater, then I came back up spitting the liquid that I had swallowed. My teacher had positioned me back to a pond. After I shook my head and opened my eyes, I watched him grin. He had a harmless little snake in his hands. I saw him place the reptile gently back on the ground. A final lesson ended this training with the old sage.

"The killer instinct is something that the warrior has 24 hours a day. You had access to it at some point, but you are far from being able to incorporated it into your daily life."

"If I understand you correctly, we must constantly be on guard?" I said, clinging on a root to join him.

"Yes, you must always be ready to react, but without becoming paranoid. Do you understand?"

"Yes, of course," I said, twisting the bottom of my shirt to let the water out, "from now on, I will always be ready to adapt, no one can get me by surprise."

"I'm glad you understand. Come, let's celebrate," said the master pushing me into the water as I emptied the liquid dripping from one of my shoes.

Chapter 18
Giri

That day was particularly hot and humid. The rainy season, *tsuyu*, was nearly here. My clothes stuck to my skin. I was walking past many salarymen, Japanese office workers. Most had taken their ties off and kept their jackets on their arms or, as many did, folded them neatly into their small briefcases which gave them the appearance of seasoned businessmen.

The old master wanted me to accompany him to one of his friend's antiques shop to look at a rare piece he had found. He told me to meet him at the foot of *Hachiko*, the famous dog statue that took guard of Shibuya. A multitude of people are photographed in front of this icon of fidelity. Arriving early, I took advantage of this moment to observe the thousands of people crossing the most famous intersection of Japan. As soon as the traffic light turned green, a tidal wave of people masked the white lines that paved the street.

"It is always impressive to see this show," my master's familiar voice said.

"The incredible thing is that all these people are moving without knocking each other around, without any tension. Back home, I think there would be daily fights in this environment."

"Why is that? Is it so violent in your home country?" My teacher asked in a puzzled air.

"With the amount of people that cross this intersection, it is impossible that people don't run into each other. In many countries, fights would surely break out. Here, it never happens, or at least very rarely. Why is it that you are so tolerant?"

"Perhaps there remains some *giri* in us," he said.

"*Giri* is the sense of duty and honor the *samurai* had, if I am not mistaken."

"That's right. It is what gives true followers the will to deepen their knowledge of things. Without *giri*, a practitioner of martial arts is limited in his progression."

"I do not see the need for it today. At the time, it was convenient to keep some discipline in the ranks of soldiers. Today, this has become useless."

The old master looked at me and nodded. He cast a glance around him and sat down on a low wall near the statue of *Hachiko*.

"For many people, the sense of duty is the tie that binds one person to another or to a group. It is a motivation to accomplish what must be done. For a soldier, it is to defend his country, and for a firefighter to extinguish a fire, it is the duty of these modern warriors. For the practitioner of martial arts, it's more than that. Whoever has *giri* will be sure to do everything he does perfectly. He will not do it to please others, but because it's part of what he must do."

"I still do not see the relevance to modern martial arts."

The master smiled before interrogating me.

"If I give you a goal and you think: I have achieved this goal, what will you do then?"

"I'll move on with what I'm currently doing to achieve it," I said with some level of embarrassment.

"Precisely what the vast majority of people do, whether it be in martial arts or for their work. Most of them are content with mediocrity. They do not realize they could do better."

I interrupted my teacher.

"Mediocrity? I think you are being a little hard here."

He looked at me without flinching and continued speaking as if I had said nothing.

"One who is inhabited by *giri* knows there is a difference between what is, and what he believes. *Giri* leads us to surpass ourselves, not to be satisfied with what we have. If there is a possibility to do better, we must do so. In what you call modern martial arts, too many people are just collecting techniques. They are convinced that the more *kata* they have, the better they are. They are champions in certain ways to fight. They do not realize that they are totally incompetent outside their area of expertise."

"Does this way of thinking fall within the sense of duty or honor?"

We were there for several minutes and, on some occasions, people passing in front of us stopped and bowed to greet my teacher. He returned the favor by nodding each time. I was surprised to see how famous and respected he was.

"This is where it gets interesting. What differentiates duty and honor?"

He looked at me in silence. Perhaps he hoped for an answer that did not come. He continued.

"Duty is what needs to be done. Honor is the way to do it."

Images of *samurai* committing *seppuku* sprang to my mind. I saw these warriors kneeling and opening their bellies with a sharp knife. He continued his explanation.

"For most people, working is a way to get money to survive and especially to satisfy desires rather than needs. A luxurious car, leisure travels, or the latest cell phone are their main objectives. If with a minimum amount of effort they can access all of this, they will be happy. It is desire, or simply working in order to receive, not *giri*. Whoever has *giri* will try by all means to accomplish their task as perfectly as possible. He will do everything to provide a quality product or service. This is the sense of honor. This is because many people will do anything for the company that hired them to succeed. For honor, they have a duty toward those who trusted them."

"And in martial arts?" I asked, thinking I knew the answer.

"When teaching such a simple technique as moving using the points of the triangle, most people start talking after five minutes. They are convinced they have mastered this movement which seems so easy to do. They never question their competence in the matter. Whoever has *giri* will try by all possible ways to integrate this knowledge in the depths of his body and soul."

I thought it was a bit much. To embed something deep in my soul...

"Sense of duty and honor are unfortunately not taught in most *dojo*. Most students will never be aware of *giri*."

"Here in Japan, people have this moral value, right?" I asked.

The old master turned his head to *Hachiko* and stood silent for what seemed a long time.

"Yes, I think something remains. It's a small part of the legacy of the *samurai*. When a disaster happens, everyone is involved in the reconstruction. They do not expect the government or someone else to do the work for them. It is not uncommon for employees to work overtime without being paid for it. They do it for the company, just the way the *samurai* were acting with their masters."

I felt a certain nostalgia in the voice of the old master. It was the first time during our conversations that he wandered as boldly between martial arts and modern life. As had happened so often, I had the impression he had read my mind.

"Budo is life. We need to project what martial arts teach us into our lives every day. Martial arts should inculcate a code of honor and discipline. In reality, even if a certain... say, ethics is present in many practitioners, I can't say the same about honor."

"What do you mean?"

"Nothing very philosophical. Just that people tend to rush through what they do. Unfortunately, here too, people are beginning to think this way."

"Especially young people, right?" I said staring, waiting for approval.

"Exactly."

"What brought this change in attitude?" I asked.

"Times change. Not so long ago, it was not uncommon to see three or four generations live in the same house. The grandparents took care of the young and transmitted more traditional values. There was a level of respect that we find less and less today. The countryside is underpopulated and in big cities, families are dismembered. People no longer live, they survive. And not to mention the internet that has not helped the cause."

There was increasingly more longing in the air. Obviously, the old master was from another era.

"It's getting late. We have to go see my friend," my teacher said, standing up.

The traffic light had changed to green. No sooner had I set foot on the white line of the street that a strong shoulder slammed into me.

"Idiot! Watch where you're going!" Called an aggressive voice.

Looking back at the person, I saw that I had run into the only Westerner around.

Chapter 19

A brief moment

Training in a *dojo* is not the only way to evolve in the world of *budo*. The true practitioner of martial arts knows that his training is 24 hours a day. Budo is above all a state of mind. Limiting it to simple physical actions is now unthinkable for me, but I certainly would not have said that a few years ago.

My teacher had invited me to eat at a traditional restaurant. The kind of place where tourists would never think to set foot in. The hot sun was not able to remove the moisture that clung our clothes to our skin. Each step that brought me closer to the restaurant made me pray there would be air conditioning.

"Stop complaining. We must learn to live in the present, not to suffer it," said the old master.

"Yes, but we got to admit that this... heaviness is unpleasant."

Curiously, he wasn't bothered by the temperature. Instead, he seemed fresh as if he had just stepped out of the shower.

"It must be because I was born in a colder country," I said to justify my discontent.

"The country is not the problem, it is a matter of attitude."

"Don't tell me my attitude is what's making me sweat so much, while you are fresh as a rose."

"No, it's not just that. There may be a 10% genetic factor, as for the rest, you are just capricious."

"What, so I'm sweating for fun?"

The old master looked at me laughing and pointed at a building on our right. Some kanji adorned the façade. He walked to the curtain that hid an entrance lurking in the shadows. Most people sitting inside seemed to know him. After leaving his shoes at the entrance, he addressed them using formal Japanese. Everyone laughed, saluting me. I do not know if I should run away or laugh with them. A tiny old woman came to bow to my teacher and pointed to a small table in the corner.

I usually managed to read the menu well enough, but here I felt in unfamiliar territory. As I was about to ask him what was written, he told me to leave it up to him, he would choose for us both. Then he began to speak as if he continued an already started conversation.

"In *budo*, it is important to seize the moment. If we do not capture the moment, it will not come back. Of course, a similar experience may come up sooner or later, but it will never be the same."

Naturally, I was totally lost. He frequently spoke like this, as if it were an already initiated dialogue. I waited for him to go on.

"Every moment is an event in itself. The decision or lack thereof can influence the future. It is the same in a confrontation and in life. Each attack requires a decision. It can come from the intellect or instinct."

Finally, I began to have a line of thought. He spoke of combat and that, I could understand. The old lady came to take our order while bringing hot tea.

"Hot tea? Could we have iced tea instead? I feel that the air conditioning is not working."

Master glanced at me sneakily and went on as soon as the waitress was gone.

"The present moment can not escape the laws of physics, but your mind can."

"What physics law are you talking about?"

He replied as if it was an obvious answer.

"I'm talking about time, of course. When you see your opponent's fist heading towards your face, you can not stop time and freeze his punch in mid-air. However, how you're going to perceive this attack will decide how fast you will see it come."

He stopped talking to bring the small cup to his lips. He closed his eyes, letting the amber liquid flow in his mouth. He set the glass down keeping his eyes closed.

"What I just did was training. I captured the moment. I stretched it to savor this moment."

"I think drinking tea is a little less stressful than receiving a punch."

"Yes, but it is the same present moment, the same drop of time is flowing. It all depends on the perception you have at that time. Take a sip, and isolate your mind while doing so."

I brought the cup to my lips and closing my eyes, I let the hot liquid fill my mouth. In a moment I forgot where I was. All my attention was focused on the liquid. Its soft texture slipped on my tongue, the smell tickled my nostrils, and I felt the movement of my throat muscles helping me swallow. There were so many steps involved in taking a simple sip of tea. The most extraordinary thing in this experience was the feeling of freedom and being nowhere that would contradict everything my body was feeling. I seemed to feel the gaze of the old master. Then I put the cup down, opening my eyes.

"Now you understand a little better what the present moment is."

"I have already done this, eating something while appreciating the taste, I mean. But it did not have the same effect as now."

"You did nothing but eat, you were not ready to seize the moment."

"I felt that time stopped, I could stay in this state for hours."

"Capturing the moment is a meditation exercise in itself. But we must be prepared before we can enjoy and reap the benefits."

The lady placed several dishes on the table. My bent legs were not fond of this uncomfortable position. I watched the old master, who like all other people sitting on the ground, seemed relaxed in this position. Once the lady left, he pointed to a dish containing blue jelly.

"Try this, and tell me what you think," he said.

Several heads in the restaurant turned in my direction. My first impression of the jelly was that it did not taste much. Then an unpleasant taste filled mouth. My teacher grinned at me and winced.

"Do not panic, use this opportunity to practice the exercise I just taught you."

Chapter 20

The beginner

I could not really say when we had this conversation, but not so long ago it came back to mind. A memory well hidden that resurfaced for some reason. We were returning from a regular class given to a group of students. I was walking the master home, hoping to absorb some of his wisdom.

"You performed particularly well today. I think that with a little perseverance, you will soon be able to say that you are no longer a novice," he confided to me.

"What, you still consider me a beginner?"

"Hmm ... More like an advanced beginner."

My shoulders were crushed under the weight of those words.

"When I teach a technique, do you understand it correctly after a few minutes of practice?"

"It depends on what you've shown, but generally I'm doing pretty well."

"When training in the *dojo* with other students, does it not frequently happen for you to stop doing a technique and wanting to help your partner and teach him something other than what I showed?"

Something told me that this was a trick question.

"Yes, but this is simply in order to assist my companion. It's always for a noble cause. When I see that he can't do it properly, it is best to help right?"

The old master just smiled. I nervously swallowed my saliva. He continued talking.

"Generally speaking, people change the technique when they do not have the skill to do it as it should be. Doing so, we can miss out on important principles."

Thinking about it, I had changed what he had taught at least twice. I had not noticed that I had changed the technique. Of course, I was careful not to tell him of this fact. The old master continued.

"Fleeing difficulty is not the best way to progress. On the contrary, we must learn to face these obstacles. They are what make us grow the most. It is not uncommon to see slightly more advanced students spend more time trying to correct others rather than training. This is usually related to a self-esteem problem."

Only the sound of our footsteps on the sidewalk broke the silence of this warm summer evening. Down the street, a man walking a brown Labrador walked in our direction. The master leaned forward to pet the animal. He complimented the beast's owner on the beauty and rarity of the breed in Japan. Resuming our journey, the master asked me a question.

"When you practice with other partners, what percentage do you evaluate your concentration level at?"

I was going to say one hundred percent, but it was not true. Ninety percent, maybe, but in all honesty, I think it was less than that. My mind often happened to wander. Less than fifty percent, no, it was certainly more than that.

"Sixty-five or seventy percent," I threw out shyly.

I found the question rather strange.

"Why all these questions?"

"To know what martial arts practitioner class you belong to."

"What? There are categories?"

"Everything in the universe can be classified," he said.

"What are these groups?" I asked, expecting to have an obscure answer I probably would not understand.

"All this is, of course, personal, but the first category is what I call the collector. It is the prerogative of beginners. Some can practice martial arts for fifty years and they will not leave this level. They constantly refer to what they know. If a technique is similar to something they have already seen, they do not notice what is different. For this reason, their minds wander quickly away from what they should be doing."

I saw where he was going with this. As soon as I saw the master teach something that seemed familiar, my attention slackened. Why bother doing what I already knew? My teacher went on.

"This level of learning is related to the intellect. Attempting to reproduce the technique, understanding the theory of movements and the mechanics of the moves. Once that is done, the practitioner of this stage is generally content with that. The more techniques he will have in bank, the more he will believe he is a good martial artist. The collector depends on his partner to train. He lacks the ability to see beyond things. He reacts to his partner's movements without having the competence to anticipate what's next."

I did not feel comfortable listening to this. I had the impression he was talking about me.

"And what kind of person do we find in the second category?" I risked asking.

"We find the assimilator. He who has understood that the technique has much more to teach. That it is not as basic as it seemed at first glance. At this level, he realizes that simply placing a finger differently changes the result of the action. He knows he is far from mastering his art. He will be more focused during classes. He does not spend his time helping his comrades, he will seek to understand and identify the details he has not yet seen. This condition is linked to the body, he knows that his mechanics have faults. He has the ability to work by visualizing the image of an attacker. He may know the result of his technique before experimenting on his partner. He has to be able to execute it properly and develop his vision of various possibilities. He will not be satisfied until his body has assimilated everything. He is not there to look good for his comrades, he is there to learn."

Thinking about it, I could predict the reactions of my partners even before making the sequences. This thought comforted me a little.

"Finally, there is what I call the connector. At this level, the practitioner may enter a trance that is not quite mystical, but allows him to connect with the divine. He has the ability to modify the technique without losing its main essence. This condition is linked to *kokoro*, the heart, his emotions, but it's more than that. He relies only on himself, he does not fight against anyone, he only adapts to what the universe sends him."

"You are in this category, aren't you?"

"I think I can say yes, but believe me, I had to work hard to achieve such results."

"Is it at this stage that you can ask for help from your deceased teachers?"

"No, that can be done at all levels, provided we are sincere in our approach."

When talking about sincerity, I interpreted this as belief, or faith. He continued his explanation.

"At this stage, we need to increase our ability to connect to the opponent, the things around us and emotions that float in the air. When we are in harmony with all that, we do not defend ourselves anymore, we simply find ourselves at the right place executing the appropriate action."

We had just entered a small alley where an impressive number of vending machines offered exotic concoctions. I put money in one of them and when I was about to press the button of a well-known brand of cola, the old master spoke to me.

"Are you sure this is the right action to take?"

Chapter 21
Master in the making

One day, in a class with a group of students, someone asked my teacher if he had always been a martial arts master. The old man smiled at this. That morning, he seemed particularly cheerful.

"No one is born master," he said, amused.

As he was about to grab a sword, I could not help but return to the subject.

"How does one know that he is a martial arts master?" I asked innocently.

He stopped, put his hands on his hips, then turned in our direction. He made us sit on the ground. Slowly, he came to join us. Back straight, legs bent, his posture did not reflect his actual age.

"The question is, what is a martial arts master? Am I a master? I do not know, this is not a title that can be awarded."

"Well, we are giving you the title of master," I said without hesitation.

"It's not that easy. There must be criteria that separate a master from a senior instructor. A master should be different from a teacher. The teacher shows what he has learned. He has codified knowledge that is passed down from generation to generation. The master must be able to evolve the style of the school he teaches, he must have the power to bring his students to progress beyond simple technique."

"What could there be beyond a technique?" Asked a student I did not know.

"The essence of *budo*," the old man replied. "In martial arts as in life, there are different steps that, when completed, make us better people. When this path is presented to us, we must have the ability to see and the courage to take it."

"You are mixing ordinary people and fighters together. Why is that? A master is so far above most people," I commented.

"Because above all, a master is a human being like everyone else. Someone could be a master and not practice any martial art."

He was silent for a moment. I would have had a multitude of questions to ask him, but I knew he was looking for a simple way to make us understand his point of view.

"Let's go back to basics. To be a balanced martial artist, there are three aspects to develop. First, you must make sure you have a powerful body. In most schools, they will make you do an impressive amount of push-ups, sit-ups and various exercises. It will push you to the extreme in order to perform better."

Listening to him speak, I remembered the physical training that I suffered during my martial arts career. The master kept talking.

"Secondly, we develop our speed. To do well in competition, you must be quick. Finally, we will teach you the technique. How to attack, how to block a punch, and arm locks and such. In short, everything concerning hand-hand combat. To visualize this, imagine a triangle where each side represents one of these aspects. At first, all martial arts are focused on these three bases, a powerful physical body, speed, and good technique."

I observed my companions' reactions during this lecture. Most nodded, acknowledging this mode of learning. I had already discussed all of this with him, but hearing it again, I understood the full scope of this teaching better.

"This triangle is that of the student. The beginner. Unfortunately, some practitioners remain novices all their lives. The reality is that from about thirty-five years old, the body is less efficient, speed will decrease and depending on family or professional requirements, we will have less time to devote to the art. In many schools, the skill comes down to an accumulation of knowledge using the memory. As we age, memory tends to go," the master said, laughing.

I recognized myself in this canvas. Around the age of forty, I still practiced other martial arts in parallel. I found it more difficult to do fighting sports with my younger students in their twenties. The body didn't follow as well as it used to.

"This is the same for daily life, is not it?"

I asked this question for the other students' sakes. I already knew the answer.

"Exactly. In your work you need to be fit to excel, you must act quickly to be profitable and you must do the tasks as they should. Here, we find the technical aspect."

I imagined office workers aching, tired, with a bad back from sitting so long. I saw them struggling to focus, accumulating work because this first triangle was lacking. The master did not give me time to deepen my reflection.

"To counteract aging, we must take it up a notch. Attempts to gain speed result in failure, so we compensate with timing. By moving at the right time, there is less need to be fast. The lack of physical performance will be offset by what we might call feeling, or instinct. Relying on our inner voice. The fight does not pass by the intellect but by experience, by intuition, a hunch based on the reality of space, knowledge and current capabilities."

"In everyday life, how could this be translated?" I asked without being fully convinced of the relevance of my question.

"Timing is doing the right things at the right time. In life, one must learn to plan ahead to make up for the lack of speed. We must avoid unnecessary steps and get directly to the point. High skill allows us to get results."

The old master looked at me as if waiting for my approval, and then he continued.

"Physical ability deteriorates with age, it must be offset by precision. If the punches become less powerful and slower, we must decrease the striking surface to get maximum efficiency. We must reach the right places rather than striking on more extended areas. One well-placed *koppo ken* to the temple could result in sending a bigger opponent to the morgue."

A student raised his hand.

"How can we adapt this to everyday life?" He asked in a barely audible voice.

"We must learn to save our energy. Do not sulk over your problems, go directly to the solution. Most of the time, people lose so much energy trying to find the right way to address them. They know the way, but because it scares them, they try to postpone going to it, or they keep looking for other ways, to finally end up returning to the first solution. People procrastinate and the more time passes, the more they get anxious. We must learn not to waste this energy."

At that moment, I saw images of the teacher defending himself against various attacks. He was not fast, but he always managed to counter everything. He kept his movements to the bare minimum, in the right place at the right time. He used his energy perfectly.

"As for technique, it is more difficult to do. We must agree to be guided by instinct. Do not confuse this with doing anything, anyhow, on impulse. It may seem strange, but the special feeling we develop in this case is something almost mathematical. We do what needs to be done and not what we have studied."

I found those words paradoxical. I waited impatiently for the rest.

"Over the years, and with adequate training, we manage to run the right automations at the right time, even with attacks that we have never learned. The feeling is also to be able to improvise using logical parameters. At this point, we do not try to do something, the response is done on its own."

A student intervened.

"*Sensei*, the technique is something that is learned. Once acquired, can we learn more from it?"

"In martial arts, when assimilating a technique, it becomes a specialized tool. The maneuver is done in a particular context. It is a programmed response to a specific attack. The technique used will be different if the attack is done with a punch or with a knife. Each attack has a proper response. This standardization refers to the memory in order to be effective. If you are attacked in a way that you have never learned, searching in your memory to find an adequate response will make you lose precious time. The instinct does not go through the memory, it develops through experience, understanding, and assimilation of the bases."

It intrigued me to see how he could transpose this into daily life. As he had done parallels with daily life and martial arts on other levels, I waited impatiently for what he could say on the subject.

"When you get out of college and start working, there is little chance that you can apply your new-found knowledge as is. The study program was created months or even years before. The standards, the technologies have changed or evolved in real life. If you trust what you have learned without adapting, you're doomed to stagnate at the same position."

I saw the minutes flying by, I wanted more time to dig into the question of what differentiates the master from the teacher.

"Can we further deepen the principle of relying on intuition?" I asked.

"Yes, this is where begins the stage of mastery. We must learn to connect to our opponent and what surrounds us."

I had discussed this with him before, but I never got tired of this subject. Each time, I learned something new.

"This link allows us to know what our opponent will do next. It is a game of chess where we know in advance what will be his next move."

I started telling the other students about a time when we were training with the *bo*, this stick of almost two meters long. A Westerner had gotten angry during the class. The master who was speaking to an old friend of his had his back facing him. The man tried to go around his training partner and was sweeping the air with his stick. He lost control of his weapon which flew behind the master's head. If the stick hit, it would hit very hard. Without turning, the master quickly inclined his body forward to avoid the impact. He cast a quick glance at the man and resumed the conversation with his friend.

"This is a good example of connection, is not it?"

"Yes, that explains it quite well." The old man nodded in agreement.

I understood the difference between a high level teacher and a master. He continued talking about the other aspects.

"We saw that lack of speed is compensated with timing. To do this, we will add the control of time. Of course, I am not talking about time travel. We have to develop the power of slow motion vision. We must learn to see the movements unfold slowly. This way, it becomes easier to respond appropriately. Racers are familiar with this phenomenon. In a fight, if you are stressed, you'll feel all actions will be accelerated. Slow motion vision is only a way of perceiving and analyzing information. With specific training, we can change our method of collecting information and at a more advanced stage, it can cause a person with us to perceive it too, to see actions unfolding slowly."

Time passed quickly. I knew he would soon end the class. I questioned him on the last aspect, and paused for a moment before answering.

"As I mentioned before, our body's lack of capacity is compensated by precision. As for ability, we add the control of energy. This is more psychological than esoteric, of course. We can even affect an opponent to the point where he will doubt himself. At this point, we capture the mind of the attacker, it creates confusion in his mind. We can also move in a way to render the opponent ineffective. Naturally on top of this, we can add the use of *kyusho*. Some of these pressure points cut the motor action of muscles. The opponent can not use certain parts of his body anymore. This is done quite well, it only requires a little practice. The psychological aspect is a little more difficult to affect."

The old master glanced at the clock. The class was over. He offered a final piece of advice.

"Remember one thing. No matter what level you are, there are two secrets to never forget in order to progress."

I must have been undergoing a distortion of time, he did not speak fast enough to my liking, I was eager to hear these revelations.

"The first is consistency. Never stop training. If you can not do it on a regular basis, go to a park, or move the furniture and do some exercises to keep your mind and body alert. And secondly, *ishiki*, be aware of what you are doing. Learn not like robots. Ask yourself questions and do not hesitate to ask for help."

Ishiki, this small word that meant consciousness. The more I progressed in martial arts, and the more I understood its importance. After the end of the class, I told the old master how much that word was important to me.

"That's great. So you're conscious of the fact that the floor needs vacuuming," he said.

Chapter 22
Reading between the lines

We were visiting a calligraphy exhibition in one of the populous districts of Tokyo. I managed well enough to speak Japanese at the time, but as for writing, I was illiterate. Of course, I knew the *katakana* and *hiragana*, these simple phonetic characters created for children or to adapt foreign words, but my ability to read the language stopped there.

Several halls were decorated with dozens of *kakemono*, scrolls hanging on the walls, through which some paintings, *emakimono*, managed to infiltrate themselves, breaking the harmony of the writings. These huge pieces gave me the impression of plunging into a timeless universe. I followed my teacher who was walking from calligraphy to calligraphy.

"It's amazing the amount of talent that can be found here," he said.

"Is it because the characters are well drawn that you think so?"

"Yes, that too, but limiting it to the beauty of the brush strokes is a bit simplistic. It's much more than that, it is in the poetry of words chosen and the way they are arranged and coordinated with the strokes. Each work is a poem, a story, a thought that reflects the human soul."

I loved watching the shapes of Kanji on paper. The object of my admiration was limited more to the aesthetic appearance rather than the poetry. The focus my teacher had admiring one of these works showed that his understanding of these writings differed totally from mine.

"See how the brush work is fluid."

"It looks like water flowing."

The old man turned to me, eyes wide with astonishment.

"You surprise me pleasantly. This poem draws a parallel with life parading as a long quiet river. The words speak, but the brushstrokes also say something. The author has given to each of his strokes the illusion of water that roams to the rhythm of the hourglass."

An elderly woman approached us. She was dressed in a traditional *kimono* adorned with delicate wings of cranes. She spoke to my mentor who bowed respectfully to greet her. I followed them, trying to decipher some words from an old dialect which was no longer used today. They discussed for several minutes before one of the calligraphies. She showed him different Kanji while explaining her choice of characters. A man came and interrupted the conversation, someone was asking for the lady at the entrance.

"It is a poem based on her first and only love," my teacher told me.

"What does it say?"

It intrigued me to see how we could say something so personal with so few characters.

"On your narrow path
two lives have walked a long way
to eternity."

"Wait, that's a *haiku*," I said, a little surprised. I didn't think I would find those here.

"Yes. It is superb. This is Japan, *haiku* are everywhere. There are some engraved on stone in many places," he said.

"You said this was a love story. I see no romance in this poem."

"Really, you must learn to read between the lines. "On your narrow path" says more than enough. The chance that their destinies intersect was minimal. Her husband could have died in the war before marrying her. The mere fact of missing a train could have prevented their meeting."

"Okay, but "two lives have walked a long way", I guess this refers to the years they spent together."

"Yes, but it is not as simple as that. If you look at the features of these Kanji, you see that they are losing some of their fluidity, they become irregular on the word "long". Their existence was not always rosy. They probably had many obstacles they overcame."

"You can tell this by looking brush strokes?"

"The lines are alive. They inspire the rhythm, the speed, and fluidity. By drawing more tremulous lines, the artist expresses the difficulties they encountered."

I never imagined that we could give as much information through the shape of the Kanji. Western writing does not transmit information with the form of the letters.

"The final line means they will always be together," I said.

"Yes, that's right, but if you notice the last brushstroke, it gets thinner and disappears completely, as if the hair on the brush had ran out of ink. That's where her lover died."

"I guess we have to be a calligraphy expert to perceive those things."

"No, we should simply open our heart," he said without looking away from the piece.

"Do all the calligraphies here hide this much emotion in their writing?"

"No, this lady is truly exceptional. She is a great artist, I admire her enormously."

Our tour continued for several hours. Some scrolls, which reached two meters high, were adorned with small characters that covered them entirely. Others showed only two or three characters drawn in a stylized manner that I would have been unable to find in a dictionary.

Yet this did not prevent my guide from reading them. I knew he was highly educated, and that he was obviously a scholar. Before one of the calligraphies, some young Japanese people were trying to understand the meaning of the Kanji without success. My master read it out to them as if it had been in the morning paper.

We arrived before a calligraphy that interested me particularly. A brush stroke had given birth to the character of *katana*. Different Kanji surrounded the blade lying on the parchment paper.

"I see that this one has attracted your attention."

"Is this what I think it is?" I asked, whispering as if the artist's work demanded silence.

"Yes. It is a poem about the *katana*."

"So...?"

"So, what?" My teacher asked, enjoying keeping me on the fence.

"What does it say?"

He laughed and focused on the work as if seeking the best possible interpretation for my limited comprehension.

"Even when the moon is full, its crescent always pierces it."

"What relationship does it have with the *katana*? I see no connection."

"The author has played with words. You know that *tsuki* is an attack with the tip of the sword. The Kanji used here refers to the moon. The two words have the same phonetics. We can only point our gaze towards the moon."

I should have expected something as poetic as this. I was lost, but fortunately for me, he had not finished his explanation.

"In the hollow part of the palm of the hand, there is a crescent shape you use to press against the tip of the handle of the sword. This part of the hand is called *mika*, which is translated by the crescent moon."

"I understand we need the crescent moon for it to become full."

"That's right. The purpose of the *katana* attributes meaning to the writing. One who does not know the sword, renders this calligraphy meaningless. I wonder who has written this. He must be an elderly person. He must have been a weapon master at one time. This makes no sense, the signature is that of a modern name. I would be unable to tell if it is a man or a woman. That's strange."

My teacher suddenly turned and went to meet one of the organizers of the exhibition who pointed to a young girl with blue hair. Dressed in a purple *hakama* and a white *kimono* top, she contrasted totally with the rest of the people present at the scene. I saw him talk for several long minutes with her. When he came back to me, I took the opportunity to tease him a little.

"So that's what a wise old fencing master in Japan looks like?"

"Very funny. She is the granddaughter of a sword master. Her grandfather often taught her sword philosophy. She can not use a sword, but was very close to her grandfather who had recited this poem to her in various contexts."

"I do not quite see in what context we can use this."

"When there is a goal to be reached, one must start with just a small part of the objective."

I had forgotten the richness of the Japanese language, he frequently played with it on several levels. It is a culture where writing has led people to think in images and not to align words linearly to express ideas. My master continued.

"To summarize, we can say that our actions describe our state of mind."

I did not see the connection between these words and calligrapher. It took me years to successfully grasp this, that is, if I understood correctly.

"What do you mean by our actions describe our state of mind?"

The old man looked at me with a complacent air.

"If you are asking me, it just means that you're not ready to understand. Even when the moon is full, its crescent always pierces it. Do not worry, one day you will understand. You're still in your first moon quarter."

Chapter 23
No sense

Training is training. Some sessions are similar and others leave an indelible mark. Several years had passed since I started training with Master. It was the end of autumn. It was unusually cold that day. Master gave me a very early appointment at the station. We were going to the Gunma region. He wanted to walk in the forest there. I was beginning to know him well, I had packed my bag with a change of clothes in case we wouldn't catch the last train back home.

As expected, he took the opportunity to visit a friend who lived in a charming country village. After taking a bus that dropped us near a narrow isolated road, we had to walk several kilometers. Arriving at the home of his longtime companion, I saw *daikon* hung on wooden poles. The two men bowed repeatedly. They spoke rapidly, using old Japanese expressions that I could not translate. After the presentations, hot tea was well received. Served by his wife, an elderly woman who stood with a straight back, the soothing liquid helped to forget the pains of the trip. The lady must have known my teacher well. Upon meeting, she went to snuggle against him, hugging each other. It was the first time I saw such a gesture of intimacy in people of this age. This couple had to be very close to my master to accept such proximity.

We spent the rest of the day visiting the man's fields. A man who was around ninety years old. The master told me he had even escaped from a Russian prison camp during the Second World War. I was impressed with the idea that someone so old could still do this much work. He always cultivated his land himself. His wife, a little younger than him, was part of a crafting circle. One of the rooms of the house was full of her work. I was entitled to a gift, a beautiful ape she had handcrafted. She had noticed my smile, watching this little creation with a mischievous face. The rest of the evening, which I was afraid would be boring, had proven itself very pleasant. I liked the stories the couple with such rich experience told.

When my teacher told me that we would spend the night, I asked him why he had not warned me that we wouldn't return the same day.

"Learning to adapt is part of martial arts. You're no longer a child we have to hold by the hand. I guess you planned a change of clothes, right?"

"Yes, I have what it takes."

"You see, you are no longer a child, I need not tell you everything."

A small kerosene heater helped temper the cool of the night. At the first light, the master knocked on my door and told me that breakfast was served. A table full of vegetables and fruit welcomed us. After a hearty meal, we borrowed two bicycles from our host who waited leaning against his motorcycle. We made our way to a mountain a few kilometers away. A small road leading to a temple nestled at the top. Lined with statues, the road kept climbing. It wound through gigantic trees. Many people holding hands had fun surrounding one of the biggest trees there. The effort required to reach the top was worth it. A magnificent building leaning against a huge rocky outcrop greeted us with its frescoes. A *Yamabushi* monk bowed crossing our way. My master exchanged a few words with him and the two men laughed. I did not understand what they said, but the look that the priest launched me left no doubt.

"Come, we'll leave the bicycles here. Do not worry, nobody will steal them."

After climbing a stone staircase and passing under a huge rock leaning against a rocky formation, we sneaked our way into the forest. We struggled to cross the first difficult meters, but then a path presented itself to us. The entrance seemed intentionally concealed.

"This path is a sacred way. We will walk in silence for a few kilometers. Consider this training," said my teacher.

I found that walking in silence was not quite the ideal type of training to improve in combat, but since that was what he wanted, I could only oblige.

The cool morning breeze brought us air of a rare purity. Shattering the tranquility of the place, the songs of birds accompanied us. I felt intense energy that emanated from the ground. Trees offered us their serenity. The few streams we crossed were supplying us with water. Far from civilization, the nature here had kept all its rights. One part of the path that was on the edge of a cliff, made me feel a little uncomfortable. It was clearly not the case for my teacher who progressed briskly, moving from one rock to another when the ground became uneven. Subsequently, we skirted a kind of swamp where the insects were legion. I could not drive away all the mosquitoes that assailed me fast enough. They seemed to spare the old master.

"Stop scratching, it'll get worse," he told me.

After two or three hours of walking, we reached a small statue that time had eroded in multiple places. My master clasped his palms speaking softly, then he clapped his hands twice, nodding.

"So you had good training?" Asked my road companion.

"Yes, of course. A walk in the mountains is always nice."

"You mean, you did not train much?"

"Doing what? We took a beautiful trail. What could I have done more than repel mosquitoes when we got near the swamp?"

"I was not talking about training physically but developing your senses. What is the noise that intrigued you the most during our walk?"

"Birds, there are many here."

"You did not notice a growl near the second stream?"

"No, nothing like that."

"You did not see the bear standing two meters away from us?"

Upon reflection, I thought I heard a strange sound, but I had not paid attention to it.

"Now that you mention it, maybe. But I'm not sure."

"And when we went on the trail over the cliff, did you notice that the wall was hot? There are many hot springs in the area."

Naturally, I had not noticed any of that.

"And the delicious floral scent of..."

"No, I did not smell it," I said without giving him time to continue, "now I understand what you meant by considering this training."

"You must develop all your senses. How do you think the *ninja* could survive so easily when they hid in the mountains?"

"I was mostly thinking of staying quiet. You must admit that I did not make much noise while walking."

"That must be why so many crows fled upon our arrival."

I preferred not to answer this last comment.

"You have to learn to listen and see better. You have to notice the smells that surround you. Your body is constantly in contact with the soil, with stones, and tree roots. Be aware of everything. Modern civilization is not the appropriate place to develop our senses. The less information the brain captures, the happier we are. Public places are not always clean. We do not want to see what is around us, for fear of feeling guilty of all the ugliness. In most countries, if someone asks for help, most people will pretend not to hear it and divert the eye. We must not let our senses atrophy."

"How do we do that?"

"Work them separately. The first week, as soon as you wake up, concentrate on the sounds that reach you. First, those who are near you, then the more distant ones, trying to locate and identify them. The rest of the day keep your attention on the sounds. If people talk on the train, unravel the conversations. You have probably already been in a noisy place such as a bar or nightclub?"

"Of course."

"Even if you have trouble understanding your immediate neighbor, if someone says your name far away, your brain will filter out the rest to inform you that we are talking about you. We can significantly increase our hearing ability with a little practice. It can be helpful if someone attacks you from behind."

"And I do this exercise with all the senses?"

"Yes, the second week you can work the sense of taste. Bring your tongue over your blankets to feel the texture. Taste your fingers."

"Ew! I hate putting fabric in my mouth. I tried as a child and I hated it."

"Stop complaining, this is training. Analyze what you eat, savor it and identify the different tastes. If you do not know certain tastes, invent your own ranking system. One day, it could prevent you from being poisoned by expired food or a deliberate trap. Most people are accustomed to sweet or salty food, and food that do not taste much. And that's not counting those who no longer take the time to enjoy the food because they are too rushed. Did you know that the *ninja* did not eat certain foods during missions so that their presence would not be detected by some easily recognizable odors? The scent of our skin can betray us if we are not careful."

"You're saying that what we swallow can change our transpiration?"

"Yes. If someone has a fine nose, he will detect your odor."

I did not know what to say. Thinking about it, it made sense. We are what we eat.

"To be honest, food is just fuel for me. I need to function, so the taste is more or less important. But with what you just told me, I'll probably revise my position on it."

"A warrior who does not control his senses is doomed to lose a fight sooner or later."

What could I add more? The master continued his lesson.

"Then you can work your visual acuity. How do you move at night? Does the sun bother you? Can you further develop your peripheral vision? Have you become aware of how you look at an opponent in action? You should be able to highlight the weaknesses of your vision. In stressful situations, do you experience the tunnel effect?"

I knew he was talking about the phenomenon where the tension or stress reduces our field of vision. For example, this is what makes it so during a police car chase, the drivers focus on what is right before them. They do not see the vehicles coming from the side.

"Then you can do the same exercise with the sense of touch. Learn to recognize different textures. Evaluate temperatures with your fingertips, feel the vibrations of the floor when someone walks by. And with a little practice, collect air changes on your palms. This is useful for blocking an attack that your eyes have not noticed."

"As for insects, I saw that you did not have a single mosquito on you. How did you do that?"

"That's more difficult. They are living things, you must be able to make them feel as if you're one of them. You must successfully identify yourself as one of them."

A bunch of questions assaulted my mind. How could we impersonate one of them? It was amazing what the master could do with his mind.

"Teach me that, I want to learn how to get them to think I'm one of them."

"I think you're not ready for that," threw out the old man smiling.

"In the meantime, I suggest you use this."

He handed me a small bottle, telling me that it was bug spray, a home recipe. I was fooled. He had no meditation technique to protect against insects. He had used a product to repel bugs. I opened the bottle and held it up to my nose. I found it curious that the product did not have a smell. I poured some on my wrist, a transparent liquid flowed out. I hesitated a moment, then I put a drop on my tongue.

"Water... This is only water."

"Mosquitoes also need water," said the old master with the most serious face in the world.

Chapter 24

The art of moving

When we do martial arts and we are able to escape almost all attacks, we can say that we move well. Our skills are at their zenith when the opponent is successful in touching us once out of five times only. We rely on stamina to compensate for what we can not avoid. By reaching such results, we can not call into question our ability to move. Yet we should still examine the subject.

That day was raining torrents. The wind blew raindrops even under the umbrellas. Nothing could be done to avoid them. My pants were still dripping when I entered the *dojo*. Fortunately for me, the tarp that covered my backpack was completely sealed. It is with eagerness that I put on my training pants. The master arrived a few minutes later.

"Was everyone surprised by the *tsuyu*'s mood swing?" He asked.

All raised their hands. Usually during *tsuyu*, the rainy season, the sky let water fall on us sparingly. It rained often, almost every day, but rarely a deluge accompanied by strong winds as there had been during that day. I found it amusing that the old man spoke of Mother Nature's mood swings like she was alive. The master looked at everyone and smiled.

"Well, in that case, put your wet pants back on."

"You're kidding," I said.

He did not need to add another word for me to understand that he was serious. I knew that silence was the best thing to maintain. His oblong eyes sufficed at making my soggy pants a little more comfortable than they were. This training took place before I had had the courage to ask him to take me as a disciple. To this day, nothing surprises me more than him. He made us perform an incredible number of exercises requiring our legs to move smoothly. Even if the first movements proved themselves difficult, the following ones just seemed to get easier. On the contrary, I could not tell if it was because the heat from my body had dried my pants up, but a strange feeling of freedom allowed me to dodge attacks as I had never done before.

"We must be the masters of our movements, regardless of the circumstances," the old man said, "you do not decide when you will be attacked. It may be that you have several layers of clothing during winter and a few if you are attacked on the beach. You must be able to dodge without taking the time to stretch and warm up your muscles. You must avoid any assault without injury. This is where it starts to be art, we call it *taihenjutsu*."

The teacher made us do basic exercises, including one where we took a step to the side. It was a bit as if we revolved around a square tile.

I called this action a triangle shift. Some of my friends simply backed up. The master took a *bokken* and struck one of the students who fled rather than sticking close to the attacker. Each time, the student stepped back too far to be able to control the attacker. The master gave him the sword and asked him to attack. Proceeding thus, he found himself next to his opponent's wrists. From there, he simply caught the two opposing arms to gain control of the weapon and the assailant.

"Moving is a game of chess. We must place ourselves at the right place to bring the enemy to use the piece we want."

"I think it's mostly a matter of speed. When I was competing, few people were able to touch me," I said.

"This may be because these people did not understand *budo*," the old man said.

"No, I assure you. I am fast. I can dodge any attack."

"Okay. If you manage to avoid two of my five attempts, I will consider you as someone of superior level," said the master.

At that time I thought I was better than everyone else. The master got into fighting position. In my mind, the challenge would be easy. How could such an elderly person reach me? I only had to monitor his shoulders, as they would move, I would just deviate from the path. I was ready, I was just waiting to see him jump. Suddenly his body found itself almost stuck to mine. A sharp pain in my stomach made me fold in half. I still had four chances.

"What's wrong? You underestimated me. Next time will be harder for me to touch you," said the master.

I shared the same opinion. He took me by surprise. Master positioned himself again, ready to pounce on me. Except now I was ready. He was trying to worry me by giving himself an aggressive air. But it was not enough to impress me. I waited and then suddenly he released all the tension in his body and smiled. It took a few seconds before I could get back up. The pain would not leave my aching stomach.

"What? Do not tell me that a simple smile distracted you. This time, it will be more difficult or even impossible for me to reach you. Unless..."

How? Why? His last words worried me. No, he was just trying to impress me. I would just throw myself aside to avoid the aggression.

"I'm ready, you will not get me this time," I said.

The old man stood before me, he remained in his position for several minutes. What was he waiting for, why was he not attacking? If he hoped to wear me out, it was a lost cause. I stared in his eyes to prove that he did not intimidate me. Then he began to move slowly, idly, almost lazily. He came towards me but my body could not react. My muscles could no longer respond. His fist came up to my nose. Then, I felt the pressure of his knuckles crush my nostrils. For a moment, I was certain that my nose was broken. But even before the first cracking sound, his fist stopped. He had spared me. He snapped his fingers and told me to take back control of my body. I immediately recoiled. Looking at the other students, I understood that I must not have been the only one impressed by this demonstration.

"You used to hypnosis, right?"

"Yes, *saiminjutsu*. Do we go on with the attacks?"

I did not wish to get hit again. The pain of the last shot in the stomach made me wiser. I decided to abdicate.

"No, I understand. Speed alone is not enough to just avoid a hit. How can we be sure that we are in the right place at the right time?" I asked.

"With experience we come to find the appropriate position. A location where it becomes more difficult or requires a little more time for the opponent if he wishes to reach us. In this position we can counterattack easily if he hits us. Ideally, we should try to control his structure."

I was in my early days with him, I did not understand what he meant by that.

"Punch me," he said.

I hastened to make his face my target. Despite my speed, he easily dodged the blow. I had the impression that he had moved slowly. He made the same movement we had seen at the beginning of the class. Then he put one hand behind my elbow and kept me off balance by stretching my arm. I could not counter his movements effectively. Also, the side of my head was offering a fully open target. I would not last long in a real fight. He was depriving me of my support, my body could not stabilize quickly enough to retaliate. Now I understood what he meant when he spoke of controlling the body structure.

"How many kinds of body shifts are there?" Asked a student.

"There are as many as we need," replied the master.

"You mean we can move anyway we want?" I asked.

"The movement doesn't matter if it brings you strategic advantage. If it does not put you at risk and brings you a step ahead of the opponent, we can say that it does the job. Your moves must not pass by the intellect. They have to be natural. Natural and logical," he hastened to add.

A student asked to speak.

"In another martial art that I practiced, there was much talk of *tai sabaki*, the art of movements. Are all movements *tai sabaki*?"

"Yes and no," said the master.

I suspected that the answer could not be that simple.

"The first kanji, *tai*, is that of the body. The second, *sabaki*, is often interpreted by movement, actually translated more by manipulation or handling, in this case, the manipulation of the body. Naturally, we imply the prevention of an attack. In that sense, all actions that can be done to avoid receiving a blow are *tai sabaki*. Some martial arts have codified a number of ways to move to integrate them into a more rigid educational structure."

"It sounds too simple," I said.

The old man looked at me and smiled.

"However," I was right, it could not be that easy, "in older martial arts, the word sabaki can mean something amplified, by exaggerated movements. You get used to performing large movements to then shrink them in real life."

That explains why I found some positions illogical. In a context where we exaggerate the movements to teach the body how to move well, the relevance of this teaching was justified.

"Do you have any further questions on the subject?" Asked the master.

I hesitated a little, then I ventured to submit one.

"Do we need speed if we want to be effective? I always have the feeling that you move slowly, and yet you are never there to receive the attack."

"There is one thing we need to understand when doing martial arts."

I expected a secret that is revealed only rarely in *budo*.

"What is it?" I asked.

"Speed is an illusion."

Chapter 25
The power of water

I had not yet taken the time to visit the sea. I decided to enjoy a day off taking a walk on the shore. I contacted the master to offer him to accompany me. To my surprise, he agreed. I had not imagined that this walk would turn into a learning session so beneficial for me. We were walking on one of the countless beaches of the archipelago. I found the master a little pensive, but I told myself that it had to be the beauty of the ocean that put him in this state.

"It's so peaceful."

"Yes, that's what it wants us to believe," he replied, "it lulls us in its illusion to better deceive us."

"What do you mean by that?"

"That," he said, at the horizon.

"Why do you say that? It's only the sea. It has protected Japan from foreign attacks for millennia. It has fed its people for so long."

"Yes, but it has its mood swings. It can cajole us to the point that we forget everything, but it can also prove devastating."

"How pessimistic of you," I said, "you're too negative."

"No, I'm not negative, I'm just a realist. We must appreciate it while being wary of its temperament."

The master laughed.

"It needs a shrink, it is bipolar."

Children playing with a ball on the beach shouted in chorus *"Abunai"*. Without looking, the master leaned forward, letting the ball fly to my forehead. He grabbed the rebound and returned it to the young people. The children had just shouted to warn us. A moment of silence was followed by a multitude of *"sumimasen"* that rang in our ears.

"Did you do that on purpose?"

"What?"

"Letting the ball hit me."

He smiled. As was his habit, he continued to speak of the sea as if nothing had happened.

"Water is powerful. In martial arts, if someone hits us, the element of water will absorb the attack backwards then, as the undertow of the wave comes crashing on the shore, we return the attack to the abuser who always allows a fraction of a second between two attacks."

I knew the principle of absorbing the blows of the opponent. This approach was based on the instinct of fear, a survival instinct that drives us to retreat in the face of danger. By backing up like so, the attacker leaves openings available, doors that can be exploited.

We had often discussed this subject. I do not know why he wanted to re-explain this principle.

"The beauty of the water," he went on, "is that it teaches us to swim in society."

I found this parallel a little strange. But, he was like that and I had learned to accept these strange discussions. Once again, I did not understand where he was going with this.

"What do you mean by swimming in society? I'm guessing you are talking about relationships."

"Yes, that's it. Like the ocean that can sometimes be totally calm, water teaches us to give a voice to people, to listen without arguing. The more one tries to convince us, to sell us his ideas, the more water seeps in. A good lawyer knows how to use this strategy."

The master understood that I was lost.

"We have two eyes to see, two nostrils to capture smells, ten sensitive fingers to differentiate shapes and textures, two ears to hear, but we have only one mouth to communicate. We are made to gather information, but instead of that, most people keep talking without listening, without seeing or feeling what is around them."

All this did not really help me understand where that conversation would lead us.

"When a *tsunami* hits, the water invades every corner the wave seeps in. It breaks everything in its path, but it also causes a lot of havoc as it retreats. It brings with it a large part of what is on its way. The human being is like that wave. With his words, he can destroy what he attacks head on and then continue doing damage even when he has left."

A few days earlier, one of his politician friends had been slandered by a competitor. He had been accused of corruption and even fraud. But the next day, the accuser had retracted and apologized for saying that his source of information was not as reliable as he had thought. That strangely resembled the scenario my teacher was trying to explain. The link was obvious to me.

"You are referring to your politician friend, aren't you?"

"That's right. He is a good person, someone who works hard for his community. Someone who puts his community before his own interest."

"Even though his opponent has made amends, the damage is done. Is that what you think?"

"Yes, like the wave that leaves traces long after its passage, slander leaves an indelible mark."

"You mentioned lawyers who can use this strategy, what did you mean by that?"

"If he is clever, he will make the person in front of him talk. He will divert his words to then throw them to his face. As the human being likes to show that he knows everything, he will easily fall into the trap, the attorney will encourage him to say as much as possible. Then he will return his words against him by mixing the words and things he said. The goal is not to tell the truth, but to destabilize the person being interrogated."

"This is different from what is done in martial arts."

The master looked at me, presenting me the palm of his hand forcing me to back off a little to avoid the push.

"On the contrary, it is quite the same. When someone attacks you and you draw back several times in various directions, he has to change and use various strategies to reach you. Every movement increases the risk of the opponent turning his own movements against himself."

The master went silent. We walked to a small rocky formation on the tip of the beach. He sat down on one of the stones. The sun had begun to tilt solemnly before leaving the scene. Its golden highlights offered a magnificent spectacle. I thought back to this discussion that I had just had with the master concerning water. A strange conversation that left me pensive. I have never forgotten this magic moment, the silence and the calm that had brought me this visit to the beach. But after a while, I thought that silence was something that could be broken. When I began to question the master on another topic, he simply said...

"How many mouths do you have again?"

Chapter 26
Kiaijutsu

We were returning from training at one of the exterior *dojo*. We were strolling through the narrow streets leading to the train station when a truck honked with all its might. The driver did not seem happy to be cut off by a girl who had not made her stop. She was fixing her eyelashes at the same time as she was driving.

"All right!" I said, "she knows you're there, stop honking."

"He did not honk," said the master, "it is a preventive *kiai*."

My teacher was referring to this projection of energy that can be done in different ways. In martial arts, we often hear *karateka* crying out profusely when doing demonstrations, breaking boards or simply to distract an opponent in a fight.

"A preventive *kiai*... Are you kidding? Finally, he finally stopped his racket. I do not see what is preventive by that. He does not think about the collateral damage done to my poor eardrums."

"I think the lovely girl will remember this little incident. The color of her face changed completely when the truck driver warned her. Applying makeup behind the wheel is probably over for her."

"Speaking of *kiai*, last night I was on the web and I read a martial tale. It was said that a master of taichi one day dropped a bird on the ground with a *kiai*. What do you think? Do you believe it to be true?"

"If it's on the internet, it must be true."

I looked at him, wondering if he was really serious. After all, he did not even have a computer. Maybe he was sincere, but something inside of me doubted it. He did not give me time to cogitate further.

"What do you know of *kiai* jutsu?"

At that time we had not broached the subject very frequently. I could thank the imprudent person who had not made her mandatory stop.

"To be honest, not much. It is the cry that we let out during competitions to distract opponents. Oh yes! I was also using *kiai* when I was breaking planks of wood during demonstrations. I had the sensation that it brought me more strength."

"And the noise impressed the spectators," said the master, smiling.

"Um, yes that's true, but I did not do it for that."

"Of course. Tell me, what does the word *kiai* mean? Can you explain it to me?"

"It's easy, it can be translated as something like uniting energy."

"That's right, but can you be a little more specific?"

"It unites our body and our will for a short time."

"And do you know what kime is?" Asked the master.

"It is the concentration of energy at the impact. It's a bit like the tip of a whip that snaps."

"You are not wrong. It is sometimes referred to as the penetrating power, but in reality it is more about the right moment to capture. When deemed appropriate, all our energy is released into a split second. It is a moment when our will, our physical ability, and emotions are perfectly synchronized. In a split second, these three energies explode at the same point."

"Yes, but regarding this martial art tale about the bird..."

He did not look at me. He continued walking without stopping his explanations.

"Limiting *kiai jutsu* to only this is a bit simplistic. It is by far more interesting than that. Kiai is a transfer of energy. Sound is an energy wave. It's not just sound that can carry *ki*."

I tried to imagine how this art can be used other than with the voice, but I could not see how. Once more, he gave me the impression to read in me, that he possessed the strange power to enter my mind.

"Remember all the times I've destabilized you by focusing my intention in my eyes."

"The eyes! We can project *kiai* with our eyes!" I said excitingly.

"A fight starts with observation. A skilled swordsman will gauge his opponent without being charmed by him."

"Not letting ourselves be charmed, what do you mean by that?"

"The eyes are the mirror of the soul. If you master the art of piercing into your opponent, you already have a huge advantage over him. Most people betray themselves by their own look. By projecting his *kiai*, the true warrior knows he has chosen the right time to do so. His conviction leaves no chance to his assailant. His accuracy and stability is at its peak. The *kiai* will effectively create a loophole in the defense of his enemy."

I understood what he was saying very well even though I knew I did not have the ability to put this into practice. He followed up quickly.

"We can also produce *kiai* with the body. The image that is projected must be strong. Our body occupies the space of the other. It's important to project great energy from the *hara* center. By doing so, you enter the animal part of the opponent. Where are born doubt and fear."

A memory of the master who seized the space before me came to mind. Without knowing why, the only idea I had in mind at such the time was to run away. I could outline no attack strategy at that time. All I could do was keep trying to escape as he closed the gap more and more between him and me. A question came to mind.

"A *kiai* lasts only a split second, doesn't it?"

"Wrong. It may last several seconds. I am not talking about yelling until we run out of breath. I mean to occupy the thoughts of the enemy long enough to make him lose hope of winning."

"Can we train to resist *kiai*?"

"Yes if you are dealing with a fighter who is just making noise. But if you fight a true master, your chances of not losing your concentration is minimal. To get there, you must master the void. Allow your emotions and your intellect to be completely disconnected. And that, believe me, it is not within the reach of everyone."

"What is the best time to project *kiai*?" I asked.

"Only the *kiai* knows. We do not decide the moment, it is he who chooses us. But if you really want a point of reference, we can say that the moment your opponent is preparing to swing down his sword is a good time."

"Because he is focused on his action."

The master looked at me and smiled. I knew that my answer had satisfied him. He continued his lesson.

"There are several kinds of *kiai*. We can hit a body with a shockwave attack, which I think you know how to do well. They use this in police training in the West. Then comes a double *kiai*, where in the same attack, a second wave will prevent the other to retaliating immediately. Personally, I like the *kiai* aimed at disturbing the mind. Some of these are so powerful that the opponent finds himself completely unable to react. His legs become limp, his hands begin to tremble, his breathing quickens as if he can not control it anymore. It is a *kiai* that opens the gates of hell."

Panicked shrieks reached my ears. They came from a tree in front of a house that bordered crumbling down. A cat advanced step by step on a branch. His target was a high-perched nest. I could not see what kind of bird it was, but the twittering left no doubt about the threat prowling around the nest.

"Hey! Get out of here!" I yelled, clapping my hands.

I took a branch and threw it towards the feline who seemed unimpressed by my warning. The danger was just a few centimeters away from the nest. The first claw swings were about to intrude when a dull sound was heard behind me. It sounded like a growl, very short, very dry. The cat froze and fell. Immediately, a sharper sound awoke the animal from its torpor. He turned and fell on his front legs to then run away at full speed.

"It... it was you who did that, wasn't it?"

"If you write this on the Internet, no one will believe you."

Chapter 27

The Basics

A few of us were conversing with the master after a class. Sitting on the *tatami*, we were discussing all kinds of topics that day. One of us asked why we had to practice the basics all our lives.

"Because everything is found in these principles," he replied, "however, be careful not to confuse the *kata* of a school and basics."

"What do you mean by that?" I asked.

"It is not uncommon for teachers to require that their students know all their school's techniques by heart. The basics are not the *kata*, they are the essence."

"But why are they so important?" Asked a student with long black hair.

"Because they reveal what is fundamental," said the master, "they teach us how to move, how to synchronize our movements and in which direction we should direct our defense strategy. They do not teach us what we should do, but they point the way to achieve it."

"Yes, but once we have assimilated how to move, the rest is robotic repetition," she said.

"Our body tends to change its way of moving depending on its mood. What might be called bad habits, happen constantly. The basics are there to bring us back on the right path."

"Yes, but those moves are rarely used as they are taught to defend ourselves on the street in real situations. So, what can they bring more?" She asked.

"It's a bit like basic math. If you do not know how to add, subtract, multiply or divide, how can you hope to assess the surface of a structure? We need to make very accurate calculations. The basics give us the tools and it is up to us to go beyond what has been learned. But if the basics are all crooked, do not be surprised if the structure of the building is erected inadequately. The building will crumble at the slightest tremor."

I liked when the old master gave us concrete examples like that. He had a gift for bringing martial arts to an every day reality.

"You have already said that we must adapt our martial art. Every practitioner should evolve according to his stature, his physical strength, his emotions and even sex, because we women have a lower center of gravity. Is it possible for a rigid basic training program to harm our martial personality?"

"No," the old man said, "whether you are a sculptor or a carpenter, you will need to know how to make a straight line with a saw. The difference between both will be how the line is made. Furthermore, the transfer of knowledge should not be altered from generation to generation. Imagine if every person changed the basics in his image. What would remain of the technique after a few hundred years?"

"Is it possible that it could be improved?" Asked one of the students.

"I highly doubt it. These principles have been through times of conflict in Japan. They have enabled many warriors to survive. In many martial arts, people grant themselves the privilege to change that. Most often, these are people who have never had to defend their lives in real situations. If you want to do something to leave your mark, invent a martial art of your own. But do not mutilate what has existed for centuries. Who are we to claim to be better than the creators of these old styles?"

The master's tone quickened. Obviously he did not like those who allowed themselves to modify traditional techniques. He paused for a moment and went on with a more moderate tone.

"When one believes that he has mastered the foundations of a martial art, he can reach a higher stage of the same basics. They can be performed at different levels. For example, we can explore the overflow principle."

A few years earlier, he had made us work on these techniques which involve bringing the opponent to the point where the stability of his structure was compromised. When punching, there is a specific distance where we have to stop. A few millimeters further and our stability becomes shaky. He continued his explanation on the subject.

"By forcing your assailant to exceed his limits, the forces of someone with a strong stature and one with inferior physical abilities are balanced."

"Yes, but what if the person is flexible and we can not destabilize him?" She asked.

"That's why some basics teach us different ways to hit. If grabbing is not sufficient, we will make use of our fists, feet, elbows, knees, and even fingers. But even these attacks need solid bases to be effective. If you know black belt holders of different styles that have lost fights in the street, there's a good chance that they would tell you, if they are honest, they felt that their strikes did not affect their opponent."

I thought about those words and actually I had already talked to friends who had experienced this feeling of inability to neutralize an opponent with their fists. The master continued his explanations.

"It may not seem obvious to most, but these basics teach us many things. When we take the time to do them well, we quickly realize that the angles occupy an important place in our defense system. A good angle gives us better management of distances, especially during attacks with a sword or a stick."

The master's teachings included a lot of work on angles. Against a sword attack, we must not remain in a distance where the weapon can touch us. We should not move too far away either. The angles allow us to maintain security and distance that allow us to take control of the situation.

"Must we practice quickly?" Asked one of the students.

"If you can do them correctly, yes, but this is not the case for most people. It is better to go slowly so that the body molds itself in the basics. We must be aware of each of our joints. One knee pointing in a direction different from the punch and we just lost twenty percent of our power. Some basics are connected to various ways of moving. It is easy to rotate the pelvis to the way of the wind element on an earth element technique, but if the basics are not well assimilated, they will make a poor fighter."

Saying this, he stared into my eyes. He was talking about one of the problems that I had trouble to correct. I had practiced martial arts based on wind before meeting him. A good part of my movements were based on this martial past. The old man resumed his explanation.

"It is obvious that on a battlefield, the foundations are not used exactly the way they are taught. We adapt them to our current needs. But if we can break a board, there is a good chance that the boat will take in water," he said, laughing, "when we master them well enough, we have to mold them to the situation. The basics are used for all kinds of situations. We must look at how we can adjust unarmed combat to a fight with weapons. A basic wrist lock can be applied to control someone attacking us with a sword. The lock will not be identical, the direction in which we will move will be totally different, but the fluidity of the movement, the stability of the approach, all that has been gained by practicing the basics will ensure that we are victorious."

For a moment I had the impression that the master was worried about something. He looked at us one after another before continuing.

"Of course, even if you do these exercises repeatedly, if your heart isn't into it, do not expect the spirits of old to help you in your fight. Only a pure heart can reach a superior state. You can fool your teachers or lie to yourself, but you can not fool the *kami*."

He was reluctant to talk about the spiritual level. Now I understand why he seemed worried about it. At that time, I myself did not understand his teachings on *kokoro*, the heart, too well. To say that the spirits of old would not help us was beyond my vision of martial arts. It was only much later that I assimilated the importance of this teaching. He hesitated, then continued on the topic.

"In a fight where everything is hopeless, you can connect to the spirits of the *kami* if your heart is ready for it. Be careful, remember the words of one of the greatest swordsmen of Japan, *Miyamoto Musashi*: "Respect the gods, but don't rely on them when you're in trouble."

"Doesn't that contradict what you just said?" I commented.

"Being connected does not mean we should expect the *kami* to do all the work for us. They are an inspiration. They will guide you in your movements. Many people who are interested in Asian or Indian culture seek *satori*. The quest of enlightenment can be done through meditation and can also be accomplished by working the body. Practicing the basics with the proper state of mind is a very powerful form of meditation."

"Is that why you do not make us meditate?" Asked a student.

"If you have the right spirit and your heart is pure, you are meditating during each training session. You must simply ask the spirits to help you in your quest."

A few years later, I began to understand this strange relationship we could have with these ancestors. One day, I was training with another senior Japanese instructor. He did not seem fit whatsoever. He was visibly tired and stressed. He seemed dissatisfied with the techniques he was showing. I was watching him the moment he took a break to go have a look at the picture of an old deceased master. He made a short prayer, and from that moment on, it was not the same teacher that stood before me at all. His teaching was light years away from what he made us do at the beginning of the class. From this point on, I regularly started asking the *kami* for help. In times when I was tired, when my ideas were intertwined, I used those connection principles. I often surprised myself at how I taught powerful things, techniques I had never seen before.

Chapter 28
Bread and games

We were walking past a Saizeria, a popular Italian fast-food restaurant with a Japanese touch. The chefs in these establishments are microwave specialists. The value attracts many clients, especially young people knowing that they will be served in record time.

"Let's grab something here," said my teacher, "I am a little hungry."

"What, in a restaurant like this? I thought you hated junk food."

"From time to time, we must accustom our stomach to eat any kind of food. If a disaster occurs and you are sick because you are too sensitive to what you eat, there is a good chance that you will not survive. We must harden our stomach and thus deal with any eventuality."

I had never thought of that. It is true that in case of emergency, diarrhea was not a good thing. A young girl, of barely sixteen years old, led us into the non-smoking section. In this type of restaurant, it was not uncommon to see teenagers working very late at night. The master took the menu and quickly turned the pages. Then without asking me if I was ready to order, he pushed the button to call the waitress.

"Hey! I have not even looked at the menu."

"No need," he said, "I'm sure you know it by heart."

He was right, I knew that I would have a salami pizza. He chose a seafood doria, a rice dish with béchamel sauce and a little grated cheese that covered some shrimp here and there. As in many places, they offered the drink bar for a ridiculous price. You could have coffee, tea, juices, and soft drinks at will. I did not mind serving myself several cups of coffee. The master looked around. Through a young clientele we found some seniors and salarymen, those office workers in their customary suit and tie. There was not a table where at least one person was holding a cell phone in hand.

"Panem et circenses," the old man said.

"What? That's not Japanese."

"No, it's Latin. It means bread and games."

"And what do you mean by bread and games?"

"It is an old Roman expression that says that if you feed your people and you give them enough interesting things to do or to watch, they will not care of the way you rule them. If they are fat and having fun, what more could they ask for? This is an excellent way to prevent uprisings and revolutions."

"Is it because people are using their cell phones that you are saying that?"

"Partially. Most people do not care who governs them, and how they spend their money. Of course, they will criticize them for a while, but once the new video game or the latest TV show is out, the change of subject will be done instantly. Priorities are not the same for everyone."

"Fortunately, people who do martial arts do not think like that."

The old man looked at me with a raised eyebrow.

"Do you really believe what you just said?" He asked. "For most practitioners, *budo* is a hobby and not a way of life."

His tone was bitter, I could feel a hint of regret in his voice.

"Is it so bad for people to have fun and not to care about politics though?"

"Doing so, they deprive themselves of consciousness. They no longer see what manages their daily lives. They are in a latent mode where they let time pass until they die."

I really did not expect him to believe in such a philosophy.

"Yes, but it was always so, no? In your days, people read books, is that not the same thing?"

"A real book provides tools for reflection. The result is often an awakening, a life philosophy. Books teach us to be closer to our emotions. Getting through a book takes time, it requires a quiet time to appreciate them. Browsing through a book is quite an effort. In a book, we can easily go back to revisit a passage which we have not grasped the meaning. Most people do not bother to go back on a video. People are too quick, they are like soldiers who are in a hurry to move, just to go wait somewhere else. Today, newspaper articles must be short otherwise people will not read them to the end. There is a lack of interest for everything. The human being is at a point where it flees, they want to take refuge in a timeless place where they will be safe from any problem."

I felt a little bad. I came to realize that I was one of those who preferred shorter articles, those being a little less well documented. I merely read the news superficially.

"The Romans had understood that we must not let the people think too much. If they are hungry or are bored, they become easy prey for corrupt politicians or invasive religions who wish to take charge of these poor spirits left to themselves."

The young waitress arrived with our dishes. A plume of smoke rose from the doria. I took the knife and cut my pizza into a multitude of small points. Then I went to the counter and refilled my coffee and a cup of tea for my master. He continued the conversation as if it had never been interrupted.

"People read the headlines, a disaster in a particular place, the space shuttle exploded, one hundred people died in an attack. Twenty minutes later, most return to their hobbies if they do not have thoughts occupied by their work."

"But we must work if we want to eat."

I could not see what he could answer to that. I underestimated him.

"Poverty in rich countries has increased. The middle class is decreasing. People have become accustomed to a higher lifestyle and must learn to adapt. Most of them have lost their sense of values, the fight for survival. How many will turn to suicide as they lose the little comfort they have acquired?"

I was not sure I wanted to swallow my slice of pizza.

"The interesting thing about all this is that people who have never had anything would never think of committing suicide. Their happiness is not calculated by their possessions, but rather by the relationships they have with their family members and entourage. They will be ready to fight for their happiness," he said.

"When I was traveling in Mexico, I went to poor villages where family houses consisted of single-room cabins. The poverty was extreme, but they were incredibly rich. Seeing the joy a mother had talking to her children, I understood that the concept of happiness was not the same everywhere."

"This is why bread and games are important. Occupying the people is the best way to ensure the tranquility of the leaders. They can pass laws without anyone noticing."

"What can be done? Prohibiting the use of video games?"

"There is not much we can do. We must wait."

"Wait for what?"

"With some luck, the next generations will not want to adopt the lifestyle of their parents. So maybe there is hope for the future."

"But if it stays the same or gets worse, what will happen?"

"It will be a minority who will lead the world. Big companies and some powerful politicians will pull the strings quite easily. But that is science fiction, it could certainly not happen in real life..." he said, dipping his spoon in his doria he had let cool down.

Chapter 29
Rhythm

"Whether you like it or not, rhythm runs your life. From the very moment you open your eyes in the morning, you are the victim of a tempo that will guide your actions throughout the course of the day."

I had barely set foot in the *dojo* when the old master spoke of the importance of rhythm, not only in combat but also in everyday life.

"Whether it is because you are late, or simply that you have nothing to do, your body, your mind, and your emotions will follow the pace dictated by your agenda or the stress of the moment."

I had never considered my getting out of bed that way. Was he saying that we do not control our lives? That morning, we were a dozen students in the *dojo* taking the last class of the year. A few days earlier, as was customary, we cleaned the whole building from top to bottom. All that could hold the building had been spread out on canvases outdoors. Each object had been washed individually. The walls were exposed. Even very highly-perched fluorescent lamps were dismantled and rubbed one by one. In Japan, spring cleaning is done at the end of the year in order to start the New Year off right. I think I gave the master the idea to focus the class on rhythm, commenting on the work we had done cleaning the *dojo* at a very fast pace where no one was wasting any time. The old man continued his reflection.

"All our lives, we are subject to different paces. As in battle, this tempo can change in a split second. We must learn to adapt to these sudden changes without losing sight of our objectives. We must acquire the pace that is needed when it is needed. In the words *Miyamoto Musashi*: "When one has completely learned the theory, he must detach himself from it. The way of tactics is a free way." We must remain free, regardless of the action that is imposed on us. Many people become confused during such a change of pace."

I had the bad idea of wanting to comment on the subject.

"I know change of pace well. In sports competitions, I used it regularly, I moved slowly and then sped up like lightning. The problem is that the opponents get used to it quickly and it becomes easy for them to not get confused by the speed variation."

The master looked at me without saying anything. I felt I should have kept quiet. I expected the worst.

"OK, place yourself in combat position and try to adapt. If you can't block my hand, you'll get hit."

He positioned himself at a distance close enough for me to touch one of his hands. He took an aggressive posture in the manner of a boxer. I was prepared that, true to himself, he would remain almost motionless. Instead, I felt that his body was moving at a frenzied pace. I was convinced that he would try to increase his speed, but it seemed impossible for it to increase as he already moved so quickly. I could easily block him in this battle mode. I was in my old element, an athletic competition. I expected an explosive release from one of his arms. But instead, his body had the impression of slowing down, his shoulders relaxed, he seemed about to abdicate. Before I could realize what was happening, I received a strong slap on the head. If he had wanted to hit my nose, it would have been easy for him to do so at that time. I had seen his arm unfold yet I could not react quickly enough to prevent it from reaching me.

"I'll do it again, see if you can adapt."

The result was the same. My skull had become a percussion instrument. Each of my attempts to counter his attacks resulted in humiliating failure.

"I don't understand. I feel delayed. I see, you hypnotized me!"

"I did not need to do that," he said, smiling, "your brain is able to grant an accelerating change of pace, but when it faces a slowing down of pace, it becomes more difficult to synchronize with the movement. The adrenaline takes a while to drain. The body is ready to react quickly while hardly being able to counteract slow gestures. You had the idea that I would attack you by increasing my speed and you remained a prisoner of that thought. Your mind has to stay free, let it adapt, do not try to anticipate."

"But you already said that a fight is a game of chess where we have to position our pawns in function of the blows ahead."

"There is a difference between knowing what will happen and assuming what will happen. Human beings are natural synchronizers. They usually try to harmonize their actions with the things surrounding them. If someone raises his voice, your biorhythms will accelerate. On the other hand, if the person you are with is quiet, you will probably relax."

Music emanating from the back of the *dojo* cut the words of the master. He took a few steps and pointed a finger towards a cell phone which let out a rather boisterous ringing sound. The owner ran to turn off the disturbing device trying to apologize. Master blasted the awkwardness of that student away.

"You have just heard a good overview of rhythm. Music is the best example of its power. The type of melody you heard is a good indicator of the rate at which your personality syncs."

There, I was lost again. I did not understand what he was insinuating. This sentence seemed devoid of all logic.

"A person more prone to aggression will probably tend to listen to rock rather than classical music. Whether we are sad, or happy, the melody we hear will influence our glandular functions. If what you hear is always fast, leaving no room for the slightest oasis of calm, you will be more prompt to react and take less time to think."

Now I understood what he meant. And thinking back about me, let's say, slightly more rock and roll days, I saw again some impulsive behavior that I had at the time. I never made the connection with my mp3 player. Was it indeed possible that this could affect me? My lifestyle matched the music I listened to.

"In combat as with negotiating with other people, we must learn to de-synchronize our mind from our body. Even if you move quickly, you should be able to be peaceful, relaxed. Even if you appear to be calm, your mind must be able to function at full speed."

The master continued on the same subject for a long time before we practiced the exercise he did with me. He concluded by explaining that the change of pace is used to disturb the heart of the opponent. I realized many years later that when he spoke of the heart, in this case, he implied destabilizing the will and determination of our opponent. For several minutes, I tried to reproduce the technique he had demonstrated, but it was useless, it could not be done.

"Is it possible that some people are naturally immune against this change of pace? I can not copy what you've done," I said, "he manages to counter me every time."

The master gestured to my partner to try with him. On the first attempt, my partner received a pat on the head.

"The problem is you," said the master, "you move quickly, then you stop too abruptly. You must quickly slow down without stopping suddenly. Your movements are not natural. But the biggest problem is that your intellect is not synchronized with the rest. Your face expresses the same thing no matter the tempo you use. Your opponent sees a body, but it also collects emotions and intentions. Your spirit does not follow your body."

After several tries, I understood what he meant. From there, all my attempts on different students led to victory. The master allowed a break.

"Everything in the universe has a rhythm. Electricity, tides, the moon, your boss, everything is subject to this phenomenon. If you manage to decipher the tempo of what is around you, you gain a little more control over your life. Whether it be to negotiate a contract with a multinational or just to argue with your children, the knowledge and mastery of rhythm makes your life easier."

My teacher had the talent to sow seeds that even though sometimes took time to germinate, bloomed into magnificent flowers that accompanied us throughout our lives. It was only after several years that I understood everything that rhythm implied. The best thing about it is that to this day, I regularly discover new functions it imposes. The master had completed the class with a few words that proved to be a trigger for me.

"Used well, the change of pace brings the opponent to confusion. Doing so, we drag him away from own rhythm."

A question came to my mind.

"Must we always be aware of rhythm in everyday life?"

"We mustn't go overboard. Just remember this: Either you follow a rhythm, or it is you who sets the tempo."

Chapter 30
Lack of balance

"If this goes on, we will have to get you a walker."

I regained my balance and attacked again, this time with a roundhouse kick towards the old man's head. He hardly stepped back letting my foot swing past his face. As I was about to put my foot on the ground, he leaned lightly on my shoulder. Pushing me in a very specific angle. I felt transported to my left, away from him. Taking the necessary distance from him was not a problem, turning my back on the other hand...

The moment I opened my eyes, I saw a bird passing between the branches of the clearing.

"How... how did you do that?"

"Making you fall, or making you fall asleep?" My teacher responded with a question, smiling. My thoughts were still a little confused.

"Um, both!"

"To make you faint was easy, I just hit one of your plexuses, which you have rendered particularly vulnerable by standing on one foot. Oh right! You were standing on one leg because I used your poor sense of balance against you."

It was the first time that we addressed this issue. As everyone who practices martial arts for a long time, I thought I mastered my own movements. But in an instant, he had sown doubt in my mind about my stability.

"You're saying I can't control my body?"

"Not just your body, you must find balance both in your head and in your movements. You put so much power into your attacks, it becomes easy for me to counter you."

The old man approached me.

"Seize me in *uchi komi*," he ordered.

My right hand grabbed him by the collar while my left one grabbed the sleeve by his right bicep. This way of standing, so dear to the *judoka*, came from the time of the *samurai*. The right hand gripped one of the straps that held the breastplate of armor, while the other hand prevented the opponent from drawing his sword.

"Now try to destabilize me," said my mentor.

However I forced, feinted, pulled, pushed and even raised, there was nothing to be done to take his balance. Worst of all, I had the feeling that he did not use any force, he merely moves slightly while changing the angle of his arms. After all these useless efforts, I released my grip.

"Okay, I got it. Where do we start?"

The old man looked at me and nodded. He gave the impression of not knowing where to begin. Maybe I was too desperate a case.

"What is balance for you?" He asked me.

"It is being able to control my body without being offset to one side or another."

"Well done. You are quite right about that."

My ego joyfully welcomed the compliment.

"You're not wrong if you act alone. I am sure you can easily walk on a beam, but in martial arts, balance is something that is done in pairs."

I really could not see how anyone could do that in pairs. He did not give me time to meditate on the subject.

"A fight is not done alone. We must learn to use our opponent from all points of view, even to stabilize ourselves. We'll do a simple exercise. You'll walk with your eyes closed around this big tree, I want you to notice every oscillation, every little imbalance that your body will suffer."

I executed without question. After three laps around the tree, he stopped me.

"I never realized that focusing on these imbalances, we could feel so much."

"This exercise is a good way to help you understand the micro imbalances that an experienced opponent can feel."

"This is what you did with me earlier, isn't it?"

"Yes, but now you're going to repeat the same exercise using this."

He held out a branch, more like a twig, of about twenty centimeters long. I began to walk slowly, touching the tip of the twig against the tree. The change was amazing. How could something so frail manage to stabilize me so?

"It's unbelievable. How do..."

He did not give me time to ask my question.

"Balance is something fragile, but also something easy to handle. It's only a matter of timing. Even before your body is carried away by one of those tiny imbalances does it compensate by leaning against what you're using as a crutch."

"It does not make any sense, a twig can't support my body's weight."

"The twig does not need to, it simply indicates that there is a loss of balance. It amplifies your acuity while helping you regain control. That's what I did with you just now when you gripped me. You took the twig's place."

"Yes, but when I attacked you with a kick, I did not destabilize you."

"That's right. This is where *ishiki* comes in. Whether you train with a small branch, or use your partner to stabilize yourself, little by little you begin to become aware of these shortcomings not only on yourself but also on your opponent."

It seemed too simple, there had to be something else to it.

"But..." I added, waiting for a follow-up.

"But it requires developing good biomechanics knowledge of the human body. Grab me."

As I had done before, I grabbed him in uchi komi.

"I'll break your posture, try to resist and understand what I do."

In a split second, I found myself falling to my left, I could not do anything to prevent it.

"How did you do that? I feel like you did nothing."

He approached me and again, he grabbed me like a *judoka*.

"You have to understand how the body works. What will happen if I raise your right arm?"

"I am slightly deported to my left, but I'm still stable."

"OK, but if at the same time I place my right hand on your shoulder and I move it slightly backwards..."

He barely pushed my shoulder a few millimeters back.

"I find myself arched backwards, with my weight on my lower back. This is what you did to me, isn't it?"

"Yes, but in a combat situation, it is done too fast for you to realize what is happening. That is why we must use our twig to stabilize us. Try to throw me anyway you want," he said, grabbing me firmly.

Even though I tried to get close to him to make him fall, I could not position myself properly. Not only could I not control him, but I felt he was manipulating me like a puppet.

"Where is the twig?"

I did not understand how he kept me at a distance.

"How do you react so quickly to my movements? I myself do not know what I will do from one moment to the next."

"It's simple, I increase my balance using you. Observe how I position my right arm."

Instead of holding his right elbow in front of him, as is usually done, his right hand gripped me by keeping the palm facing down. His elbow, parallel to the ground, pointed outward. I came to understand that his arm was like a lever. He did not need to see that I was trying to project him. When I approached him, his outstretched arm pushed his body back automatically, making it impossible to grab him conventionally. He made me do several exercises that gradually led me to better feel not only my own imbalances, but also his.

"Earlier, you talked about balance being as important in my head as with my body. What did you mean by that?"

"If you aspire to win a fight, you're probably going to use more energy than necessary to achieve your goal. The roundhouse kick you used against me was so powerful that you had no choice but to sacrifice your balance. Wanting too much isn't better than not enough. When the desire is too strong, it borders on obsession, which in turn leads to a loss of control. We must learn to find balance."

I had read something like that when informing myself on Buddhism. This training with my teacher was the first in a long series on balance. Even today, when I walk along a wall, I enjoy how simple contact with the tip of a fingernail on its surface can change the way I move.

Chapter 31
Bugei

As I did on occasion, I was accompanying my teacher on his walk with his dogs. The night tore the day's last rays of sun. The scorching summer heat seemed not to affect his pets who were walking at a rapid pace. The conversation had drifted on the subject of different categories of martial art practitioners. Of course, we had discussed this many times, but each exchange on the subject brought me new understandings.

"You've already told me that when you took part in competitions with your students, you always came back with an impressive number of trophies."

"That's right, but my students worked hard to achieve these results."

"According to you, what was it that made your team so good?"

I had never stopped to analyze our victories in this way. I was content to reap the honors. Thinking about it, a particular point stood out.

"I think part of our success was based on the training I was having them follow."

"What made them so good?" Asked the old man.

"Automatic reflexes. I forced my students to constantly repeat the most appropriate sequences. I also taught them ways to retreat to better counter-attack. The opponent was sure he had just taken control, but at the last second, we exploited the doors he left open because he became too confident."

"So you think the secret of victory rested on automatic reflexes?"

"Yes! For sure."

"I believe you. One of the best ways to optimize the speed of a fighter is to save time on the development of the response."

"What do you mean?"

"It's simple. When a fist comes towards your face, the eye perceives it. The image is transmitted by the optic nerve and goes to your brain, where the electrical impulses are transformed into information. The answer to this analysis is something like: "Oh no, is a fist coming up in my face, I must do something." After seeing the danger, the brain establishes a strategy. This mechanism takes time. Then, through the nerves, a the speed of one hundred meters per second, the brain sends orders to the muscles to react. Only once this process is complete will the arm move to try to block the attack. Needless to say, the defender has a delay on the attacker."

I had never seen an attack in this light. I wondered where this conversation would lead us, until something clicked in my head.

"This is where automatic reflexes are taken into account."

"That's right," he said, "they allow us to save time by avoiding developing a strategy to protect ourselves. Avoiding having to choose between various options, the body reacts more quickly."

I suddenly realized that had I insisted more, we could have performed better during competitions. My teacher went on.

"These automatic reflexes are so effective that they may become hazardous when used in combat sports."

"What I was teaching was a martial art though."

"If you say so."

These last words were frustrating. He had just implied that I did not practice a martial art, but a combat sport.

"What difference is there between the two? I do not see it, both are made to fight."

At the time, this statement was the only truth in my small, beginner's brain.

"There is a huge difference," said my teacher, "in traditional *budo* where there is no competition, the ultimate goal is survival. This is what we call *bugei*, it is what I am conveying to you."

"That's what I taught my students, to survive an attack."

"Oh yes! Did you show them how to take out eyes or break a knee?"

"Well, yeah… sort of."

Passing under a street lamp, I could see the old master's look staring at me from the corner of his eye.

"And did you practice the automatic reflexes of sticking nails in the eyes or destroying a joint?" He asked me in all seriousness.

"Of course not, I'm not crazy."

"That's why you were teaching a combat sport. Imagine a competition where one of the participants has no other options, without thinking, he would sink his fingers into the eyes of his opponent. These practices related to survival were all removed from combat sports to avoid such accidents. It's a good thing, otherwise it would become a carnage."

I understood where he was going. Thinking about it, most of the techniques I had shown at the time was politically correct. If I compared them with what he was teaching me, my old martial art was a game of confrontation. The old man suddenly crossed the road to go to the vending machine on the street corner. He admonished a young man who tried to extort a bottle of alcohol from one of the machines. I had already noticed adults scold children who were not their own. The teenager looked down at the ground while the master talked to him. He did not raise his voice, but I guessed that his every word bore fruit. The young one bowed several times and then walked away.

"It's part of my martial art, to protect people, sometimes against themselves."

"Why did you sermon him? He could not buy anything anyway, he would have needed an identity card proving that he was over 20."

"You never know, it's technology, and technology is far from being reliable," said the man that did not own a PC.

"That's why you do not like computers?" I asked.

"I have nothing against them, they can be useful sometimes. But too many people stop living and thinking for themselves with these machines. It's too fast, too thoughtless. In the past, when someone wrote a letter, they took the time to weigh the words, to choose the right ones, the most suitable expressions to charm, explain, or lecture. Today, people have lost the sense of the value of words, they write without realizing the weight of these writings. How many people send emails under the emotions of the moment and regret it later? Spreading thoughts on paper is no longer a way."

I took advantage of his last words to bring the conversation back to martial arts.

"A way, just like the do of aikido, kendo and other martial arts?"

"That's right. Again, there has been a filtering of techniques just like in combat sports."

"What do you mean? There is no risk of bad automation, since there is no competition in most martial arts that end in do."

"Yes, but do means the way, the spiritual path. Many of these arts rely on certain gestural coding to create a meditative state. It is difficult to enter this state when violence is the ignition of the technique."

I had never considered these martial arts in this light. Thinking about it, it was quite logical. He continued his explanation.

"These arts are using one of the paths that can lead to *satori*."

I knew this Japanese word could be roughly translated as enlightenment, or understanding of the universe.

"To achieve this, the student must perform many repetitions taking great care to recreate the same gestures. It is meditation done with the body and mind. But the *mantra* is especially made by the body. Once the choreography is well understood, the mind finds the path to peace."

"Then why is it that you do not make me repeat the movements in the same way with the same accuracy?"

"Because no aggression is completely identical. Each of them is different. If the foot of the attacker is not in the same angle, the response will not be the same. Each circumstance is unique and the goal is not to reproduce a situation, but you learn to adapt to each of them."

At that time, I had already realized that if the attack differed in the least, I had to adjust myself to what my opponent gave me. The old man continued.

"In *bugei*, it is not we who decide which technique to use. It is the technique who chooses for us. We should react according to the situation. Establishing a strategy in advance brings a risk of losing the fight. If everything does not go as planned, we may be destabilized, so I am teaching you to react rather than try to predict. We can anticipate contexts, but to know exactly how the opponent will attack, that's more difficult. Sure, we can get him to punch or kick in the way we want, but there will always be some minor variations that we will need to be wary of."

It all seemed so simple said like that, but in *budo*, and especially with my teacher, I had learned that nothing is as obvious as it seemed. A question came to mind.

"In all this, what is the best martial art?"

"There are no better or worse. Only what is needed to meet the expectations of practitioners. If someone is happy when training in combat sports, then good. Whatever we choose, it has to match the needs of the moment."

"The moment... Martial arts are something that last a lifetime, they are much more than a moment."

"You're talking about one life or many?" Asked my mentor.

I did not want to go in that direction. He continued his explanations without insisting on the subject of past lives.

"We are no longer in a time of war. Most people do not feel threatened. For them, whether it is in do arts, or combat sports, it's important to fill that little something missing in their lives. For those who wish to defend themselves against real attacks, they will continue to search until they find the right martial art."

"Yes, but there are so many teachers who sell their style with the idea that they are the best, that their students can face any situation."

"You can not save humanity. This is where the practitioner's judgment comes in. It is for this reason that martial artists must ask the right questions and should not hesitate to ask their instructor. If the instructor pushes back the answer to later, hesitates, or ignores the question, then the student should seriously question his skills. And if he has an answer, the student will have to learn to judge its relevance. In true *budo* there is nothing useless. Each movement, each technique, each angle can be justified in a combat logic."

"I remember one of my first teachers kept telling me that I would understand later. Today, I know he could not give me an answer because what he showed me was visually spectacular, but from a strategic point of view, it was completely absurd. At the time, I did not have the competence to see it, but now it's different. The sad part is that he still teaches a lot of people."

"They will remain with him until they realize that he is not good and what he teaches can even be dangerous."

"Yes, that's right. What can we do to help people avoid this?"

"You can not do anything. We are the sum of our experiences, good or bad. You had several teachers before me. You have left them all at one time or another. What tells you that one day you won't realize that what I teach is totally wrong?"

Although I could not see his face clearly in the darkness of the evening, I guessed that the old man was having fun at my expense.

"That won't happen," I said with assurance.

"Oh really? What guarantee do you have of that? You sure seem confident."

"You've never hesitated to answer any of my questions. Now I am not learning any more techniques, I am mastering principles and basic mechanics."

Chapter 32

Hat

I often happened to converse, or rather should I say, philosophize with my teacher. Those moments of exchange often took place when we were eating together. I loved those moments even if sometimes he managed to push me too far, to highlight my faults and my character traits which I was not very proud of. I think he liked talking to me or at least answer my questions, which I must admit, were not always relevant.

That day, before going to a *sobaya*, a noodle restaurant, my teacher walked into a store that offered seven or eight floors of clothing for all tastes.

"What are we doing here? I did not know you liked to shop."

"I think I'm going to buy a new hat."

"I've never seen you with a hat."

"Not knowing when I'll use it is not a reason for not wanting to get one. You never know, it could be useful one day."

I followed my teacher who set his foot on the escalator.

"It's a bit like *budo*," he said, laughing, "once we set foot on the first step, it is difficult to go back, one can only to be carried away. The trick is knowing where you are going."

That's what I liked about him. I never knew what to expect. Comparing the escalator to the progression of *budo*, only he could initiate such a subject.

"I think it's very different. In martial arts, we must make efforts to improve, but here one can only to be carried away."

"Yes, but to get here, there was a huge chain of events," he went on.

"I do not see which ones. You needed a hat, we walked past the building and you took this opportunity. It was not a coincidence, it was the result of a wish."

"I never said that I needed a hat. I said I thought about buying a hat. It's not a necessity, but an idea like that."

We were on the third floor when he left the escalator and headed for the men's shirts section. I did not know if he was talking aimlessly or if he was trying to guide me somewhere.

"Why did you compare the escalator with *budo*?" I asked.

"For no particular reason. It just came out like that."

It was the first time he spoke just to talk, but I felt there was actually more to it.

"Browsing stores is a bit like doing martial arts."

I did not see the connection between the two, but I let him go on, I felt it was going to get interesting.

"In both situations, we must be free to make the most of it."

I do not know if I've mentioned it before, but I was sometimes a little confused listening to his explanations. Just like in this case.

"Free of what? Nobody prevents you from doing martial arts or buying anything."

"If you do not have enough money or if your wife finds you something else to do rather than come help me choose a hat, do you not lack freedom?"

"It is difficult to get something when you have no money in your pocket, I know that very well. As for the spouse, I consider it normal to give her time. I do not see the connection between the two."

"It's quite a coincidence that we are here to shop or to train in martial arts. If you do not have the freedom to choose the appropriate moment, this moment will not return. What that tells me the hat that should have been mine has not been sold in the last few minutes because I was waiting for you while you were in the bathroom? Maybe when you went to visit your mother-in-law you missed the martial arts class you needed the most to improve. That class might have held the key, the trigger that happens from time to time."

"Yes, but these techniques will always be there. Surely I should be able to learn them later."

"The technique yes, but the feeling of the moment that accompanied this teaching is unique, it will not return. The technique is a robotic series of movements, without the emotions that give it life, it is not much."

I decided to bring the conversation back to shopping.

"Okay. But once you get to the section of the store you're interested in, if you have money, you only have to pay and leave with the item you want. It does not require as much effort as *budo*."

"I quite agree with you, but it's so easy to buy a poor quality product. Observe this shirt, it looks very much like the one you see there. Yet there is a huge difference in price between the two."

He took the most expensive one and brought it close to the cheaper one.

"Compare the two."

To the naked eye, I did not notice any difference. For me, aside from some differences in the design of the fabric, they seemed identical.

"It's like *budo*," he said, "most people have trouble seeing the difference between low-end and quality product."

He opened the cheap shirt.

"Look at the coarseness of the stitching. Just like *budo*, if everything is not sewn properly, you expose yourself to weaknesses."

"These are just small pieces of thread that we notice once we are wearing the shirt. We only have to trim them, it won't show."

"Unfortunately, this is what too many martial arts teachers do. They do not realize the difference and do not hesitate to cut what exceeds without wondering why there are so many."

I had to find a point where I could argue.

"What is the relationship between freedom and these shirts? I do not see the relationship with the circumstances you mentioned earlier."

"Quality requires more effort. To acquire it, its future owner had to work harder in school, force himself to get a better job. He probably had to, in many cases, study without going out to party with his friends. He made a choice. He did not let himself be influenced. Then he had to find work that suited him best. He perhaps turned down several jobs before finding the right one. Then, gradually increasing his salary, he developed his affinity to see the difference between a cheap shirt and one of quality that stands out. There was a whole set of circumstances that lead to this refinement," he said, holding the most expensive shirt in his hands.

Wow! If there was a speech I did not expect to hear from him, it was that one. I hurried to defend the working class to which I belonged.

"Maybe that person had a richer family that motivated him more in his life. Maybe he did not have to work while studying. Perhaps with his parent's credit card, he never had problems putting gas in his car."

The more I spoke, the more I felt the pressure rise in my face. The old master looked at me, smiling. He had manipulated me.

"You're playing with me, aren't you?"

He seemed particularly proud of having fun at my expense.

"Budo can not be bought, it is deserved. You can buy yourself a quality shirt without knowing why it is better. We can buy ourselves techniques, but we can not buy *budo*. I assure you that one of the essential conditions for good progress is freedom. Budo is instinctive, when we feel the need to do it, we must do it. This means that our mind is receptive to the present moment."

"The choice of training when we feel like it, the possibility of attending a maximum number of classes if we want..." I said to myself while decompressing slowly.

"The freedom of which I speak is done on several levels. It is also that of thinking."

"We are always free to think, as far as I can tell."

"No, you're wrong. Many people who wish to follow the path of *budo* have often practiced several martial arts. In most cases, they continually refer to their past acquisitions. They are hindered by a knowledge that they have carried for a long time. They do not learn, they just try to validate what they already know, even though in many cases the baggage is poor."

The old master placed the shirt back and headed toward the escalator.

"We should not be content in remaining a prisoner of a plateau. It takes effort to go further, higher."

"You were talking about freedom, but modern living no longer allows us to put as much time in martial arts as in the old days."

"So you think they had no obligations, families to feed back then? Training after spending ten hours working in the field, this is not what I call total freedom."

"But in this case, what prevents us from becoming as good as they were?"

"Apart from the fact that they had to use their techniques on a battlefield in real situations?"

"I used to work in the field of security, I had the chance to use my techniques quite often."

"So, in theory, nothing prevents you from reaching a high level. But never forget that you must listen to your instincts. Consistency and freedom are essential in order to progress. If you feel the need to train, then do it, do not wait."

We had just arrived at the hat section. The old master took a quick glance and headed back to the exit.

"You did not take the time to examine the hats, you came here for that. You barely even looked at them."

"My instinct tells me that it is not the time for me to buy one, after all. I like my head to be free."

Chapter 33
Mystique

I was watching a video one of my friends had shared on the internet. It was showing a Western teacher who was demonstrating a simple technique. In its approach, there was something specific that stood out, but I could not put my finger on it. There was a touch of mystery in its execution. I admit that my curiosity was piqued. I had to show this video to my teacher.

"I do not understand why it gets me worked up. The form is basic, nothing should surprise me, although there is something that intrigues me in this."

I brought my tablet. The old master examined the video, then smiled.

"When looking at a demonstration like this, there are two aspects to be considered," he said, "there is the container and everything in it. First, there is the art. It can be good, excellent, or completely absurd. The art is the content. Once removed, only the container remains."

I thought it was a rather simplistic way of speaking of the one who performs the technique, but looking at it that way, it made sense.

"What is the thing that attracts you to this person?" He asked me.

"Everything. He gives the impression of being powerful, his way of expressing himself is... I would not say fascinating, but intriguing. Even his walk has something special about it."

The old master nodded, frowning.

"Are you certain that his technique is good?"

He had cast doubt in my mind. I looked at the delivery a few times. My teacher was waiting patiently for several minutes when he asked me to replay one of the sequences of the video.

"Do you not notice something strange in the way his partner attacks?"

"No, I do not see anything," I replied. I was a little worried about not detecting a flaw in the technique, if there was one.

"Look carefully," he said, "his partner's punch does not reach all the way to his face. It changes path slightly. If he had continued, it really wouldn't be pretty to look at."

Such a pretty technique! It felt a little funny to hear.

"It's true! How did I not notice that?"

"Because it is hidden."

"Hidden? We can clearly see the arm change course. What I do not understand is, how did I not see this before?"

"There are plenty of ways to hide things. How would you describe this man?"

I hesitated to call him a master with what I had just realized. I was trying to find various qualifiers when a word popped into my mind.

"Mystical! I would say he is mystical."

My teacher seemed pleased with my answer.

"You're right, that is the best feature we can grant him. Everything is present to produce an impression of mystery, a feeling that many martial artists seek. Yet there is nothing magical about *budo*. It is not uncommon for teachers to give themselves an... occult look."

Hearing these words, I became aware of certain details I had not noticed that now leaped out at me.

"A wisp of smoke in the background, they are burning incense."

"It adds an image of spirituality," said the master, "even if one does not realize it at the time, our subconscious records this kind of staging, but there is more. Observe how the students are watching him. They are completely bewitched by his character."

"That's right, they seem to be admiring him."

"The way they admire him has influenced your perception. Do you find his way of speaking natural?" He asked me.

"I find it captivating."

"This is because it is studied. We immediately can say that this man must have had very extensive public speaking training. His tone of voice, intonation, the pauses he takes are well-timed, it is likely that this man has taken a course in theater or public speaking. See how his actions reinforce his words. All his actions are reflected, studied."

I looked at the video again and already I considered the individual less fascinating. Merely realizing that his attacker had allowed the technique to work had disappointed me to no end. The master went on.

"Do you have other demonstrations by him?"

"No, it's the only one I found."

"It's very similar to a marketing promotion. They show just enough so that people would want more. You knew that there were some marketing firms that take *dojo* owners in their charge and help them grow their customer base, right?"

"No, how do they do that?"

"They completely transform the personality of the teacher. Generally, they draw a different aura around him. From his speech to his way of dressing outside the *dojo*. With that, there is even professional monitoring done with the members of the organization."

How could he know all this? He does not even own a computer and I doubt that he lets himself being run by one of these firms.

"A few years ago, I had a student who was approached by one of these agencies. They completely transformed his appearance, they also worked his verbal skills and body language. His school grew to a few several hundred members in the span of one year."

"Wow! That is good. It never hurt to be able to make money with what we love."

"He became bored quite quickly. He could not teach the techniques the same way as before. He had to make it easier for his students. If a student leaves a class by failing the last thing he learned, it is statistically proven that he is more likely to give up. So to avoid losing students, he made the techniques much easier to perform."

"That's not right. People can not become proficient in these conditions."

"That's right, they can't. As they are capable of performing these techniques, they think they are good. That is the danger," said the master.

I thought back to the many times I had left my teacher, frustrated of not being up to par. Difficult times in which my ego took a hit.

"We must live well," he went on, "earning money is not bad in itself, as long as it does not influence the quality of learning. We teach from the heart. The goal is to help the student grow. We must never lose sight of that goal."

His wide-open eyes stared at me intensely. He seemed to expect a reply that did not come.

"Many people lack spirituality. This age deprives us of the gods that were so important to our ancestors."

I realized he was talking about nature spirits, the ones so dear in *Shinto*ism.

"Most people seek a belief system that they can attach themselves to. Nowadays, there is a lack in this area to fill. Unfortunately, many people exploit these vulnerabilities. It is no coincidence that there are so many sects that emerge everywhere around the planet. It is not for nothing that young people let themselves be sucked in by various fanatic groups."

I broke down the video again, but this time there was no more admiration in my eyes. The master saw my disappointment.

"We should do martial arts naturally. In this case, it is obvious that this man is not, this is a character. A particularly successful character, but still a character. Nothing like what a sincere teacher should be."

A short generic giving information on the school followed. The professor laughed.

"Look at his title, he borrowed two titles from different schools to unite them in a single word. For a beginner, such a title can be impressive. Any experienced teacher will giggle at seeing this. It is not done in any martial art. The marketer that made him take such a name is obviously not aware of traditional martial arts. But nevertheless, this prestigious title will surely draw him a great number of students."

"I'm lucky to have found you," I said, "I could have come across a charlatan like this myself.'

"I'm only here to help you repair your bad karma."

Chapter 34
The spirit of the blade

That day, we had to be close to thirty participants in the master's class. We were practicing with the sword. For training, we used *bokken*, wooden replicas of *katana*. To be honest, at that time, I was rather proud of the way I was manipulating my weapon. I managed to overthrow the harshest attacks, I managed to redirect the opponent's weapon against a second assailant. There are times like this when it seems that everything we undertake succeeds. I moved at the right time in the right corner, using the ideal distance, what more could we ask for from a swordsman?

I should have known it was all too good to be true, the old master did not miss the opportunity to deflate my ego, which, I must admit, was beginning to take on worrying proportions. When my opponent tried to poke me with the tip of his weapon, I flipped my blade around, and with its dull side, I managed to almost drop my training partner to the ground.

"Bravo," said the latter, "I would like to be able to do the same."

"It will come, don't worry. It is only a matter of practice and, of course, a bit of talent."

I had just set foot in a trap that would lead me to my incompetence. My teacher was behind me when I said those words.

"Yes, I must admit that you have a certain ease."

I was not expecting a compliment from him, I did not know if I should be flattered or terrified.

"You're a good technician. Maybe someday you'll know how to wield the sword," he said.

Nobody was moving in the *dojo*. All were listening attentively.

"You are saying that I do not know how to use a sword?"

"No, I never said that. In fact, you are manipulating it well... like a technician."

What more could he ask for? Technique is the secret of handling weapons.

"Is that not the requirement to develop good control of the *katana*?" I asked, not knowing where he was going.

He made the students sit on the *tatami*. He took my *bokken* and weighed it. With one hand, he held it parallel to the ground and shook it with small jolts. He placed his other hand on the handle, raised the weapon above his head and with a powerful swing, the wooden sword split the air, hissing. His gaze went around the congregation and stopped at me.

"What is the relationship we should have with a sword? What happens when we hold it in our hands?"

I was hoping someone else would answer. All the eyes were pointing in my direction. I felt trapped. Every second of silence seemed endless. I had to give an answer.

"It's simple, the sword has to become an extension of our body."

I looked over at my companions who nodded and I was satisfied with my answer.

"Good answer," said the old master.

I do not remember how I felt, but I guess I was smiling stupidly, proud to have discovered this obvious fact. That's when I had the impression that my ego was being deflated with a *katana*.

"Yes, that's what we tell children when handling a sword. The weapon must become an extension of your body. It is easy to understand and all, this concept is immune to idiots. It is a technician's response."

Some days, my teacher did not use white gloves. He might have been a master, a wise man, he was nonetheless human. I understood this much later. It is with frustration that I was replaying his last words in my mind. Then he continued.

"Weapons, swords especially, have their own life. We must learn to listen to them. But still, they are just accessories. Use them as a simple tool and allow yourself to get rid of it if necessary."

"What do you mean by that?" I asked.

"If necessary, we can throw our sword at an opponent's face, using it as an object to distract him."

"To get rid of it this way... No sword school worthy of the name would teach such a thing,' I said in a slightly offended tone.

"You are right. These schools teach the way, and not survival. In a situation where only this gesture can save your life, there is no hesitation. Our school teaches *bugei* and is not an institution where spirituality reigns. This does not mean that there is no spirituality in our art, on the contrary, but the ultimate goal is to survive while protecting our physical integrity, our family and our village."

In a few words, he had described the warrior spirit. He continued.

"The sword is more than that. It has its own life. When we work it at a certain level, the swordsman must be guided by his blade."

"Is it not likely to cause him to kill without reason?" I threw out raising my voice.

"Like humans, there are good and bad blades. Bad blades love blood, while a good blade simply seeks to protect its master."

He attributed emotions to a piece of metal. At the time, I was completely overwhelmed by the remarks. I let him go on without saying anything.

"The most difficult thing when handling weapons is to develop such sensitivity that we come to know what they want. From this point, you can move released from the technique."

The old master looked at me. He saw that I did not understand what he wanted to convey.

"Take your *bokken*," he said.

He raised the weapon above his head and hit me quickly. I just placed my blade on the side as I had learned. My *sensei*'s blade slid to my right without reaching me.

"What you just did is a technique. A well-programmed robot could do the same. Now attack me as you will."

I place myself in *hasso no kamae*, a natural posture that offers plenty of mobility. I moved forward crossing my legs to force my teacher to recede. He waited calmly and held the sword in his right hand. He did not seem concerned about what was to come. By the time he moved to adjust his position, I projected my blade horizontally, towards his head. He turned his body counterclockwise and blocked my attack with his sword vertically, tip down. His slightly curved arm offered him the necessary strength to fight my impulse. He had no technique, he was content to hide behind his blade.

"Impressive," I said, maintaining the pressure of my sword against his.

"That's nothing," he said, lifting my wooden sword making me lose balance. I found myself on my lower back which was arched. He took my *bokken* handle with one hand while doing a leg swipe. I fell on my back, with two swords pointed at my throat.

After a few moments of amazement, the students began to applaud. The old man did not seem moved.

"Technique is necessary," he said, "but it is only one step in the mastery of the sword. You must learn to communicate with it, to listen."

The end of the class was announced. After the ending ceremony, I turned to my teacher to ask him one last question.

"How can we achieve this?" I asked.

"Achieve what?" He replied, smiling.

"Communicating with it."

"We need to listen, talk to it, respect it. You must learn to converse with it."

"But if we throw it at an opponent's face, are we not disrespecting it?"

"How can we show disrespect to a piece of metal?" Master said, stepping out of the *dojo*.

Chapter 35
Who am I?

We were walking in some alleys in Asakusa. The autumn sun slowly warmed the bitumen still cool from the night before. I rubbed my palms for better or worse, trying to root out some heat. I looked at my teacher who seemed to be in no way affected by this temperature.

"You do not seem cold. My fingers are freezing."

"You only have to send more blood into your hands."

As I was about to ask for an explanation, we walked past an elderly lady accompanied by two small children on the corner of the street. Curved back, she walked with difficulty. The younger of the two toddlers clung to her coat. I could hear her telling an old Japanese tale.

"Poor woman," I said, "I feel bad for her."

"I have more pity for you than for her," replied my teacher.

"What do you mean? Why do you say that?"

"Can you not see how radiant she looks? She is with her grandchildren, she takes pleasure in telling them stories. Her physical ability is currently the least of her worries. Can you say you're this blissfully happy now?"

"I'm good, I feel good. I am happy."

"My question is simple. Are you happy or is something missing in your miserable existence?"

He was being hard on me. Then I wondered what it meant to be truly happy. I was doing what I loved, I was surrounded by wonderful friends. Of course, I missed my family at times, but I think I could say that everything went for the best in my life. And yet...

"Do you not have the impression that something is missing, that there is a void to fill, but you are unable to see what it is?" Asked the master.

This devil of a man had seen right. I had always felt a void without ever knowing exactly what it was. My master gave me no time to answer.

"Do not worry about that void, most people feel it."

"What makes me feel this way?"

"It can be many little things. The feeling of not belonging or having no purpose. The feeling of being useless is much more present than one might believe."

I loved philosophizing with my teacher. I knew I would be served that morning.

"I think a lot of people need to feel valued. Many will do so through their possessions. The most beautiful house in the neighborhood, the most luxurious car possible and anything that can demonstrate their professional success to others. But the money probably will not fill the void felt by most individuals."

"In any case, it isn't my type to display myself with all those things," I replied.

"Oh really? And if you won the lottery, would you not buy you a sumptuous residence?"

"No, I would go to the countryside, far from everything, and I would build the best training ground one can dream of."

"I think you're telling the truth, because you have a goal: To become the most competent possible in martial arts. Budo is a fertile ground for developing self-esteem. Most people look at a black belt with admiration, great respect and in some cases an undeniable fear. It is rewarding for those who have reached a good level."

"I have worked hard to get to where I am and I'm proud of it."

"The vast majority of practitioners will never stand out. Human beings seek the recognition of their peers. Almost all occupy the same kind of functions throughout their lives. All these years will go by in total anonymity. It will be difficult to emerge from their lot by their actions alone. They will try to attract the attention of others by displaying their wealth."

I thought back about some of my friends who fit in this frame perfectly. Then some of his words came to mind.

"You mentioned people who have the feeling of being useless."

"There are people who have more awake consciousness and stronger personalities, the feeling of worthlessness frequently eats them. They feel that their existence is useless, that they could perhaps do more. Some find their ways in jobs where they can help their fellows. Whether through military presence, humanitarian work, or simply volunteering for the less fortunate, these people fill in part, or in full, this gap in their lives."

"Do you mean to say that the anonymous beings you mentioned earlier are useless?"

"Many people are only a cog that can be changed on demand in a society based on consumption rather than human values."

I have already learned the hard way that no one is irreplaceable. I used to have a well-paying job where I was replaced by someone who was paid less.

"But how can we know what we lack, what is this void we must fill?"

"It is hard to find. We must ask all sorts of questions and we must especially be honest in our responses. For many people, confessing that they are not happy or that they could be better off, is confessing their failure. Life is a fight, you have to take risks. We must dare charge forward. But most people are afraid and ashamed of failure. What would have happened if I had said no when you came to see me?"

"I would have harassed you until you accepted me."
"And why is that?"
"Because I wanted to improve."
"Is this is what we call having a goal?"
"I think so, yes."

I realized that for years, my aspiration was oriented towards martial arts. So what could be that void that occasionally came to torment me? The old master continued, preventing me from feeling sorry for my miserable fate.

"It's fine to have a goal, but you have to do it for yourself."

"Nobody ever asked me to do martial arts," I said as if he was blaming me for something.

"I know," he replied, "I was rather talking about the intention to impress others, to try to find the recognition of peers."

There he had touched a nerve. At that time, I was still looking to stand out from other practitioners. Today, I do not care. I know the level I have reached and I have nothing to prove to anyone. The master seemed to have a lot to say on the subject.

"Most people have not learned to be happy. They are only used to fulfilling desires. They are working to have enough money to fill the fantasy of the moment, then, very soon after, this desire gives way to another. It is not by overlapping desire with desire that we build a balanced personality."

"Is this why so many people behave like spoiled children?" I risked.

"Yes. In poorer countries, people who have almost nothing are often happier than in rich nations. They have come to appreciate what they have. The values are not the same. When we come to break away from these desires, we become free. Think of all your friends who have once been unhappy, or even depressed because the woman or the man they wanted did not like them back. Whether it be the desire of possessing objects or people, desire makes them sad, if not unhappy. If you have what you want and you can afford it, then good. Otherwise, you must learn not to be touched by those things."

I thought of some friends where the purchase of gadgets of all sorts followed each other at an alarming rate. These friends told me I was lucky to go to Japan as I did. Yet they spent much more money than me in a year. I possessed neither a car of the year or a premium phone that came with an exorbitant contract. It was a matter of choice.

Chapter 36
A matter of choice

When I presented myself at the *dojo* that day, I really was not in a good mood. The master soon realized this, but did not mention anything. After the class, he walked over to me and invited me for tea at the kissaten on the corner of the street. We often went there. The owner always showed a radiant smile when she saw him. Of course, the place no longer had any link to a traditional tea house. It also served coffee and sandwiches. I liked the tea, but I had the impression that coffee would have a more calming effect on my agitated self. At that time, I was far from being disciplined. My fury manifested itself regularly.

"So why is it that you're displaying such a negative aura?" Asked the old man as if he was talking to a child. For a second, I had the impression of standing in front of my father.

"To be honest, during the whole training session, I was cranky."

"What terrible thing has happened for you to be in such a state? An international arms dealer attacked you?"

I did not even realize the absurdity of the question.

"It is one of my friends. He enrages me."

"Enrage?! That is quite a strong word. How was he able to manipulate you to this point? He must have a very strong hold on you."

"Manipulate me? He did not manipulate me, he does not control me."

"No? Then why are you like that?"

"He says he came to Japan to train martial arts."

"I understand how maddening that is. Coming to Japan for that, what can be more frustrating?"

The master had fun at my expense. It did not help my mood at all.

"Instead of attending your class today, he preferred to go sightseeing."

"That is what has put you in such a state? What will happen when we kidnap your wife and children?"

I did not stand up to his sarcastic comments. It was better that I remain silent rather than be rude. He did not give me much relief.

"I think I understand. It was you who funded his trip and you're shocked to have wasted your money this way."

"Of course not, it is not I who covered the cost of his holiday. I do not have the means to do that and if one day I happen to get rich, do not count on me to pay for him."

"In that case, if he is paying for himself, why are you angry?"

"I find it unfortunate to come such a long distance with a very specific purpose, to finally do something else."

"Is this the first time he comes to Japan?"

"Yes, he's been here for almost a week. It is he who trained with me for the last two times we came to the *dojo*."

"Where is he now?"

"He went to visit Kyoto."

"And you are furious that he did not invite you, is that it? You wish to visit this city. It's beautiful in that area, you know."

"Absolutely not. I'm not a tourist, I am here to learn, to be able to acquire everything that you will teach me."

"How can it affect you so that he takes a few days off?"

I came to realize that since the beginning of our conversation, my teacher took up the defense of my friend. I did not understand why he did so. How could he excuse such a behavior?

"Why are you defending him? I do not understand."

"Because it's his choice. Not everyone is as, um... well, as determined as you are. He is paying for his trip, and may dispose of his time as he wishes."

"But he does not realize what he is missing out on."

"We can practice martial arts for various reasons. Each has personal motivations and interest levels of their own. You said it yourself, he has made a long journey to get here, it's normal that he wants to see the country."

"Maybe, but it's beyond me."

"The problem is not from him but from you. It is you who is possibly a little too uncompromising."

"That is not a problem, it's a passion."

"You think everyone should share the same enthusiasm as you do. So why do you not do music or calligraphy? You should also have these passions. No, really, I do not understand why you do not put as much effort in these areas."

The lady returned to serve tea to my master. As I was about to order another coffee, he put his hand on my wrist and asked the lady to bring me hot tea.

"It will calm you."

"But I want coffee," I said, offended.

"Yes, but I have a passion for tea, I want to share it with you."

"But it's my choice, I'm the one who decides."

"Oh!" Said the master, smiling.

Chapter 37
The music of *budo*

The more I evolved under the supervision of my teacher, the more I noticed the depth of traditional martial arts. Arriving to his house one night, I had him listen to a song on my music player, the song Over the Hills and Far Away, by the band Nightwish, I expected him to be critical about this type of music. To my surprise, he said he liked it, that they had a lot of talent. He added that if it had been *budo*, these people would have been accomplished martial artists.

"How can you make such a parallel? Music and martial arts are two completely opposite worlds."

"They are different in the acts, but not so different in the emotions involved."

There was no way I would leave it there. I had to deepen the subject. I came to help walk his dogs. The time was right for such a conversation.

"You're saying the emotions are the same?"

"The same emotions, or rather, a similar journey. We should perceive martial arts the same way we do with music."

"I do not understand."

"It's simple, you'll see. The first step is to learn the technique. It can be done robotically or with the highest concentration."

He had just see-sawed from music to *budo*. I expected both subjects to overlap and that is what happened when he went on.

"Many people begin playing instruments hoping to become virtuosos in a few months. They are dreamers."

The relationship with martial arts was particularly easy to establish. How many beginners believe becoming a Jackie Chan or Bruce Lee a few years of practice?

"In *budo* as in music, it is not everyone who has the ability to fully enjoy a performance. Most customers in a restaurant can
hear background music without realizing that it is a masterpiece. The first stage of this journey is enlightenment. See what is grandiose, differentiate what is superior."

At that moment, I understood the analogy between the martial arts universe and music better. Often, when a technique is performed without spectacular movements, many people believe it to be inefficient. They feel that something is missing. If we repeat the same identical sequence by letting out a few shouts, making big gestures and giving our face an aggressive expression, they will think that the technique is much more efficient, without realizing that we have done the same thing.

"To master music, we must learn to listen and not just be content with owning it, we must feel it. We must acknowledge that each partition, each technique is unique. Each of these creations has a purpose, for its creator and the listener. You can hear and not listen. One can look and not see. Although a technique's only goal is to create a diversion, it has its reason to exist. This Awareness leads us away from the mere collector. Even if one has thousands of music discs, it is possible that quality is lacking. Nothing touches the soul. We must be aware of the depth of the work, the technique's possibilities. We should know why we want to listen to this work at a particular moment or why a certain technique must be used at this time."

The master spoke with great emotion in his voice. He was not trying to transmit his knowledge, he was trying to awaken my conscience, and he succeeded.

"Finally, we must realize the potential of the work or art, learning to apply this and interpret music that touches the soul. It is necessary to see which technique will be realistic and functional at the time when it is needed. The music notes separately might mean nothing. Together, they become powerful, capable of transporting us to internal worlds. It is the same with techniques."

An ambulance lighting us in all its red glory forced us to place ourselves on the edge of the street. The master continued to talk without making anything of it. I had to approach him to not miss any of his words.

"In 1951, Professor Ichiro Oga discovered three lotus seeds in some ruins in *Chiba* prefecture. He planted the seeds, and the oldest lotus flower in the world bloomed. Be aware that the work and the technique is like those little seeds. Taken from the past,

they open the future to us."

The ambulance turned the corner of the narrow street, further down. The master was silent. I felt unable to endure this silence, this darkness in my thoughts.

"If I understand correctly, the understanding of music has multiple levels?" I said quickly.

"Just like martial arts techniques. The first step is to know your body, learn to move properly in order to develop good *taijutsu*. Practicing our scale of movements, forcing ourselves to make numerous repetitions to master the basic gestures. Then we shall see the *kyojutsu* hiding both in music and techniques."

The principle of *kyojutsu* was to show a false reality to an opponent. If he were certain of reaching your face with a punch, that's probably what he would try to do. With that we trap the aggressor.

"How can there be *kyojutsu* in music?"

"There are lots of subtleties in major works. The music leads you where you do not expect to go. Then comes the tactical aspect. The reason that prompted the composer to create these notes. What is this little move that makes all the difference in a fight? Why did the author decrease the tempo at this point in the piece?"

I thought back to some music that was able to calm me. Then to other pieces who produced the opposite effect. As for martial arts, there were sequences that could make us aggressive and others who brought us a contagious serenity.

"In your opinion, what is the best musical piece of all time?" I asked.

I expected him to cite works of the classical repertoire or to name some traditional Japanese compositions. His answer was quite different.

"There is no better or worse music, there is only what makes us feel good when we need it most."

Chapter 38
Out of our shell

It had snowed that day. Several trains had been delayed. The sidewalks all dressed in white offered an opportunity to practice my balance techniques. Some merchants were sweeping the immaculate thin carpet and tiny piles were accumulating on the side of doors. This area in Japan was not used to having snow. For many people, the day promised itself harsh. As something good comes from every evil, we were very few in the *dojo* that morning. I was hoping that the master would reach the *dojo*, but I could not be sure of it.

One of my friends asked me to explain a technique I had already done, but which I had forgotten some details.

"I do not remember, I would have to have my class notes to answer you. I'm sorry, man."

"At your level, you should know it all by heart," he said.

"Are you crazy, there is far too much material for us to remember everything."

"It is mandatory, mastering everything is the goal that we must achieve."

"Unfortunately, I don't have enough brains for that. I'm not here to train my memory, but to develop my skills. I prefer focusing my efforts on refining the way I move rather than trying to remember everything. Do you think the master remembers it all by heart? Come on, it does not make sense."

"You are free to waste your time," he said.

"How much time do you spend memorizing all this?" I asked.

"A great deal of hours, but I'm sure I'll get there."

"This is why you stagnate," I said in a dry way.

"What, I am stagnant? Who do you think you are?"

"Someone who practices martial arts and does not content himself with analyzing everything little thing."

The tone was rising more and more. Fortunately, the old master entered the *dojo*. He shook off the thin layer of snow that covered his shoulders.

"What is going on?" He asked without taking the trouble to put his dogi on.

My friend hastened to reply.

"We do not agree on some points," he said, "some people think it's not worth the trouble to learn the basics."

"That's not what I said. There is a difference between assimilating the basics and remembering all the techniques the master teaches."

The old man's look wandered from my friend to me. Then he knelt on the ground. All of the other students present did the same and grouped together around him.

"I understand your dilemma," said the master, "if you ask me if I know all the *kata* that make up our style, I will answer yes."

My friend looked at me by displaying a wide smile, but his victory was short-lived.

"I know them, but I can not remember any of them. Besides, I do not want to remember. We must learn, practice them, but without being a slave to the technique. One should not become a collector."

"Then how are you able to show them to us?" Asked my friend.

"I consult my notes when I want to teach a specific technique as it is transmitted in the manuscripts."

I felt sorry for my friend. I ventured to affirm the importance of the basics.

"Yes, but we must learn the basic techniques. I think it is mandatory to know the techniques that offer the main principles, the most essential things, is it not?"

"Yes," said the master, "the techniques are like an egg shell. They are indispensable to give birth to the bird. It must be strong in order to protect the life it creates. However, one day or another, the bird must break out and stand on its own."

The image that had drawn the old sage was powerful. This illustrated the need for basics well, but also the idea of not remaining prisoner to them.

"How long should we train doing these techniques?" Asked my friend.

"Our whole life," answered the master, "we must always return to these basics. We must practice, explore and dissect them in order to understand them. But we can not afford to constantly refer to our memory to improve. In a real fight, we must react and not seek the ideal technique to defend ourselves. Besides, it's good that I do not have to remember all that. I do not have a good memory..." he explained, "and it's not because of age!" He hastened to add with a sneer.

I cast a glance at my friend. He gave me a little nod to say he understood. A question came to mind.

"Can we one day master them sufficiently enough to not have to do them anymore?"

"It would be rather pretentious to believe that we no longer need these *kata*," said the old master, "what I'm trying to tell you is that we do not train martial arts by constantly referring to our memory."

Another student raised his hand.

"In the style of karate I used to practice, we had to learn the material of each belt by heart. We had to memorize them in order to go up to the next grade."

The old master did not seem surprised by this remark.

"Yes, but there is a huge difference between those schools and ours. Here you learn more in one year than most styles do in ten. We have so much material that trying to remember everything is a waste of time. Take notes, describe the techniques and practice them thoroughly. When that is done, forget them until the next time you will do them. Remember the key points, the movements, postures and a few basic principles."

"But if we do not know the techniques, how can we note them down?" Asked the student.

The old master looked at me. I knew he wanted me to answer this question.

"Personally, I always take notes when I have time. Whether it be on paper or on my little tape recorder, I try to describe what we did. Then when I have a little more free time, I copy them into a final draft making sure that I can read them myself. It's a bit like I am doing the training again. It helps me understand so much better."

The old master nodded. Then he rose, and after changing into his dogi, he knelt for the class opening ceremony. Before he pronounced the official words announcing the start, I think I heard him say the following words.

"Repeating these techniques is the work of a lifetime."

Chapter 39

Tyrants

Several years had passed since I had started training with my teacher. Age did not seem to affect him. Of course, his physical flexibility had decreased slightly over the years, but his cognitive abilities compensated for his agility. His martial and even spiritual knowledge never ceased to improve. En route to his residence, I met an old friend I had not seen for a long time. He was going through a bad patch, I was sorry for him. I finally arrived at my teacher's place and had I barely set foot inside when he joined me.

"Do not take your shoes off, it's too nice out, we will walk a little."

I expected to take the dogs out on our hike, but they stayed in. He walked them especially in the evening after sunset. It was late April, neither too hot nor too cold, a perfect time for a walk.

"I met one of my friends that I had not seen for several months," I said, "he was rather depressed. His girlfriend left him."

"He is lucky. It's a good opportunity for him to learn something."

"He's lucky?"

"This is a good chance for him to study his tyrants."

"What do you mean by that? I know his girlfriend, she has nothing of a dictator."

"You told me he was depressed. If this is not because of a tyrant, then what makes him feel like that?"

I found it strange for him to react like so. I did not see the connection with a tyrant.

"What is a tyrant for you?" He asked me.

"It is someone who persecutes us. A dictator, a sadist who harasses us to the point where it affects us."

"Being depressed is a disease, but it is a tyrant who has brought us in this state."

"Yes, but I'm positive that his girlfriend is not a bully, it's just that they are perhaps not meant to be together."

"A tyrant is not necessarily a person, it can be a situation, a combination of circumstances. No matter what it is, we must take the opportunity to learn. Tyrants are excellent teachers. We kneel to them or we fight them."

Turning the corner, we came face to face with an old temple. Setting one foot in the temple courtyard, I had the impression of entering another world. It seemed that the street noises were unable to cross the boundaries of the sacred enclosure. An invisible wall cutting us from the outside world.

"Excellent teachers... You have a funny sense of humor today."

"I'm serious," he said, "imagine that you work in a place where you have to rub shoulders with many colleagues. One of them is always on your back. You dare not replicate because he has been there longer than you. He harasses you, he keeps making your life hard. It becomes increasingly difficult for you to go to the office in the morning. You do not do anything about it. Then one day, a new position opens up elsewhere. You apply for it and eureka, you change your location, but the victory is short-lived. You have to face another colleague who starts doing the same thing."

"It is because there are butts that are not kicked that such situations exist," I replied.

"Although you may be able to defend yourself, it is not the case for everyone. Generally, when we flee a tyrant rather than face it, there are chances that the same scenario will happen again and again, indefinitely. Tyrants are predators looking for weak victims. It is likely that our imaginary employee finds a way to attract the same kind of tyrants who terrorized him at school. Tyrants have the curious ability to constantly enter the lives of anyone trying to escape them. Many battered women who manage to escape their abusers fall into the hands of similar, and sometimes worse men."

I understood very well what my master meant, but I could not see how my friend could learn from his break-up. I told him my view on the subject.

"If your friend is in such a state, is it possible that this was his first real romantic relationship?" Asked the old man.

"No, he has dated other women before. Each time, the break up ended in disaster."

"If this situation had the objective to teach him something, and believe me it does, what would it be?"

I did not know what to answer. The only thing that came to mind is that he had to learn not to be touched by this kind of situation.

"I think your friend is dependent on his relationships. Maybe he should consider becoming more independent."

"I remember hearing she found him too present, too perfect even. Maybe being a little more independent would help."

"Yes, he is a prisoner of his desire to possess," he said, "we do not possess a companion, we have to deserve one. These people often forget to let their partners breathe. A tyrant who receives the backlash," added the master before becoming silent.

"I read that in Buddhism, desire is one of the biggest barriers that cut us from the path to happiness."

We arrived before the main temple where three thick ropes hung from the ceiling. Master clasped his hands together then waved one of the ropes which rattled a bell at the top. I turned my back to him to leave him alone with the *kami* of the place. After a few moments, I heard the sound of his voice once again.

"A lot of civilizations have been invaded over the centuries. Some of them emerged stronger from these trials. Others have kept the soul of conquered countries."

I never thought that a simple discussion on a depressive friend could take us this far. I did not give up on him.

"There must be tyrants who have nothing to help us evolve. If I get kidnapped on a trip, I do not see what such a situation can bring me except making me want to stay at home."

"You can feel sorry for yourself and hope someone will save you, or you can take the necessary steps to escape. When you're away, you must take the opportunity to develop your sense of observation. They put a hood over your head? Learn to collect as much information as possible with your ears, by the movement that your body undergoes. Are there any sounds of railways or boats that could give you clues of where you are? Are there any animals that bark or make other noises? Anything you can capture may be helpful. You can cry about your situation or take the opportunity to see what it can bring you. Even when you're in your cell, collecting information continues. How many guards are there? What is their routine? Can you make friends with one of them or otherwise enrage them if necessary?"

"My kidnapping just turned into a professional internship on intelligence, is that right?"

"In a way, yes. In addition to all the information you can gather about where you're held, it is necessary to learn to assess the situation. What is the best time to attempt an escape? What are your chances of success? If you do not do it, what are your hopes to get out alive? Your tyrant instills survival in you. You have to feed yourself even if you do not like the food they give you. Knowing the character of each of your captors is essential. And finally, you must have the courage to seize the opportunity when it presents itself. Information, threat assessment, strategy, timing, a good tyrant can teach you so much. Most people do not dare attempt in fear of failing to escape. Some survive and others perish."

"Can we learn from all tyrants?" I asked.

"Yes," he said without hesitation, "there are only two options. Giving in or facing them. Tyrants are reluctant to return when they were beaten once."

Chapter 40
Submission

I do not quite remember how the subject was brought up, but that day we had a conversation about submission. Actually, it's coming back to me, I think I remember how this discussion began. It was initiated by pain. Intense torture had made me kneel before my teacher. He had used a stick which he had pressed on my forearm. The suffering he inflicted gave me the feeling that my bone had shattered into pieces. With my other hand, I tapped repeatedly on my thigh for him to release his macabre embrace. I felt my heart would stop beating so much it hurt. It had been a few years since I became his disciple, and I had yet to see any techniques on the control of pain. It would have been helpful during that moment.

This training took place in one of the outdoor *dojo* he loved so much. That day, I could detect no mercy in his eyes.

"You'll break my bones. I'll never write again," I said in a slightly aggressive tone.

"You mean you can no longer have fun playing video games," he said laughing, then releasing his grip.

"It's not funny, you almost broke my arm."

"Do not worry. I only pressed without hitting. It is true that if you had had a weakness in your bones, it could have broken."

"That's what I said, you almost crippled me."

"No, I only made you submit yourself to me. Or rather, it is you who has admitted defeat in the face of pain."

"I did not submit myself, I had no choice."

"We always have options. There are lizards that will sacrifice a leg or tail to escape a predator."

"Yes but my limbs don't grow back."

"There are circumstances where we have no choice, we must be willing to sacrifice a limb to survive. But here you had nothing to offer, you could only face submission."

I did not understand what he meant. How could anyone handle something like that?

"It's hard to endure so much pain, it's almost impossible."

"The human being easily surrenders. I hope that no extraterrestrial civilization will attack us," said the master, "with people like you, we can not win."

How could he insult me like this? I preferred to dig into the issue rather than trying to defend myself. For the time being...

"Why do you say that men easily capitulate?"

"Because it's true. In ancient times, when people were conquered by others, the men taken prisoner joined the army to invade new countries. They would never dare discuss orders and rebel against those who had destroyed their civilization."

He took my arm that I was massaging since he had released me, and pressed heavily on the lump that had appeared on my bone. An even greater pain shot out. I knew he had applied a *kuatsu*, these ancient effective medical techniques. I knew from experience that we could hit on my bones once again and it would no longer be sensitive. If he had not applied this *kuatsu* on me, a simple touch on my arm would have been torturous for the next few days. While applying his treatment, he continued to tell me about submission.

"This form of recruitment is still taking place today. Girls abducted in Nigeria helped terrorists carry ammunition. They had no choice, they have abdicated and in the circumstances it was the right thing to do. But when we arm men and the number of fighters exceeds that of the conquerors, it would be easy for them to revolt, yet this does not occur."

"Fortunately for me, I'm not like that, I would rebel."

"You think you would not submit? Today maybe so, but would you have said the same thing a few years ago?"

"I think not, but I always did what I wanted to do."

"Did not you already tell me you had missed seminars because your ex-girlfriend had planned other things?"

That was a low blow.

"It is normal for couples to spend time together. We have to think for two."

"Yes, but was it done on both sides or was it especially you who had to make these compromises?"

"Back then, I lacked confidence. I did not want to displease my companion."

"Did she abuse of your servitude or was everything split equally so?"

"Well... Maybe not, but..."

"This is what we call submission. It is a dependency that has the power to make all the decisions for us. Human beings do not like responsibilities. This dependency allows man to detach himself from responsibility. For many people, it is easier to live like so. Many religions have understood this principle and uses it to guide their...let's say, disciples. It's okay to allocate roles in a couple but everyone must collaborate. If one does something, it has to be done in harmony and not in submission. It is quite normal to share tasks. I know what it is like, believe me."

"To be honest, I agreed to her requests because..."

The master smiled at me.

"I agreed to her requirements in order to buy peace. I did not want to deal with my relationship failing," I added.

I really did not want to talk about my personal life with him.

"You said it's human nature to be submissive, but there are people who revolt."

Saying this, I thought about Afghan warriors who fought the Russians and then the Americans for so many years. I shared my thoughts on the subject.

"Yes, there are some who rebel. They are usually people who have experienced poverty though. People who have suffered and have nothing to lose. In civilizations where the lifestyle is, say, more comfortable, the resistance drops dramatically."

"But what connection is there between resistance and the pain you inflicted on me?"

"You preferred submitting yourself instead of measuring yourself to a very tolerable pain."

"Tolerable pain?! Are you kidding, no one could resist…"

"I'll prove it."

"There is no way I am applying this arm lock on you. I am too human for that, I'd be afraid to break your forearm."

"We will not try on me. I'll just do it again on you."

I thought he was joking. When my arm was once again trapped in the vice, I had only one desire: to cry for help.

"Stop moaning," he threw at me, "I do not want a whiner for a disciple. Instead of panicking when you feel pain, feel it, feed yourself off it. Tell yourself that this is only information and you can tolerate it. The more pressure you feel, and the more determined to advance you will be."

It is without any warning that he tightened his grip. The pain surprised me, but I focused on it. Strangely, it gave me the energy to resist. The more pressure I felt, the more I was determined not to yield. I had enough of living a life of submission.

Chapter 41
Living in fear

"One who is never afraid has psychological problems. We all have at least one phobia. We must not conceal it. We must learn to control and even use it to our advantage," said the master.

The subject had been raised by one of the students stating that he did not know how he would react in a real fight. He had done a lot of sportive fighting competition, but he had never fought on the street. He agonized at the thought of not being up to par and it was unusual to have these fears.

"How can we control this?" He asked.

"Some may advise you to see a good psychologist," replied the master.

He had just opened a door that I was certainly not going to let close itself.

"You think it's the only solution?" I asked.

"There are other possibilities. You could, for example, do a clean-up of your principles, in your thoughts and way of life."

With him, I expected strange, or aberrant answers from time to time, but he had overcome his own limitations.

"I do not understand. How does this cleaning of ourselves help overcome our fears?"

"In ancient times, in many cultures, you had no choice. You had to go into battle or were executed. In the best case, you were imprisoned for disobedience. But these rules were mostly for low-rank soldiers, those who were put in the front line, the first to be killed. But for true warriors, often from father to son, they had to learn to control their fears. In feudal times, confrontations often ended in death. The *samurai* were good soldiers because they were not afraid of death. They had tamed it and had even made it a glorious way to leave our world. Ending his life in battle, sword in hand, there could not be a more honorable exit. They were not afraid of dying."

"But this is the heart of the problem," said the student, "how does one go about dominating this? Wanting to die with prestige is unfortunately not part of my culture."

"By erasing doubt. We must first learn to differentiate fear from doubt. Do you doubt yourself, or are you afraid of the consequences of the fight, afraid of what will happen to you?"

I had never made the distinction between the two, between fear and doubt. It is true that it can be easy to confuse them, the boundary between those two ideas is thin. The master went on.

"Doubt is a slow poison that can lead to insecurity which itself leads to fear. First, we must learn to differentiate these states. No one can predict how they will react until they have faced a real fight."

"Is it possible that there are people who feel absolutely nothing?" Asked the student.

"Aside from a psychopath, no. Just think about how you feel when the police stops you when driving your car for a routine check. If you have committed a crime, you know why they are stopping you. Stress will be better managed, but if you do not know why he ordered you to pull over, you will likely have all kinds of speculation. Your heartbeat will increase. You will even get the impression that it is harder to express yourself. All this nervousness for something as insignificant as a burnt rear light. It is not even an attack and it already affects your vital signs. So what do you think will happen during a real confrontation?"

These words had brought back memories of the few occasions when I was stopped for various reasons. Each time, I would almost panic at the mere sight of the flashing lights. He did not give me time to rehash those unpleasant memories that had caused more pain to my wallet than my body.

"To a warrior, the first condition is whether he is in the right. If the fact of undertaking this fight is legitimate. If you have provoked someone for no reason, if you looked for trouble without any justification, you may feel uncomfortable assaulting someone. But if the other person unjustly attacks you, you'll probably have less remorse when you see the first drops of blood spill from your retaliation."

"Yes, that's fine, but there are people who like to fight for fun. They do it for no reason."

"On the contrary, they have one. They need to prove something. They would not pick on a child, or a woman unable to defend herself. They look for a challenge and are justified by the act. Yours will be to use your killer instinct, telling you that nobody has the right to undermine your integrity. But before you get there, you have to clean up your programming."

It had been a long time since we had talked about the killer instinct. I had almost forgotten that phrase. As for programming, I was burning with impatience to hear the rest.

"If you doubt yourself you must know why. What is the reason? Are you afraid of not hitting hard enough or with the necessary precision? Do you think your opponent is too fast for you? Do his tattoos, shaved head, and piercings give you the impression that he is powerful, or even evil? On what do you base your doubts? Identifying and isolating them is an essential step to control them. You have instilled these uncertainties in yourself. Why is that? I do not know, but we can reprogram ourselves the other way. The first step is to be fully aware of our weaknesses."

"What about fears?" I asked.

"Fear has no justification like doubts do. It is simply there. It happens like that and it is unclear why. However, even if we do not find an explanation for our behavior, there is a way to go around it, to get over it."

"Is fear easy to ignore? Some people are unable to replicate when they are scared."

Raising this point, I thought back about when friends told me when they actually had a gun pulled out on them. They said it was impossible for them to move, because their legs were trembling too much. Fear had frozen them in place.

"We must reprogram ourselves. We have to visualize ourselves in the worst situations by imagining how we would react. Then we replay the same scenario in our heads and this time we react in the right way. This exercise should be done every day for a few weeks. The subconscious will come to take for granted that this new program is the procedure to be adopted."

"This is neurolinguistic programming," said one of the students, "It has been developed in the seventies."

"Ah," said the old master, "in martial arts, it is called *saiminjutsu*, and it has been used for several hundreds of years. It works well even if it may seem a bit simplistic. We must not deny fear. If we control it well, it is our defense against negligence. Fear leads to prudence."

"Have you ever felt fear in combat?" Asked the same student.

"Yes. Fortunately, some of our techniques are defensive. They focus on that emotion. When we are afraid, we tend to retreat, to turn back. One day, three men attacked me and I panicked. I was anxious about what I could do, about my reaction to their aggression."

"You were afraid of hurting them. How did it end?" I asked.

"I was lucky, they proved to be reasonable."

My curiosity was too great for me to give up.

"What do you mean by that?"

"I told them that I would maybe end up in the hospital, but they would accompany me, and that the first to attack would probably end up at the cemetery."

"And they believed you?" I asked.

"No doubt appeared in my voice. I spoke with such confidence that I had succeeded in sowing confusion in their minds. My words were able to initiate fear. I spoke like someone who had nothing to lose."

"And they retreated," I said.

"Yes. I think they got scared."

Chapter 42
Overflow

"Most people live with hope. Whether it be for a project to succeed, to be rich and happy, or simply to win a fight, hope is a tool that can easily turn against us. Addiction to gambling is a good example. They feel they are almost there. They think that with one or two more bets they will win the jackpot."

That morning, the *dojo* was crowded. People of all nationalities, cultures, and age groups were there. After the opening ceremony, we had remained on our knees, facing the old sage who lavished us with his teachings. He frequently brought up the topic of the day through stories, anecdotes, or established scientific facts. That day, he decided to talk about human psychology.

"If you believe you are above this, think again. Sure, you might not be betting money on games of chance, but this same motivation influences your life. You must meet someone and they are late, you will probably wait a few more minutes with the idea that they will arrive soon. Your favorite sports team loses the game by a difference of a few points. Until the last minute, you believe there will be a turnaround. The human being is like that, he hopes until the last moment."

I saw less and less relevance with martial arts. This class took place the third year he accepted me as a disciple. I was not familiar with such a concept. He continued on the subject.

"This hope can cost you your life in a fight."

"Come on! As if hope had ever killed anyone," I said.

The master stood up and asked for a volunteer to hit him. I jumped before him with an alert bounce in my step. Just as he motioned me to attack, I took a step forward to reach him with my punch. My arms fully stretched out, his face was just a few millimeters from my knuckles, I was sure to reach my target. Suddenly, without knowing what had happened, I lost my balance. The master took the opportunity to grab my wrist and made me do a spectacular somersault on the *tatami*.

"Why is it that I managed to throw you too easily?" He asked me.

"You caught my wrist and pulled on it. It is normal for me to have been destabilized."

"Did you have the impression that I had to use much physical strength to make you fall?"

Upon reflection, I had barely felt him grab me with the tip of his fingers.

"Um, no. You barely touched me. I felt caught in a trap."

"And what brought you there?"

"You did?"

"No, it is you who did this to yourself. Everything happened in your subconscious. You were so certain to reach me that you made the extra effort needed to achieve it. You went so far forward that you ended up overflowing from your stable position."

Overflowing from my position. The phrase was well chosen, that's what I had felt. He brought me to the limit of the balance that my body could handle. Unknowingly, I drew myself into an area that could not contain me. He gave the example of a drop of water that overflows the vase. That's what he did with me.

"Now that I understand how it works, I think it will not work on me a second time."

"Do you want to make a bet?" Said the old master raising his eyebrows several times.

His mischievous air made the students laugh. I stood before him to strike a second time. When my fist approached his face, he bent his knees causing my target to go downward. It was too late, I was trapped again. The contact my backside made with the floor was more brutal this time.

"The reality is that even if your intellect knows what will happen, your subconscious mind does not. That's who you want to influence with such a technique. It is he who dictates the compulsive gambler to continue to bet even though his rational mind recommends caution. It is also that part of you that politicians will address when they make big promises. Until the last second, you thought you could hit me."

"Are there times when it does not work?"

I was intrigued by this phenomenon. If I had seen another student being catapulted so, I would probably tell myself he was exaggerating, that he threw himself to please the master. To have experienced this personally made me see that there was something there. No magic, just behavior related to psychology.

"It will fail if the attacker is not sincere."

"What do you mean by that?"

"If he hits without any real intention of reaching his target, it will not work. That is why it is more difficult to achieve in training than in a real combat situation on a battlefield. The compulsive gambler does not do it for others. He does it with sincerity, convinced that he will reach his goal."

"Apart from martial arts and gambling addicts, can we use this strategy with something else?" Asked a student.

"All companies that invest in scientific or technological research have one day been caught by this phenomenon. They felt so close that stopping the financial abyss in which they found themselves did not seem to be an option. Hope masks a cul-de-sac. The emotional outweighs the rational. By injecting new funds, it will become fatal, yet the solution seems so close. What keeps them going? Hope. With industrial espionage, some companies have provided false information suggesting that their research focused on a product was going to propel them to the highest levels. This misinformation led competitors to disperse and spend their capital in a dead end. But this is not where it concerns us the most."

With him, I expected anything. This time he had touched a sensitive nerve that would affect a lot of people.

"Your relationships, or should I say, your dating expectations exploit this overflowing phenomenon."

Most students looked at their companions as if they could give them the answer to this riddle. The master did not let us cogitate very long.

"You see a person of the opposite sex that you like, that you are attracted to. You often think about them. Not to the point of being obsessed, but you think they would make an ideal partner for you. Then one day, while talking with you, this rare gem places a hand on your shoulder. How do you interpret this sign? If a relationship with that person is absolutely not your goal, you probably will not even realize this gesture. But if you have an eye on them, there is a good chance that you will decode this contact as an attempt to flirt. An intimate move, when in fact it was a simple gesture of camaraderie."

Listening to him speak, similar memories came back to mind.

"We must learn to be lucid and to accept the idea that there are limits to what we want, and not to get caught up in this trap during a fight, it's simple, just play defensively by merely responding to attacks from the opponent. The overflowing comes from the fact of wanting too hard. In battle, as in love, we must react and not hope."

Chapter 43

Kamae

The master had asked me to find him at the *dojo*. This fact had nothing special about it, except that I had to meet him there at 2 am. Since the last train stopped around midnight, I had to wander the deserted streets nearby. Less than ten minutes walk away, there was an old shrine. I took the opportunity to go to recharge myself. The sculptures that decorated the walls of old buildings were taking demonic airs, angry in the slanted rays of the night lights. They must have been upset of being surprised in their intimacy. The full moon provided a propitious time for malicious spirits to amuse themselves by playing with my imagination. I quite liked this strange sensation. Feeling that someone is watching you all the time knowing that you are alone is something indescribable, especially within the walls of an old shrine where every stone inscription displayed is partially offset by the centuries. Bowing respectfully, I thanked the Kami for letting me spend some time with them.

It was about 1:45 am when I arrived in the alley leading to the *dojo*. From a distance I could see light that was escaping the windows. The master was already there. I had not even removed my shoes when he ordered me to practice my *kamae*. This strange training took place at the beginning of my second year with him. At that time, I would never have dared ask him anything that could upset the teaching he deigned to grant me. I appreciated the privilege of training with him and I wanted to prove to him that I was a good disciple. Without hesitating, I took various fighting positions. Each *kamae* consisted of a posture based on different emotions, different elements. Some of them were inspired by the earth and were based on self-confidence, both physical and mental stability. Others, focusing on the flow of water, exploited the power of fear. In this state, you tend to flee, to escape. If an opponent is faster and more powerful, the fact of backing up causes the opponent to create openings that are easily exploitable. If he extends a punch, he exposes his ribs. If he kicks, a well-prepared fighter can aim for the privates or the other knee. Some of these postures express more aggression and even anger. Like lightning, the fire element allows to attack at high speed to overwhelm the opponent. Finally, the wind remains something that no one can grasp, some positions will offer the enemy the opportunity to hit emptiness. Just like a tornado that sucks everything in its path, such a *kamae* allows us to capture the energy the opponent deploys and lead him where desired by returning its power against him. It is by linking these various postures that I took possession of the *tatami*.

The different positions I knew followed each other at a cracking pace. I tried to memorize the sequences I did to vary the series of movements that I executed. From time to time I cast a glance at the clock. I felt I had been doing this exercise for a very long time, but only fifteen minutes had passed since I started. This type of training was called shadow boxing and is practiced in almost all martial arts. Different postures are used as if we are fighting an imaginary opponent. But here, there were very few attacks. I was simply trying to diversify the sequence of my movements as much as possible, but I had the unpleasant feeling of always doing the same thing.

"What are you doing?" Threw the old man at me.

"Well, I am practicing my *kamae*, as you have instructed me."

"I had not realized that was what you were doing. My masters must be turning in their graves. Poor them, if they saw that, they surely would demand that I do *hara-kiri*."

I thought that was a bit much. My postures seemed more than acceptable.

"I am executing them as you taught me. My bone alignments are correct, I am respecting the right angles, my arms are well placed."

"Hmm! I believe that a robot would do just as well. All you are doing is changing positions and not *kamae*. You confuse the two. A *kamae* lasts only a split second, a very short time, it is a transition between two techniques, between two emotions. It is not static, it is dynamic. We do not choose to make a *kamae*, it is the *kamae* who imposes itself according to our needs. Your body does a good replica of that, but your heart and your mind are not up to par. Go, again."

The second try hardly proved more fruitful. Apparently, I was a Westerner who had never learned to focus on what he was doing. I felt the anger rising in me, but it is the prerogative of the disciple to suffer the wrath of his master if he can move forward in the path of knowledge. The fire of his exasperation could only forge me.

"You make all your *kamae* with the same emotion. You should not be a prisoner. You must learn to use them and let them go when it's time."

"I do not understand. What do you mean by letting them go?"

"Whether it be in martial arts or in daily life, emotions are one of the most powerful engines that lead man towards his destiny. We should not be controlled by them."

"I never allow myself to be dominated by them."

"No? When you are angry, how many seconds does it take for you to completely change your mindset?"

"That's not the same it is normal to keep this attitude for some time."

"This is probably why a lot of angry people speak words exceeding their thoughts, words they will regret bitterly. A skilled opponent can use any of your emotions and turn them against you. Imagine a lawyer questioning a policeman on the witness stand. Juries turn their backs on him. He observes the agent who undergoes the pressure of stress. The defense lawyer smiles at him, staring into his eyes. The people in the room see the policeman smile without realizing it is just out of empathy. The lawyer takes this chance. "What makes you laugh? You find it funny that my client suffers, it amuses you perhaps?" The policeman has been destabilized, he becomes vulnerable. It's the same thing in combat, you must not remain a prisoner of an item. You must learn to let the right element take its place when it is time and allow it to leave when necessary. Imagine a businessman who is obsessed with one of his competitors because he slept with his wife. He will focus his attention on this man, forgetting the other competitors that will make him fall. We must learn to let go. The *kamae* represent an attitude. Visualize yourself trying to show your anger to someone, but your face expresses the opposite. You will not be taken seriously. If you want to have the desired effect, it is necessary that your body, your emotions, and your thoughts are aligned in the same direction."

"Yes, but here it is more difficult. I have the impression of always doing the same sequence."

"It's not a problem if your mind free. A *kamae* is timeless, it must be timeless while keeping your mind here and now."

That was not the kind of explanation which at the time could help me. The only words I understood were more or less here and now. Timeless seemed like an expression coming from an unknown language. I regained my place at the center of the *dojo*, and after taking a deep breath, I placed my leg back while extending an arm forward. Then I told myself, "to hell with elegant movements", I had to let my body and my mind work on their own. The first movements seemed to disorient me, expressing a severe lack of coordination. Then for a brief moment, I felt like an open book that invited the attacker to throw himself at it. I moved in a circular manner, I had the sensation of having become untouchable. I quickly felt my emotions turn into an aggressive energy that forced me to move forward. Then a strange feeling of fear, or perhaps I should say caution, forced me to retreat and take me to transfer my weight on my back leg and raising my other leg, resting my foot near my knee, I blocked an imaginary attack with my hand pointing forward. My positions succeeded naturally. I felt that time itself flowed in my veins. I knew that if I had a real opponent in front of me, I would perceive his attacks in slow-motion. My body, my emotions and my mind acted by gradually depriving me of all feeling. I was outside the time barrier, I was beyond the physical laws such as I knew them. Several years after this experience, the master told me that it was the Kami that had guided me during this training.

To my surprise, I had been doing this exercise for one hour. All this had seemed to last a few minutes. I expressed my amazement to the master.

"How is this possible? I feel like I only did a few sequences."

"You just entered a meditative state. We can reach deep states of mind with movement. It is not for nothing that there are sacred dances in many ancient civilizations. The body is a vehicle as well as the mind."

"Were my movements better this time?" I asked a little fearfully.

"I think your subconscious has learned a lot tonight. As for you, I do not know, maybe there is some hope after all."

Chapter 44
Predictable

The master had asked me to meet him at his home. No sooner had I set foot inside that he pulled me by the arm.

"Come, let's get something eat. I do not feel like cooking today."

Naturally, I did not have my say. When he made his mind up about something, nobody could make him change it. In less than five minutes, I found myself sitting in a small restaurant, tucked in an alley near his home. He did not give me time to consult the menu.

"I will order for both of us, that way we can save time," he said, nodding toward the server that did not leave us from the corner of the eye.

"Where are we going?"

"Nowhere."

"In this case, you must be awfully hungry."

"What makes you think that?" He asked, looking at me in all seriousness. I did not know if he was joking or if he was serious.

"You just seem in such a hurry to eat."

He did not answer and called the server. He spoke too quickly for me to have the time to know what I was eating. Fortunately for me, I enjoyed Japanese cuisine very much. Although I admit that I was rather destabilized by his curious behavior.

"Where did you say you had to go?" I shyly risked.

"I'm not going anywhere and I was not hungrier than usual," he said, not bothering to look at me.

"But then, why such haste?"

"Because we have to eat well."

"Yes, but why do it in such a hurry?"

"Because we do not know what the next moment will bring us."

I knew that I had set foot in a mysterious gear. The meal was only a pretext for philosophizing. He liked to draw me in these verbal jousts. The first few times, I was completely disoriented, but after all these years, I had acquired a taste for these exchanges.

"In this case, I do not understand. Sometimes you devour your plate so quickly that I can only finish half of my meal and at other times it takes you hours to swallow the same dish."

"There are always two sides to everything. It depends on the circumstances."

"What can determine the circumstances?"

"Why should this instant be defined?"

I could not answer that. He remained silent. I suspected that I had to find the key that would allow me to understand where he was going, but I had searched in vain, I found nothing that could justify such behavior.

"I do not know. Sometimes I have the impression that you are unpredictable."

He looked at me with a smile. I had touched an answer, but had no idea of the direction to take.

"What is predictability?" He threw at me.

"It is what we can anticipate. Why do you ask?"

"Do you know how I will spend my days in advance, or which route I will take to get to the *dojo*?"

I had already realized this eccentricity he displayed. I did not pay attention to it more than I had to.

"What for? Is being unpredictable a quality?" I insisted.

I did not expect the drastic response that followed.

"The survival of a warrior may depend on it. Some influential men have been murdered or kidnapped because they used the same route day after day."

"What is the relationship between that and *budo*?" I asked.

"We must learn not to be predictable. Often when you attack me, you do your favorite attack sequences. You're so predictable that I could read the newspaper while fighting you. We must decide on certain things that we are willing to let show."

"You mean in everyday life, or just in martial arts?"

"In everything. Most people have built their lives around ingrained habits so strongly that the slightest change destabilizes them. Living without surprise is simply waiting for death. It's the same in martial arts. If your opponent knows how you will behave, he only has to produce the necessary conditions that will lead you to do what he wants."

"It can be played on both sides."

"That's right, but even creating feints, sometimes our habits betray us. You have to train to react in different ways, not limiting yourself to what you know."

"You mean that we should do what we do not know? How can we do that?"

"In martial arts, if we perform a technique, it means that somewhere we have learned it and have assimilated it enough to be able to use it."

I absolutely did not understand where he wanted to go and he was well aware of it.

"Doing what we do not think of doing, to be guided by instinct. Do you believe that when I teach, I know everything I am showing? More often than not, I follow my instinct and most of the time it releases new ways of doing things that are not only very effective, but also usually very unpredictable. It is not because you're trying something new that it is not good. If your technical level is high enough, what will come out will be logical and functional. However, if your experience is lacking, well established techniques will likely be ineffective and will leave many openings which your opponent can exploit."

"I have met people who have tried to invent new styles of martial arts. The results were visually pleasing to look at, but from a technical point of view, most had many gaps that were easy to exploit. These people were better in marketing than in martial arts. They managed to sell their junk to beginners without experience."

My teacher closed his fist in disapproval.

"These people are dangerous," he said, "they put their students' lives at risk by letting them believe that they will turn into real fighters. In the end, we get the teachers we deserve."

I found the master to be a little harsh. He continued his explanation.

"Becoming unpredictable can take all kinds of facets. If you have a sword fight against someone who has more experience than you, there is a good chance that you will lose your life. You must then use your blade in an unusual way. Make use of your left hand, hold the sword with one hand only, or grab it in reverse, or even handle it like a spear or a stick. By changing the way we do things, it becomes more difficult for the opponent to predict our actions."

"Can we do that with all weapons?"

"Yes, of course. You can use a *bo* as a javelin or a baseball bat. We can also use a knife as a stick to hit sensitive areas rather than cutting. When we know how to hold it properly, it's faster to hit than to slice."

"With weapons, it seems easy, but how can we do that with our bare hands?"

Just as he was about to answer, the waiter brought our dishes. I expected my teacher to eat at full speed, but

instead, he took his time. He seemed to enjoy each of the noodles that entered his mouth. Halfway through his plate, he resumed the conversation.

"Without weapons, we can play with positions. Taking a defensive posture to make a surprise attack or otherwise take an aggressive attitude while being ready to retreat in order to draw our opponent into a trap."

He took a sip of tea and again attacked the still-steamy noodles. I understood what he meant by using false positions or stances. I was eager to return to the *dojo* to experiment it all. Having sucked-in his last noodle noisily, he continued his explanation as if he had never stopped talking.

"Everything that falls into our hand can become, when used unpredictably, a formidable weapon."

I was a bit skeptical hearing these last words. I searched my pockets for the first object I could find. I felt something round that escaped at my fingertips. After squirming some more, I managed to extract a small one *yen* coin.

"You think you can turn this into an effective weapon? I'd be curious to see that."

Without saying a word, the old master took the coin. He grabbed my index and in a split second, he slipped it under my nail. With his thumb, he strongly pressed on the edge of the coin. In one blink of an eye, I found myself on the ground, using my other hand to tap with all my strength against my thigh for this monstrous grip to slacken. My vision was narrowing rapidly, the pain was unbearable. The master slightly diminished the pressure.

"It is dangerous to play with money," said the old man sneering.

I must admit that I had not seen that coming!

Chapter 45
Shizen

I think the word that came back most often during my training with Master was undoubtedly *shizen*. Shi, the first syllable of the word translates as self. The second part, zen, can be interpreted as in relation, or what is right. Overall, one could say that the word means the things that can influence us. Seen this way, it does not mean much, but once these two kanji are put together, it means nature, or natural, to move naturally, naturally react, the nature of man, the word kept coming back during my teacher's lessons. One day when I was with him in a grocery store, his words made me ponder for days. As I placed strawberries in my basket, he put his hand on my forearm.

"As a bird that sits on the ground only when he knows he is safe, you have to learn to react naturally," he said.

Yes, he was like that. Some of his teachings could sometimes graze hermeticism. Though I tried to make the link between the safety of the bird and our presence here, I just couldn't.

"Why do you say that?" I asked.

"Look at these strawberries, some have mildew. I won't be eating those."

He called one of the employees of the store and showed him the product. The man apologized repeatedly by removing all of the spoiled fruit. I began to see where he was going. Knowing what you eat should be a simple reflex. Do not swallow anything. But I suspected he was trying to get me somewhere else than a debate about food.

"*Sensei*, you often talk about *shizen*. Are we not always *shizen*? If a person is tense most of the time, is that not normal for him to be in this state?"

"The question should be, is it natural for a human being to live constantly under pressure? If you're a caveman and a dinosaur runs after you, then yes, it should help you survive. But to be stressed all week long because we have difficulty managing our lives is not normal."

"Yes, but in a situation of confrontation, it is natural to be tense."

"I fully agree with that, but *shizen* has many facets. In *budo*, the first step is to learn to move well. Being stressed in a fight is something natural. If you panic at the thought of this emotional state, it means that you're afraid of what is normal. If you accept this state, you have already taken a step toward victory. But if you panic at the thought of losing control, then you are already partly defeated."

While explaining this, he sniffed the scent of *daikon*, these large white radishes that do not taste much, but are very nutritious.

"What is the relationship between moving well and being stressed?"

"Even being tense, we must learn to move naturally," he replied, "if you dodge a punch arching your torso backwards and bringing all your weight on your lower back, you will have difficulty avoiding the second attack. A tiger caught in a trap will move like a cat, even if driven to the wall. We must learn to move depending on our body's capabilities whatever our condition."

"So *shizen* is simply using our body properly?"

"At first, yes, but it's much more than that. As I told you, *shizen* has many facets. The tactics you use to defend yourself should be natural."

"I do not understand. A strategy does not leave much room for being natural, it refers to intellect, to choose the right maneuver to counter a determined attack."

"That's true, but the response you use needs to be in harmony with the attacker as well as your physical and technical abilities. You are planning to capture your opponent's arm when he punches, but it is too fast, he pulls his arm back at lightning speed. With his other arm, he manages to hit you in the ribs. What is natural? Staying there or choosing to retreat? If you have been taught to advance on the enemy as in sports competitions, there is a good chance that you will lose your fight, but if you follow the nature of things, your instinct, you probably will have the wisdom to back up, to distance yourself and maybe even retreat if necessary for your survival. We must learn to do what is natural."

I had already realized that, for years, my athletic training had not conditioned me to the idea of a strategic retreat. Combat sports teach us to advance on our opponent, my master kindly called that cockfighting. He nodded a few times as if nodding to some secret thoughts and then he continued.

"*Shizen* applies to the body, the intellect, and emotions too."

I did not realize he had connected *shizen* to these two other aspects. How could we attach this word to emotions? I tried an explanation.

"For emotions, it's easy, it is always natural. If we are happy, angry, worried, or surprised, it always remains natural. We do not choose our emotions, we live them when they chose to present themselves," I said.

The master looked at me with a smile.

"I did not know you were hiding a philosopher's soul, but you're right, we live emotions. However, we can fight contradicting them."

I began to see where he was going. His teaching was based on the natural elements of earth, water, fire, wind, and void. Each of these elements are connected to a human emotion. Earth symbolizes confidence. Water is more elusive, and is linked to fear, knowing when to back up when the opponent uses the aggressiveness of fire. Extinguish fire with water. Wind draws its power from kindness, in the absence of confrontation and fear. Wind lets go of the opponent in whichever direction it has chosen while returning his energy against him. Void is a little more difficult to grasp. I think one could say that it is all about mastering the other elements, and using the right one at the right time.

"Every emotion causes our body to react differently," said my mentor, "if you are afraid, your muscles will respond differently than if you have total confidence in your abilities. Who has not once felt his legs tremble during a moment of stress? Even if it be only to go talk to a group of people?"

He chose a good example to demonstrate the extent to which emotions could play on our glandular functions.

"*Shizen* is all that," he went on, "it is doing what needs to be done at the right time."

"That's easy to say, but how can we become so natural?"

"It starts with simple everyday life things. Knowing how to stand up, for example. Most people seek a wall to lean against, or they take breaks resting their body weight on one leg. Learning to sit properly is a good way to develop our *hara* center and increase our balance."

"That's all nice and all, but what makes a technique not natural?"

The old master sighed, staring at me. He looked at me as if I were a lost cause. Then I saw his shoulders relax.

"I think we can summarize it by saying that many martial artists do what they should not be doing. If a train comes straight at you, you remove yourself from the railway. You will do the same if a powerful antagonist hammers you with punches and kicks that you can not block. Do not stay on the track, leave the corridor and you can watch the train pass."

The image might have seemed a little strange, but it was so realistic. In sports competitions, I had often seen people stay before an opponent who repeated strikes impossible to counter. In most cases, people were content in trying to back up rather than moving out of the linear path of the attacks. It is easier to advance than retreat. I was proud to tell my teacher that I understood what he meant.

"So, we can summarize *shizen* by doing what needs to be done? I mean, finding the ideal technique to perform at the right time and place."

"You got it. Basically, that is just the idea of *shizen*. After that, you just have to add connection, good timing, good angles, good range, a good psychological condition and learn to let yourself be guided by the divine to achieve everything that is natural."

That was it, the master had just finished me off.

Chapter 46
State of mind

We were in one of the classes that my teacher gave regularly. We were practicing *muto dori*, defensive techniques against swords with our bare hands. When my partner's blade fell down on my head, I easily managed to dodge it. I began to gain confidence. I asked my friend to hit me as fast as possible. He hesitated, then went to change his wooden sword for a soft, padded weapon to prevent serious injury. I was arguing with him to keep using the wooden weapon when the old master came up behind me.

"What are you trying to prove?" He asked, staring at me with amusement.

"I think that in martial arts, we must make the training as realistic as possible. A foam sword is not very serious,"

I was ready to defend my point of view, but his answer froze me in place.

"I completely agree with you, but first I need you learn to move properly. You do not move in harmony with the sword, you run away like a rabbit."

How could he say that? I could dodge the blade while remaining very calm. My movements were done without jerking around, they were smooth and I dare say, graceful. Obviously, there was bad faith in his words. I explained my point of view, how I felt, avoiding the blade.

"That's what I'm saying, you're fleeing," he answered.

The master invited all the students to sit in a circle.

"When we do *muto dori*, we must become a weapon."

I was beginning to get lost. How could I be a sword? For a moment I had the impression of being a wreck in the middle of the ocean. I was not only helpless, but for a short time I had the feeling that all my years of training had become futile. It felt strange to feel this way because of a simple few words.

"Defending ourselves against a weapon by fleeing is easy. It's only a matter of reflexes, moving skills. Many people are content with that."

Saying this, he looked at me for a moment and smiled.

"When assaulted by a sword, our movements must have an influence on the mind of the attacker. If we only run away, then we are just playing a cat and mouse. In the spirit of *budo*, winning a fight is important. To defeat a rival, we should not be content with trying to win the fight physically A real fighter has to reach the heart and capture the mind of his enemy. This is true for both for a sword fight and a battle in the business world."

It was like him to compare a sword fight and the business world. I preferred bringing the conversation back to the sword, it was easier.

"Excuse me *sensei*, but if I manage to avoid my opponent's blade, did I not just disrupt him? He faces a failure, the blade missed its goal."

"Yes if he is a beginner, not if he is an experienced warrior. Those with experience know that if their blades don't reach their enemy, it does not necessarily mean that the opponent is good, but that they were lucky."

I had nothing to say about that. A multitude of questions came to mind.

"Then what do you mean by capturing the mind of the opponent?"

The master walked to the side of the *dojo* and grabbed a wooden training sword.

"Attack me," he said.

While placing my right leg behind my left one, I raised the *bokken* above my head. I took a deep breath. I felt my shoulders relax, I was ready to strike with maximum speed. Without warning, I stepped forward slicing the air with my weapon. I missed a little, but I knew I could attack again, it would be easy for me to reach him by slicing horizontally. I did not have time to start my second attack.

"Now tell us your impression of what you just did."

I told him what I had felt and also the fact that I could have re-attacked quickly, but I did not want to tarnish the image of my teacher, so I did not insist on the fact that he was vulnerable.

"I had the feeling that I could reach you easily, but I'm sure you would have done something to prevent the attack."

"Would you say that you acted as a hunter, chasing a prey trying to escape?"

The comparison was realistic. That's how I felt, like a cat stalking a mouse.

"Now let's do the same exercise, but this time, stop attacking me in ridiculous ways. You want to cut me in half, not to knight me."

Like before, I got in position, but his time I lowered my center of gravity in order to maximize my blade's speed. The master stood before me with a natural posture. He seemed in no way concerned with what was about to happen. I waited a little. This short time gave me the feeling of a cat stalking a mouse again. Then, without announcing my attack, my back leg quickly stepped forward, propelling my sword at a velocity that it had never had before. Master dodged the blade effortlessly. At that moment, a strange phenomenon happened. I felt that my life was threatened. By the time he moved to the side, I had the unpleasant feeling that his body was going to hit me hard, it stole the space that was allocated to me. The eyes of the master invaded my mind, sowing confusion in my thoughts. I tried to construct a strategy, but my emotions destabilized me, leaving only lack of confidence and panic in their wake.

"Can you describe to the others what you felt?"

"It's strange, I felt threatened. I now understand what you meant by becoming a weapon. It's hard to explain, but I felt helpless. I was certain that I was no longer the hunter but the hunted. No matter where I thought I could move, my mind felt that any retreat was futile. How did you make me feel like the prey rather than the hunter?"

"It is difficult to teach because it is something that can not really be explained with words. I think I can say that the first condition is to achieve a proper mindset. One should not think of escaping the attacker, but to pressurize, to drive him to the wall. Using emptiness, I created an invisible wall."

"You did not attack me, you did not even touch me."

"That did not prevent you from feeling attacked. By channeling our body, our will, our emotions, and our heart, we can get to influence the feeble-minded."

These last words were not helping me increase my self-esteem. I preferred not commenting on that. Fortunately for me, the master put balm on my ego.

"What I mean by a weak mind is just a mind that is not aware that a confrontation can be played on other levels than the physical body. As soon as we become aware that these struggles exist at a higher level, we begin to grasp the true nature of *budo*."

"Yes, I understand what you mean, but how can we get to be able to use this, to create what you have projected onto me? It's easy to say that all we have to do is unite our will, emotions, and our heart. How do we actually manage to do all that?"

"The first step is *ishiki*, consciousness. Most people who practice martial arts act as if they were playing cards. We must be emotionally involved as if we feel that our life depends on our every move. That every breath helps us not to fall into a precipice."

These explanations did not really get me anywhere. I felt like I was standing before a *Jedi* from the Star Wars films.

"It's like I'm hearing Obi-wan Kenobi order Luke to use the force."

"No, no, no, we do not say to use the force, he is said to believe in the force. In the Japanese version, those are the words of the *Jedi*."

I came to realize that when I had attacked, my eyes had met his for a fraction of a second. It was from that moment that I knew I had lost the fight. There was no doubt that he had disturbed my mind.

Chapter 47
The art of words

The Japanese language is fascinating. It contains subtleties that traditional martial arts have adapted over centuries. It is a simple means of expression and at the same time it is very complex. Reading these characters called kanji which derivate from drawings do not use the same areas of the brain that Western letters do. When looking at our alphabet, a word is a sequence of sounds that allow us to understand what it written. For example, a mountain is separated into two distinct syllables. In Japanese, the kanji represents a drawing of a mountain. The brain automatically perceives the image rather than interpreting the sounds in order to know what is written.

In older martial arts, you could play with this elasticity of the language. One day, the master explained that the name of a *kata* often contained the key to understand it. I decided to try to deepen the subject.

"I do not understand. How can the name be the key?" I asked as candidly as possible.

He chose an old technique called batsugi, borrowed from the koto *ryu* style. This school was created in the mid-1500s. My teacher asked me to demonstrate. It was very simple, easy to implement, and effective in controlling an opponent. In our language, the first two syllables were translated by the words to capture and the last meant art or skill. My partner grabbed me by the collar with one hand and tried to hit me with the other. I put my hand on his to apply a twist of his wrist. Then with my other hand, I pushed on his face, forcing him down on the *tatami* while I was doing the twist.

"Very well done. You can see the meaning of the name of the technique. We imprison the hand that holds us and using it, we redirect the body of the attacker to the ground. In other words, the art of capturing. In this technique, we work according to the attack."

Seen in this light, the name of *kata* fit with its translation, but it could not be that simple.

"In ancient martial arts," he said, "they wrote the names and a brief description of the techniques on *densho*, Japanese scrolls. They had to keep written records in order to pass down the information from generation to generation. However, they did not want to reveal all of their secrets to the enemy if the precious scrolls ever fell into their hands. How did they resolve this contradiction?"

He looked at me, smiling. I expected to be criticized despite the fact that I had done the movements well. Instead, he asked me to redo the technique. I applied a little pressure on the wrist to cause my partner to fall as quickly as possible to the ground. I certainly did not want to look bad.

"Here, the technique was performed according to the kanji that have been drawn, but in Japanese, sounds matter. The phonemes can sometimes be illustrated by an impressive number of different kanji. Breaking down the name of the *kata* further and changing the ideogram for another that sounds similar can inspire different ways of doing things or give more clarity to the proceedings. For example, ba can be translated as horse or old woman. Tsu can be interpreted by words such as location, a capital, but with the verb pass, a seaport and even pain. As for gi, one can find definitions like art, justice, discussion, doubt correct, play, flirt, and sacrifice. There are others, but I don't have the memory I did in my twenties," he said laughing.

I tried to run various combinations of all these words in my head. Rather than clearing up, everything became confused. Fortunately, he continued.

"In the standard version of this *kata*, physical power is recommended to bring the opponent down. Strong pressure must be applied on the hand of the aggressor to bend his wrist in order to control him. Now imagine that we take the word for old woman to make-up the name of our maneuver. We would link the words place and discussion. How does the use of these words change our technique?"

He asked me to hit him. As I was about to punch, he quickly stepped on me, depriving me of the space required to start my attack. I found my body weight balanced on my lower back. He placed his hand on my face and effortlessly, he made me fall. Instead of twisting my wrist, he grabbed my finger, forcing me to bend to the side if I wanted my finger to remain intact. He had used no physical strength to subdue me.

"Do you see the difference? The old woman does not have big arms. She can only talk to try to stop the attacker. To discuss, we must move towards each other. It is what I did. The old lady perhaps did not have the ability to make a wrist lock, but can control the situation by twisting a single finger."

I had found a flaw in his explanation. He had forgotten the translation of one of the sounds.

"Yes, but what about the word place, I do not understand its use in the name of the technique."

"Yes, you're right," he replied.

He ordered me to grab him again and asked someone else to get behind him and attack with a training sword. As I tried to punch, he turned his body and effortlessly propelled me on my companion who got me on the shoulder with his weapon. My sidekick and I harming each other made it easy for the master to get us on the ground. Using his hand on my face, he could lead me anywhere he wanted.

"To limit the techniques as they are written in *densho* is a serious mistake. Most of them have several layers of teachings. It is like peeling an onion, the best is hidden underneath."

"Is it like that in all martial arts?" Asked a student I did not know.

"Many popular styles have only existed for fifty or sixty years and sometimes much less. When these more recent martial arts were founded, the needs were not the same. I think in all languages, there is a saying that says necessity is the mother of invention. It was the same at the time. We had to keep track of the tools that could ensure the survival of the members of the school, but we also had to take precautions to prevent these techniques to turn against their creator. On paper, the teaching was basic. To get to understand the hidden meaning of these *kata*, one had to have access to *okuden* transmission. The transfer of word of mouth information from master to disciple. When the student was ready to receive these secrets, the master presented himself to him."

"But what about in recent martial arts?" I asked.

"These schools were not created for survival. They are usually the result of the reflections of one man who wanted to share some of his knowledge. For this reason, some techniques offer little, or no adjustment possibilities. We block the attack, answer with a kick or punch and that's it. It does not allow us to adapt if the aggressor comes at us a different way. Today, it is the sporting aspect which predominates. So why try to design something complex? Moreover, people no longer have the patience to wait to master what they learn. If it's too complicated, they give up. For the creators of new styles, the marketing aspect should dominate in most cases. They have to pay rent..."

"In the old schools, if that knowledge was not taught, it was lost," highlighted another student.

I found this idea of losing so much information unfortunate, so many martial arts schools were forged during the troubled times of Japan.

"Yes, that's what happened to several schools. Masters were too demanding in seeking good disciples. Many *ryu* have been forgotten. I do not want that to happen with my knowledge. That is why I accept so many students from everywhere. What I have acquired should not disappear with me."

That explained why the old master was so generous to me and the other students he taught. In other martial arts that I had practiced before, I received knowledge in dribs and drabs. With him, it was often more than I could assimilate. As soon as we had a special request, he was eager to respond by giving us an enormous amount of information. He continued talking.

"Take the time to understand the name of the technique. See if, by changing the kanji with another with the same pronunciation, the technique can evolve in a direction that you had not planned. You will be amazed at the results. Moreover, this exercise will develop a way of thinking that is essential in *budo*. The power of words feed your ability to adapt to all kinds of possibilities."

He made us do the same exercise with different sequences and each time the result was surprising. Changing the word within to that of direction and that of a wave for the verb align and you get a very different control of the opponent's body. At that time, I began to regret not better mastering Japanese writing. Fortunately for me, there were excellent dictionaries that might help me in this gigantic task that I had given myself of deepening the meanings of the *kata* names. A question came to mind.

"What happens if a person does not take the trouble to do what we just learned, if they do not dig to better play with the names of the techniques?"

The old master smiled at me.

"Many of them do not realize they are in a state of mediocrity. They will still be happy and convinced that they have talent."

"That's kind of sad," I added.

"No, that way they can not do harm to anyone," he merely replied with a shrug.

Chapter 48
Larger than life

During the first months my teacher had agreed to take me on as a student, he had accompanied me to the Tokyo National Museum. By the time we were about to change showrooms, someone bumped into me without turning to apologize. It was a Western man who had to be at least two meters tall. A colossus in proportion with his long arms. He had nothing in common with the skinny types that are only skin and bones. His shaved head reflected the light of day the upper windows let through generously. His bare arms showed various tattoos, including one with a skull and a knife planted into it. I could not stop staring at the man who climbed the stairs two by two. I was not really tempted to go demand an apology from him.

"He impresses you," my teacher told me.

"Yes, I would hate to have to take him on."

"Why is that?" He asked in surprise, "I do not understand why he has that effect on you."

"What, don't you see the stature of this man?"

"Ah, that's what perturbs you so much, his size?"

"With reason! Have you seen the length of his arms?"

"Yes, but fortunately he has only two," he said, chuckling.

I found his sense of humor of questionable taste at times.

"With biceps that big, the power of his fists must be incredible."

"You think that the force of a blow is measured by arm length and the volume of biceps?"

"If not, it still surely must help."

"So you evaluated that this man would be a formidable opponent simply by his size and muscles?"

I began to feel embarrassed to say yes, but my teacher gave me no time to answer.

"If I understand correctly, even before the battle would begin, this man would destabilize you."

I was a little embarrassed to admit it, but that was the case.

"Is there anything about him other than his stature that disturbs you?"

"Well, to be honest, I have always associated shaved heads with brutal people who love to brawl."

The master smiled at me.

"And I imagine that his tattoos do not reassure you either, am I right?"

"I have some distrust of such individuals, yes."

"I thought you were good at martial arts," argued the old man.

"Yes, I am excellent in competition. I'm not afraid to face anyone on the *tatami*, but in terms of street fighting, a guy like that makes me uncomfortable. Would you not be afraid to test yourself against such a colossus?" I asked.

"You and him are similar, so no, I would not mind having to defend myself against a person like him."

"What? You're saying that we are the same? Him and I have nothing in common. We're totally different."

"How many support points do you have on the ground?" He asked in all seriousness.

"If you are talking about feet, I have two, but his are larger, they must be more stable."

The old master did not mind my remarks.

"Do you figure that his skin is thicker and is better protected from impacts than yours?"

That was sarcastic, but he was right.

"Do you think his nerves are more resistant to pain than yours? You think he has no reaction like everyone else when he hits his elbow?"

"I guess it must hurt as badly as me."

"No, it's worse for him. Because obviously, he is training to develop his muscles, many of his nerves are more sensitive than those of ordinary people. The swollen muscles compress the nerves and make them more receptive to *kyusho*."

I came to realize that this armor of muscles were a weakness.

"Did you even see how he moves?"

"Well, same as everyone else... I guess. I did not really pay attention to it."

"He walks with his shoulders kept very high up, raising his center of gravity."

"Therefore..."

"Therefore his attacks are much less powerful than they could be for a man of his size. Have you noticed that he tends to walk on the tip of his toes?"

"No, what does that change?"

"Really, you have everything to learn," said the old man in a slightly discouraged tone, "if we capture the energy when he tries to hit us, we can redirect it to the project him. Because of his size, it even becomes easy."

I did not realize all these weaknesses at the time. After some reflection, I told myself that maybe this man was not as bad as I imagined.

"You let yourself get impressed by his stature and especially by his appearance. Many feel psychologically crushed in the face of such individuals. Some take advantage of this, they feel superior when the person in front of them expresses a feeling of inferiority. If you are in a meeting, act as if the other people were very small. You will notice quickly enough that their attitude will change."

Thinking back about the man, I tried to imagine myself in front of him, considering him as an equal friend of mine. By visualizing this scene, I became calmer. My master was contemplating a *tachi* blade, the ancestor of the *katana*. He continued.

"Look at this blade, it is beautiful. Unfortunately, its length makes it more fragile."

I think I got the message.

"But the length of arms, that makes a difference."

I expected any kind of explanation, except for this one.

"A tiger is only dangerous if you find yourself in front of its fangs or claws. The area surrounding its paws is filled with emptiness. You must learn to swim in that void."

That was simple. All I had to do was learn to swim in void.

"Now," my mentor asked, "would you be able to look at the same man by imagining him being of normal stature and even smaller?"

"I think so. The visualization exercises you taught me can help me do it," I said, raising my chin.

"Good," the master said, placing his hands on my chest and pushing me backwards.

I took a few steps back until I felt my back hit something massive. I had hit someone. By the time I turned to apologize, I saw the giant looking down at me, frowning.

"I wanted to apologize for having bumped into you early. I was spacing out," he said.

Chapter 49

Endurance

My martial arts career is divided into two distinct parts. Before meeting the old master, and after. Like most people, I did not put my efforts in strategic places in my youth. Yet it is without hesitation that I would have told you it was the right path to follow. I had not realized at the time that there was not only one road to follow to achieve enlightenment.

My friends and I were trained in the hard way. Physical training five or six hours at a time was normal for us. During these hours, our hearts were very rarely at rest. All we could do to torture and harden ourselves, we did. Nothing stopped us. I think I can safely say that at that time, I maintained an athlete's body.

We also practiced different hardening exercises. Getting hit almost anywhere on the body was our daily routine. What more could one ask for to create a real war machine? I remember one exercise where a companion of mine climbed on a chair and threw a five-kilo training ball down at us with all his strength. Lying on our back, we had fun jumping on each other's bellies. The heavier the person, the more we were satisfied.

After joining my teacher at his home one day, I told him about the training I used to do before meeting him. He just smiled, the same smile that an adult would do when seeing a child unwrap a Christmas gift.

"It does not seem to impress you," I said, a little frustrated at his lack of empathy for my efforts.

"Oh no, believe me, I'm fascinated. It takes determination to do what you did."

Finally, he recognized the hard work I had done to get to be so effective, but he had not finished.

"Although, it is not very useful."

How could a martial artist of his caliber not agree with this method of training that had made us real fighting machines?

"Why would it not be useful? It is important to be able to absorb impacts if we do not want to get knocked out right from the beginning,"

I was certain that he could not answer such an obvious argument.

"When you were practicing this way, I suppose you let yourself get hit on the stomach and chest, right?"

"Of course," I said proudly, raising my head.

"Undoubtedly, you're used to receiving attacks in the back while avoiding your spine getting hit to avoid serious injury."

It was with a little less assurance that I nodded.

"If your training was complete, you probably enjoyed getting hit on the legs, shins and thighs."

"Yes, of course."

"And naturally, you had to undergo conditioning by getting kicked on the side of the knees."

"Of course not," I said in an exasperated tone, "these joints are too fragile."

"I imagine you punched specific places such as the liver, pelvis and groins with great strength."

I preferred not to answer.

"I also assume that you trained to receive impacts to the face, eyes and nose."

"Of course not, it's too dangerous."

"Yet in a fight, they are the first targets susceptible to attacks."

I was desperate for a way out.

"To protect our heads, we were blocking strikes with our arms," I answered with assurance.

"But then why did you not use your arms to counter the impacts on your body?"

I felt like I was entangling myself more and more.

"Because the body is stronger than the head, it can resist violent shocks."

"Even the shockwave punch I've taught you?"

A few months earlier he had made me feel the power of these techniques. I put several layers of books on my abs, despite this, the force of the blow had sent me flying backwards. I was completely out of breath.

"No, it would not have helped. But if I understand correctly, you are trying to tell me that I wasted my time training that way. What I should have done instead?"

"Learning to move, flow, anticipate the strategies of your opponent."

His eyes gave me the impression he pitied me.

"When did you stop doing these mutilation exercises, excuse me, I should say hardening exercises?"

"A few months before starting training with you."

"Then it may not be too late."

"What do you mean by that?"

The old master got up and went to make a cup of tea. A few minutes later, he sat down and continued the conversation as if there had been no interruption.

"Many people of my era who practiced this way have developed cancers or various problems with their internal organs. And that's not mentioning the fragile bones and blood clots. The human body is not meant to serve as a punching bag. It has its limits."

I brought my hands mechanically to my stomach. He continued his explanation on the subject.

"This method of training was used to quickly form a military elite. They made up for the lack of martial experience with greater physical endurance. It was easier to replace a soldier of this type than one who would have taken years to train. Several factors come into consideration to successfully manufacture this model of efficient soldier. Initially, it is not everyone who have the genetics needed for this kind of long-term mutilation. Those that we see in videos are usually part of that elite with solid genetics."

"But then, if one does not train that way, what would you advise to survive fierce combat?"

"Like I said, learn to move. When doing martial arts, the aim is not to become the best punching bag. We should instead focus our efforts into dodging attacks. Think of all the hours that you spent training that way. If you had used this time learning to move well, you would be safer in a fight than you are now."

This was the answer I was expecting. Unfortunately at that time, my martial awareness was very underdeveloped. It was testosterone that led my training rather than my judgment.

"Okay, I agree regarding the impacts. A ten-year-old child can break the knee of an adult with an impressive musculature if he hits at the right angle. But in terms of fitness, you can not deny that it is a plus."

"You are absolutely right."

I smiled in victory. For once it was I who held the winning argument. Unfortunately, the old master had not said his last word.

"But..."

He had cut my victory short with a single syllable.

"If you spend too much time doing exercises or fitness, you are wasting valuable time."

"Why is that?"

"Because if you spend several months without exercising, you will lose this energy which regular exercise offers. However, even if you stay for years without practicing martial arts, when you need it, your knowledge will be there. It will come out of oblivion and help you when needed. So, it's better to base a defense system on martial technique rather than big muscles."

"Yes, but it can not hurt to be in good physical condition."

"On the contrary," said the old master, "It's a plus, but you can do that by yourself outside your *dojo* learning hours. It is not uncommon for teachers to spend more than half of the teaching time doing fitness. Moreover, most people mix this with real martial arts. They get home exhausted and aching because they did many pushups and think the martial arts class was fantastic because they have pain everywhere.

Did their knowledge of *budo* improve though? Of course, we must have a certain level of resistance. If after thirty seconds of effort you need your asthma pump, maybe you have to invest a little more time on your fitness, but if you want to ensure your safety and rely more on your physique rather than martial capacity, there is a serious problem."

Something inside me desperately wanted all the hard work I had done during all these years not to be useless. A final argument came to my mind.

"Yes, but the advantage of the training I did is that I am now used to pain. My body has learned to manage it."

In response, he took my hand and pressed his thumb nail at the junction of one of my fingers. Severe pain short-circuited my whole being. Shadows appeared in my field of vision. I was on the verge of fainting. I did not even have the ability to try to escape this insidious embrace. Before my consciousness completely dove in darkness, the master released my hand.

"This is the kind of pain you are talking about?" He asked quietly before taking a sip of tea.

"Okay, I get it."

What he had just done to me far surpassed in intensity everything my body had endured all these years.

"You are right about one thing, we can get used to pain, but we do not need to mutilate ourselves to achieve this. In my martial art, it is through *kyusho* that we learn to tame it. If the martial art you do causes damage in the long term, you must consider changing schools."

I have often thought back about this conversation. However, I have never regretted those years of training the hard way. My only regret is the time I lost stagnating martial-wise.

Chapter 50
Anger

I had not seen my master since his lesson about the killer instinct. What I had learned on the subject raised a multitude of questions. That day, I had to go to his home to help remove some weeds from his garden.

Upon arriving, I found him at the top of a ladder with a pair of shears in hand. He contemplated the branch of what looked like a giant bonsai. He had been staring at the tree for a few minutes, then the metal scissors barely sliced a twig at the end of the branch.

"Would you like me to get your glasses for you? You seem to have trouble seeing what you have to remove."

"Cutting branches is easy, what I am doing is adding void at the right places," he replied, carefully examining his work.

What could I say? Metal wires forced some stems to grow in various desired directions. A piece of fabric was protecting the bark to prevent it from being deformed under the pressure of the cables. A second snap of the shears sent the green glitter of the tree flying as a light breeze hurried by. He must have spent at least ten minutes examining his work between the two actions. Slowly, cautiously, my teacher descended from his ladder.

"So, why are you in this state?"

"What state? I'm fine, I have no problem."

"I did not say you had a problem, but something is bothering you. I can see it, in your aura."

I did not know if he was joking or if he really saw something, but he was right.

"It is about the killer instinct," I helped him fold the ladder which I placed over my shoulder and carried to the mysterious shed in which I had never set foot.

"I have several questions about it, to be honest."

He showed me a small round table surrounded by some chairs. A pot of iced tea and two glasses stood on it, waiting to be served. He poured us glasses and emptied his in one shot, which made it look quite delicious.

"For most people, it is something scary, something immoral. Most people associate the word killer with violence, and they are not wrong. Is it something ethical that is bothering you?"

"No, it's not that. Using this energy, I felt my emotions turning to anger. The kind of emotion that can make someone lose his head. It has already happened for me to go into an enraged frenzy. When this happens, I have no control of myself."

"The killer instinct is a feeling very close to anger. A dark rage, a situation where emotions have no room for reason. That is why we must be ready. Without serious management, it is easy to cross the border of the two worlds. We must transform this state into a cold, detached anger."

His solemn tone of voice gave me chills. I had never felt him talk with so much emotion.

"Have you ever had to exceed this limit?"

For a moment I felt bad for having dared ask this question. His past was his business, the kinds of memories that we don't share with anyone.

"Yes, it has happened to me, and believe me, I regret it to this day. At that time I could not distinguish the killer instinct from anger. When we are angry, we can commit acts that we regret our whole life. It happens on impulse. We arrive at a stage where negotiating is out of the question. We want something and everything is focused on the self. I want to win, I want you to lose, you'll see that it is I who am right and decides."

He stopped talking to have a sip of iced tea. This time, he swallowed slowly. His face was transformed, and for a short time, I had the impression that his mind was elsewhere. He went on, but I felt that it would take a less personal direction.

"Imagine you are driving your new car and while changing radio stations, you accidentally cut in front of another vehicle. The driver honks at you, you raise your arm as if to apologize. He sticks behind your car very closely. You have to turn right and you realize that he follows you. He keeps switching his headlights on and off, and you begin to find it particularly unpleasant. He continues by pressing constantly on his horn. You pull over to the side and he walks up to you with two of his friends. He begins to yell at you and tell you you're going to get the beating of your life. You are a good player and apologize, but nothing works. A first punch comes from one of his acolytes behind you. It reaches your shoulder blade, and you feel a sharp pain in addition to hearing a disturbing cracking sound. Like most people, you might be scared, but with your martial training, you do not fear them, you're angry."

The more he talked, the more I had the impression of living this situation. I had already gotten cut off several times and even had the middle finger flicked at me. I always promised myself that one day I would punish one of these ill-mannered bullies.

"You throw your first punch at one of the attackers, you see droplets of blood spurt on your car. Your attackers fit the profiles of ex-cons more than classical dance students. You manage to narrowly avoid a kick that ends up denting your door. You start to lose control. You feel like you want to beat them, hurt them, to take away their ability to harm you. The more you get involved emotionally, the less you feel the blows they throw at you. You do not realize the power of your own attacks. You manage to push two of the attackers away, only the driver remains. You beat him in the face, he falls on the ground. You get on top of him and you hit once, five times, ten times, you do not know how many times you punched. You forget the reason of the fight. The only thing that matters is that you want to hit him. At this point, is it still self-defense or total loss of reason?"

"I think I lost control of my actions long ago," I said, almost feeling guilty about the imaginary scenario.

"With the killer instinct, you can have this anger, but you must control it. Yes, you are in your right to defend yourself, but in this state, it is not you who decides, but your primitive brain. With the killer instinct, you know when it's time to stop. You know what level your opponents are. For a warrior, this awareness allows retreat when the time comes. It allows him to never use more force than is necessary. This instinct allows you to act in a detached manner, as if you were not personally involved in the situation. Your emotions do not manage the situation, but you need to perform the acts that can ensure your survival and the success of your mission. Many people lose the fight because they are reluctant to give the first blow. We must act when necessary. Logic and tactics dominate, not emotions."

"When you made me do the exercise the other day, I felt like I was living the scene in slow motion, even though I was blindfolded. Is it normal to perceive things this way?"

"Yes. When you're angry, your adrenaline runs the show, stress changes your perceptions. Everything happens fast. The first handicap comes from the tunnel effect, where your field of vision narrows to the point of not seeing what is between you and your target. The tension caused by your emotions gives you the impression that all the action takes place at high speed, preventing you from realizing what is happening. The killer instinct brings you to be calmer. From the start, you realize that everything becomes slower, you have time to see and above all to think about what you're going to do next. You make use of the same energy, but just like I taught you, the fact that you are in your right to defend yourself, you get an adrenaline surplus, which gives you an advantage."

"I understand the emotional and glandular aspect, but I still can not grasp why you are calling it the killer instinct, it's more like the energy of despair," I said.

"For many people, despair leads to giving up while the killer instinct leads us to confront the issue. Unfortunately, or rather fortunately, for most people, this instinct is hidden deep within them."

The old master stared at me intensely, without blinking, as if waiting for a reply.

"Do not confound the psycho who kills by pure pleasure and the one that uses the killer instinct out of necessity. The warrior who uses this instinct does it when it is right. If he leads a mission, he does it for his country, for a noble cause, and not out of a drunken power trip."

"This is what makes it that a mother who would never hurt a fly could kill to save her child. This is maternal instinct," I said proudly.

"Yes. She will be ready to kill to protect her offspring from danger. Her determination is unwavering when the survival of her child is in question. Now imagine that some ill-intentioned people take your parents hostage, what would you do?"

"I think I would negotiate."

"But if they are having fun torturing them for pleasure, and each day they send you a severed a finger that belonged to your father or your mother. What would happen when you find these people?"

"I think I'd kill them."

"That is not the killer instinct, but simple revenge."

Chapter 51

Kukan

"You will never succeed like this, stop thinking."

"But you said that we could think during combat."

"Yes, but not the way you are doing it right now. You're not thinking, you are desperately trying to find a way to save yourself."

The old master was right, I was not acting in a serene way. He let me know that I was reacting like a rabbit who felt cornered at the bottom of its burrow. He was right, I was thinking in a completely disorderly way.

"Hit me with all your might," he said, raising his voice.

I raised my guard and advancing my right leg, I launched an attack that would have knocked anyone out. Naturally, I had not managed to reach my target.

"Now do the same thing again and notice what happens."

The moment he moved to avoid my punch, I had the feeling of falling into a hole. A sensation of being sucked in that held me back for a split second in an invisible bubble. It was strange. The old master smiled at me knowing I had seen the difference.

"W-what did you do?"

"I used, or rather, I created kukan."

"I may be wrong, but I think we can translate this word by void, right?"

"That's right, but that emptiness can reveal itself in several ways."

"Whenever you move to avoid my fist, you leave an empty space where you used to be. So why is it that this technique was so different this time?"

"I just told you, kukan has several facets. Budo is *sanshin*. It affects our physical body, emotions, and mental perception. Most martial arts are limited to the body. No warrior worthy of the name can survive if he limits his training to muscle building,"

The master stared at me through his eyebrows, head low. He seemed to expect a reaction that did not come.

"When all we do is avoid an aggression by fleeing, we create space that is not completely empty. Our fears, our thoughts, our emotions persist in this space. We leave our desires and hopes of winning behind."

"I do not think I see that when my opponent dodges my attacks."

"And yet you perceive it all. It's as if you were hiding not to face a problem head-on."

I thought of all the times I had trouble in my life. Rather than taking the time to analyze the situation, I preferred to try not to think about it. The wise old man resumed his explanation.

"You do not know it, but this information influences your subconscious. It gives a human dimension to your fight."

I absolutely did not understand what he meant by human dimension. I let him continue.

"Kukan, at a higher level, is a state of mind where all emotions are removed from the attack zone. We create a total void bubble, a divine space."

He had often spoken of the divine and the human. He separated the two states by raising the fact that man possessed both. At that time, I had no grasp on this warrior duality.

"There is a difference between creating space with total void and simply leaving no target in front of the opponent. By producing this space of complete emptiness, the attacker that enters that area loses all his points of reference during a split second. Great swordsmen who were about to fight duels feared intruding this divine space."

To the Westerner that I was, this notion of the divine was difficult to grasp. In our culture, there was only one God. I thought he wanted me to consider myself a God. It took me time to understand and accept that the divine is present in all of us and had to learn how to connect to it. The old master continued his teaching.

"Now, do it again, hit me several times."

I knew I'd never get to touch him. I expected to feel that falling sensation again, but this time it was even stranger. I felt like I was carried away in a river where the water currents constantly deported me in different directions. I had never experienced this phenomenon since I started doing martial arts. The master told me to stop and stared at me, frowning. I knew from experience that this look meant I was expected to comment on the technique.

"It's strange, I had the impression you were sliding into the void like a ghost."

"It is not me who was in the void, it was you. I simply created different kukan around you. I merely made you move from one space to another."

The word merely seemed too insignificant to describe what I had just experienced.

"I had the feeling that you were all around me," I added.

"Because there was emptiness around you, I swam in these areas."

Yes, it was an elementary explanation. If I lived several hundred years more, I would probably come to understand. I took a deep breath trying to unscramble my confused thoughts.

"The level is too high, how can I manage to do that? I do not know where to start. Is there a more basic exercise you could teach? Something... less divine?"

During a second, I had the impression of seeing the disappointment in his eyes. Then he laughed.

"Okay, let's go for the children's class. Attack me."

Just when my fist was about to touch him, he stepped back, bending his knees. Regardless of my will, my arms began to descend and I found myself slightly unbalanced forward.

"All I did was capture your mind. The brain works on hope."

I thought I had heard it all with him, but he still managed to surprise me.

"If your subconscious mind, and not your intellect, thinks the shot will hit its target, it will make an extra effort to get there. When your fist came closer to me, I fell while remaining close enough to you to give you the hope of touching me. If I had retreated too far or too fast, you would have changed your strategy instead of continuing on your momentum."

"It's true, the whole time I had the impression I was going to reach you. I was even certain that you could not escape."

"Here it was more basic, I only created a physical void. Your subconscious did the rest."

That I could do. Later, while training at the *dojo* with other students, I was able to use this principle. Fortunately for me, the old master had not finished his teaching.

"Energy does not like void, it is always trying to fill it. Kukan is only a small portion of non-existence, a place where thoughts and energy have not had time to fill. In this empty space, we have the opportunity to slip in false information. This is called *kyojutsu*, but that's for another time."

"You mentioned that the brain thrives on hope. What do you mean by that?"

"Most people do not live in the present moment. They live by clinging on to hope. That of a higher wage, a happier life, a more luxurious car, and even to get better at martial arts. We must learn to focus on the present moment and not to allow ourselves to be divided between the present, past, and future."

"Is there a connection with *budo*?" I asked.

"Attack me," was the answer.

I sprang with all my strength to reach the old master in the face. He stepped back and knocked violently the inside of my biceps then placed his fingers around my eyes while at the same time raising his other fist above his head, ready to knock me out. I was torn between the pain from the block, his fingers that threatened me, and his other fist that was about to befall on me. The position he took was to sow total confusion in my mind. The pain he had caused in my arm kept me a prisoner of the past, his fist ready to hit me threw me into a painful future. Finally, in the center, between the two, there was the void of the present moment, a place I could attempt to escape with difficulty.

"You understand? I created kukan between two spaces occupied by your mind. In a split second, it was impossible for you to react. You knew what happened, you saw what happened, but you were disconnected from the present moment. Time is transformed by kukan."

It took me years to sort it all out. Today, I am far from being able to do what he taught me, but at least now I know that it all exists.

Chapter 52
The best

There are questions that one should never hesitate to ask. One day, one of them brought me an answer I did not expect. We were at a restaurant and I took the opportunity to ask my master why our martial art was the best.

"Who said it was the best?" He replied. He seemed surprised that I would ask him such a question.

"If isn't, why don't you practice another martial art?"

"Why did you not order this delicious curry rice I am eating now?"

"No thank you, I was fooled once. It is way too spicy for my delicate palate."

"I'm not saying that this is the best rice in the world, but I love it and appreciate its full-bodied flavor. That's what I want right now. It's the same with martial arts. I practice what suits me best."

"So that means there is no better martial art?"

"There exists only the one that allows us to evolve when it is needed."

I was not sure I understood. I thought I was practicing the ultimate martial art with my teacher, and there he was confessing he was not sure we were practicing a supreme art.

"Why so many questions? Do you think our martial art is not up to it?"

"No, it's not that. I just wanted to know why our martial art was so powerful compared to others, and there you are, telling me there are better things out there."

"I never told you that there was something better, I simply asked who said it was the best?'

"I do not understand."

"Yes, that's your problem, you take pleasure in complicating everything."

"That is completely untrue."

"If there are that many existing martial arts, it is likely that there are as many categories of practitioners. The teaching I give you would probably not be appreciated by most people. One should have reached a certain level to have the ability to grasp the subtleties of *budo*. If a person is not ready for this, they had better do something more basic, or even nothing at all."

The old master had touched a good point. Ten years ago, I probably would have found his lessons ridiculous. At the time, never would I have been able to grasp and appreciate the small detail that changes everything. He resumed his explanation.

"Since you started with me, how many techniques have I forced you to remember before showing you more?"

"It has never happened. You always taught me to learn with my body, heart, and mind, never with the memory."

"That's right. This way of transmitting martial arts is the most effective, but also the most difficult. Most people measure their knowledge by quantity. They need points of reference to know where they're going. That is why in modern schools, they have codified and stored certain techniques and *kata* into groups that practitioners must remember before moving on."

"Is this why almost all these institutions now have a multitude of different colored belts?" I asked.

"That is one reason, yes. The other advantage of compartmentalizing material this way is to give students the opportunity to get a new belt every three months. Marketing firms have discovered a decrease in interest on the part of the students passed this three-month time period. Tell me, when was the last time I gave you a rank?"

I must confess that if my motivation had been to acquire new belts, I would not have stayed with him for a long time. He was not the type to fixate on that sort of thing. I went on with a new question.

"You said there are as many kinds of martial arts as there are kinds of practitioners. Is it possible to define the different categories?"

The old master rubbed his chin nodding, looking down at the ground.

"Basically, we can separate martial arts into three main groups."

"Beginner, intermediate and advanced," I interrupted, gradually decreasing my tone of voice.

The old man turned, and looked up at the sky. For a moment, I had the impression that he had looked at me with... pity.

"The first category includes the arts that end in do," he said, "that includes styles like aikido, kendo, and some others."

"What do they have that is so particular?" I asked impatiently.

"They are made to gradually bring their practitioners on a spiritual path."

A thousand questions tormented me, but I let the old sage go on.

"The second category is combat sports. Whenever there is a possibility of competing, it is likely that these martial arts are less focused on defense in a real context. Dangerous automations have been completely banned from those systems. In the ring, there is no room for gestures or techniques that could kill or seriously injure someone."

For years, I thought I was a fighting machine that could cope with all kinds of situations in the street. On several occasions, the old master had brought me back to the real world.

"And finally, there are martial arts like ours that we call *bugei*. The goal of these martial arts is simply survival."

The pause I was expecting had finally come.

"If I understand, our martial art has nothing spiritual."

Far from being disconcerted by my words, he gave me a big smile and simply answered me with a new question.

"Why is it that the spiritual path is so important to you?"

"It leads to absolute understanding," I was very proud of my response that actually did not mean much.

"Okay, I see you still have a way to go. On the path of spirituality, the practitioner searches for *satori*. The question should rather be: what is enlightenment?"

I did not dare give him my version. I let my teacher go on.

"We seek enlightenment to achieve the highest levels of martial arts. Connection, control of time, energy, in short, everything that can lead to mastery. In the do arts, they work on meditation, they exploit very... well, ceremonious movements in order to develop *ishiki*, universal consciousness."

"If it's that important to achieve this level of understanding, why is it that we do not practice meditation and ceremonial movements too?"

"Because there is not just one path that leads to the way. If your whole life you do these series of movements and your mind is elsewhere, it becomes a waste of time. Moving is meditation in itself if we do it with awareness. If you only do meditation by spending all your time sitting on your behind, martially speaking, you shall not learn anything, but if you train with attention to detail, with awareness of the present moment and keep your heart open as much as your mind, then you can achieve this state. Instead of using the mind to access the channel, you do it through the body. The mind and body are just two different vehicles that lead to the same places if we control them well enough."

"In that case, all martial arts can lead to this level of consciousness."

"Yes, provided that the practitioner is not hindered by anything."

"What? What can stop someone from reaching such a level?"

"If when you are training, your memory is solicited more than your intuition and your abilities, there's little chance you will achieve it. If your goal is to accumulate an impressive amount of *kata*, you will not master anything, all you are doing is collecting. This certainly is not the path to follow."

Using his chopsticks, the old master dipped a ball of rice in curry sauce. Bringing the content to his mouth, he closed his eyes and seemed to savor this dish that scared me so much at the time. After swallowing his food, he continued the discussion.

"Martial arts are only a tool. What makes the difference is the one who practices. These instruments are only there to allow the flower to bloom. If you do not have the proper tools to care for your plant, it may survive, but it will remain frail. But if you feed it the right fertilizer, give it the necessary sunshine, cut off the dead branches what eats away its energy, then the tree will have strong roots. It will produce wonderful fruit."

I let the old master continue on the fact that martial arts were only tools whose quality made all the difference. A badly sharpened saw could sometimes do more harm than good. Something at the table next to ours caught my eye. I watched the young waitress set several plates of curry rice down. The customers had all chosen the same dish as my teacher. I took advantage of this coincidence to renew the conversation after my *sensei* had swallowed another bite.

"Looking at these people, I see that they have ordered the same dish as you. Yet there are plenty of people on the other side of the street in other kinds of restaurants. So that means..."

"So that means not everyone wants to eat this delicious curry rice. If you prefer Western fast food, it's your choice."

Chapter 53
Contact

On several occasions, the old master had me practice with my eyes closed. "You work too much with your eyes. You must learn to use your real eyes," he used to say. Over the years, I discovered many advantages of developing my other senses. My connection with everything around me had become a valuable asset in my martial learning. I thought I covered the subject when one day, he once again made me face my ignorance of the human soul. I noticed long ago that we only used a small part of our capabilities. That day, I was told that training would be held in one of the outside *dojo*. The very one who was near the small cave. I dreaded having to repeat that trial.

I was the first to arrive at the clearing. As always, I was there early. I did not want to make my teacher wait. It would have been a lack of respect that I could not afford. When we get the chance of being accepted by someone of his rank, it is our responsibility to do everything we can to make it work. I took the advantage of my free time to do some *sanshin no kata*. These movements introduce us to various ways of moving. They not only teach our bodies, but also create the link between the emotions and the body, in addition to requiring the highest level of mental awareness. They allow our emotions to connect to our subconscious. Of course, you can practice these *kata* like a simple exercise, just imitating the movements, but when *sanshin* are made by uniting the three cores that are mind, emotions, and body, they turn into an incredible energy source.

One hour must have passed since I had started doing these exercises in different ways. After having done them the basic way, I used trees as partners to vary the routine I performed. Rocks and neighboring obstacles became opponents to beat. My worst enemy was myself. I began to worry not seeing my master arise unexpectedly. He told me to be there, so I was there. I took the opportunity to revise my *ukemi*, these techniques used to protect ourselves when falling on the ground. Knowing how to fall had already proven beneficial. One day as I was riding a bicycle, a car did not make its mandatory stop. I hit the side of the vehicle and the shock propelled me over the hood. It is by doing a forward roll that I found myself on my own two legs without suffering serious injury.

I tried to use everything around me as a training accessory. The most difficult thing to do was to dive between two trees close together. I had to rotate to the side to successfully pass through the gap. A rock was waiting for me upon arrival, I had to project myself far enough not to fall on it. I began to worry about the absence of my teacher. Then I remembered that he had said that worrying when nothing could be changed at the time was a loss of energy. "If you can not act in the present moment, then cease to torment yourself, it will change nothing. You need to be at your best in the present moment. We can prepare for the future, but we do not live in the future," he said.

The full range of exercises I could do alone had been done. With all the jumps I did, the fauna must have thought of me as an *oni*, a demon taken straight from Japanese mythology. I took advantage of the calm of the place for various meditations both passive and active. Then I went back to physical training by racing between the trees. Instead of running great distances, I aimed an area of about ten meters by ten, and I zigzagged between the trunks, constantly changing directions. My scratched arms were proof that I could not completely control the space around me. Suddenly, my head began to spin, I became very dizzy. An image of the master flashed before me for a few moments. Even though I did not see his lips move, he whispered me to disconnect my mind and emotions from my body, to continue what I was doing. My mind told me that I must have suffered a heat stroke. I had had nothing to eat and drink for several hours. I was torn between continuing my training as the hallucination dictated, or stop and rest as common sense wanted.

It was my rational side that lost. I continued to run and move like never before. I do not know how, but I managed to separate my mind from my body. I was inside my carcass like I had been trapped in a soulless machine, a simple structure that served as a vehicle. My emotions were nonexistent, I moved, and that's all. After ten minutes, my intellect advised me to manage myself. There are still limits to respect.

I took a towel from my bag to wipe off some sweat. I think I had never done such an intensive workout. Of course, in my years of karate, I had worked hard, but this was different, I had never been so demanding towards myself as that moment. I took the time to sit at the foot of a tree and closed my eyes, I thanked the forest for allowing me to spend a few hours with it. I walked slowly along the path that lead to the small train station. As I was about to drop my card on the ticket reader, the voice of an employee caught my attention. He told me that my *sensei* was waiting for me at the kissaten near the bookstore.

Upon entering the tea house, he waved at me. He was sitting in the company of an older man I did not know.

"So our training went well?"

"Our training? I did not see much of you."

My teacher smiled and introduced me to his friend, Suzuki-san. The old man greeted me and apologized, claiming his wife was waiting for him.

"A friend of yours?" I asked.

"Yes. He is probably one of the wisest men I know."

"What do you mean?"

"He has a very healthy philosophy of life. I learned a lot from him."

I had never thought of that before. My master also had to learn. He was not born a master, but became one by working hard and persevering.

"I see you have been busy, you seem dehydrated."

He called the lady who brought me a cup of hot tea.

"Cold would not be good for you," said my teacher, "we must balance your energies. Tell me what kind of training you did."

I related to him all that I had done without rest. Naturally, I did not consider the meditation exercises as a break. I finished by explaining the heat stroke I had and the vision where he had appeared before me.

"It was not really you since you can not appear in front of me like that, right?"

"Who knows? The human mind is something vast and mysterious. It can do much more than what we might think."

"Was it you who told me to disconnect myself from my body?"

"Whether it was me or something else is not important. What matters in these visions are not the messenger, but the content of the message. It is what connects us to the divine."

These words did not help me understand, they did quite the opposite.

"Has such a thing ever happened to you?"

"Yes, very often. To this day I use this when I have doubts or questions."

"You have doubts?"

"Yes! I am just a human being like everyone else. I have no power, I do not do magic."

"So then, who do you connect with when it happens?"

"I trust all those who were there before me. My old teachers who died and their masters. Sometimes, even the *kami*."

"You... you actually communicate with spirits?"

"Yes, I ask for their advice. I seek their help."

"And it works?"

"In most cases, yes."

"Are you actually in contact with the dead?"

The old master smiled at me. He took a sip of tea that he seemed to particularly enjoy.

"What do you think?" He asked me, "can we actually communicate with spirits?"

"I do not know."

"Well, me neither," he said, fixing the cup he held in his hands.

"Then why do you talk to your former teachers? They are dead and can not respond."

"Yes, they are indeed long dead. I do not know if it's really them who communicate with me, but I get my answers."

"If it is not them, where do these answers come from?"

"I do not know," said the old master, "maybe from me, maybe the gods. The only thing I know is that when I put myself in the proper frame of mind, the solution I am looking for becomes clear."

"Are the results always good?" I asked.

"If my intellect does not interfere then, yes. That is why we must have a pure heart."

"A pure heart? You mean someone who has never sinned?"

"You are mixing spirituality and religion. In ancient *budo*, a pure heart is something different. To keep it simple, we might say that it is a state of mind that separates the emotions, intellect, and the body. If each of these are isolated, are not contaminated with the other aspects and work alone, we can sometimes accomplish amazing things. They each have a different way of communicating."

"Yes, but usually, it is preferable that these three states work together, right?"

"Most of the time, yes. But on certain occasions, you have to make the most of each of these states. By entrusting what we learn to our subconscious, something positive always comes from it. Is it just us, or a connection with the divine? Nobody can say for sure..."

"But do you attribute that to yourself, or to your subconscious?"

The old master looked at me, joining his hands together in thought.

"The question is, where does the human end and the divine begins?"

Chapter 54
The aggressive energy

I think that morning, the old master had gotten up on the wrong foot. It had been a while since I had not received such violent blows. I felt like my bones were breaking at each contact with his fists.

"*Sensei*, can we take a break? I feel that my body is about to explode."

"What's going on? You partied all night, I suppose?"

"What's going on with me? I rather need to ask you that. You keep massacring me since this morning."

"You call this a massacre? Do you want me to show you true carnage?"

We were in one of the outside *dojo*, a small clearing in the forest. It seemed that even the birds preferred to remain silent rather than to irritate him more.

"No, master. I apologize if I offended you."

He stared at me, squinting his already half-closed eyes. I had the feeling he was going to kill me only with his gaze.

"Do I look like someone who's upset?" He asked.

I felt that he had grown a foot taller. Maybe it was because I felt crushed by such strong energy. He crossed his arms over his chest as if preparing to hit me.

"Do as I do, adapt yourself to my rhythm," he ordered.

I tried somehow to imitate his movements, but I was far from his velocity. How could such an elderly person be faster than me? I panicked at the thought of not being able to follow him.

"Stop feeling sorry for yourself and strike. Move a little."

My body had reached maxed speed, it could not keep up with his pace. My attacks were powerful, but they could not reach the speed needed to hit... an elderly man.

"You do not have the right spirit," said my teacher, "you are on the defensive, you are not using the correct element. Abandon water, use fire."

"I can not, I'm not angry."

"You think being fire is to be angry?"

"Well..."

"Okay, let's take a break."

Within a few moments, his face was reflecting his usual love of life. How could he transform so quickly?"

"So you thought I was mad?" He asked me, smiling.

"You did not stop hitting me violently. I was certain that I had done something wrong."

"Since this morning I am telling to you to be like fire, have you any idea what that means?"

"It is when we are angry. We become aggressive and we can use the energy released by this emotion."

"What happens if you have an opponent who has the same ability as you, but is even more furious?"

"It will be difficult to stop him."

"Why?" He asked.

"His attacks will become so powerful."

"And disorderly," he went on, "did you have the impression that was my case?"

"No, you seemed in full control of all your means. Your face seemed to be possessed by some mysterious demon out of another world though."

The old man laughed.

"It was not the case. Only government officials have the mysterious power to transform me into a demon," the master said, chuckling.

"But then, why this expression of anger?"

"Fire draws its energy from will. An explosion of determination. We can not fully use this energy without adapting our body. In addition, displaying it openly can influence the opponent."

"Why does the body become so disorderly though?"

"It is not the energy of fire that does that, but anger. We must learn to handle fire without being dominated by the negative side of that emotion. We can be aggressive even with the intent of killing if it becomes necessary, but two seconds later we must be able to return to being as gentle as a lamb. Throughout the process, our mind must be controlled. We must not let the fire enslave our minds."

"We are back to *ishiki*, being aware of everything at any time," I said, happy to contribute to the explanation.

"Exactly. It is easy to shift from elements such as earth and water to fire, but it is more difficult to calm back down to earth."

"Concerning speed, how do you manage to be so fast?"

"It's simple, you are desperately trying to be fast, I'm just hitting, and reacting at the right time."

"I am still reacting at the right time, I have this awareness of my body and my environment."

"From what I understand, you have mastered *ishiki*?" Asked the master advancing towards me.

I suspected he had started playing with me, but I could not see the trap he was setting.

"Yes, I'm doing a pretty good job."

"If you were attacked from behind, you would feel the danger ahead of time? Would the speed provided by fire be sufficient for you to avoid any aggression?"

He kept advancing towards me, as if he was about to engage in combat. I felt threatened. I sped up my breathing in order to use the speed that fire provided. I was ready for the worst. With confidence, I stepped back in order to keep the necessary distance to be able to respond to any eventuality

"Are you ready to take a little test to see if you can counter a surprise attack?"

From that moment, I had the feeling that the old master was not mad at me, I was sure of myself. I knew I could dodge his attacks.

"Well, then turn around and try to dodge this," he said, stepping back like I was about to attack him wildly.

I felt something slither on my shoulder. I turned my head to see a forked tongue and two menacing eyes staring at me. The master laughed and clapped seeing me jump in terror. It wasn't the first time he had pulled off the snake joke on me.

"I hate those creatures!" I screamed, brushing it off my shoulder in a hysterical manner before running behind the master who was bent forward laughing, tears in his eyes.

"You should be ashamed of yourself, you scared it away. Those tiny snakes are totally harmless...I think."

Chapter 55
Budo finesse

While most martial arts teachers need to be on a *tatami* in order to teach, the old master passed on his knowledge constantly, no matter the place or the circumstances. Each conversation with him became an endless source of learning.

One day, we were sitting on a train, a passenger was reading his newspaper. An article talking about a fighter who had just won a prestigious title in the world of mixed martial arts. I had seen this athlete perform on television before.

"Have you ever seen him in action?" I asked.

"No why? Did I miss something that might help me progress?"

"He has an interesting technique. He is an intelligent fighter who knows how to exploit his opponent's weaknesses."

Pleased to be able to introduce him to my teacher, I took my phone out and found the best video I could online. He looked at the progress of the fight carefully. I felt a certain satisfaction to be able to show him something he did not know. I was proud of myself until I saw him crack a smile. The kind of little smile that makes you feel like a child.

"You do not like him. You don't think he is good? I see that you do not like what you are seeing," I said without understanding why.

"No, no, that's not it. I think he is good, very good actually."

Again, I felt a certain pride. A pride that did not last very long.

"I think he has talent... In his class."

So much misunderstanding caused me to accidentally nudge the lady sitting next to me.

"Shitsureishimasu, *sumimasen*," I stammered confusing my excuses.

"You see, that's exactly the problem this man has."

Naturally, I grasped less and less what he meant.

"He has good skills, he has a certain power to him, nice technical knowledge, but he lacks the essential."

At that point, I was completely lost. He compared my hitting of the passenger next to me, with a video of the world's best fighter at the time.

"What is the relationship between me and him?"

I think I had never stared at my master with as much interest.

"You nudged the lady even though martially speaking, you have all the knowledge you need to manage how your body moves in the surrounding space. Yet you still hit her because you still have much to learn. Your skills are still at a basic level. You're at the stage of fighting against an opponent and not with him. You fight with only what you see, not with what your physical body feels."

"Okay, if you say so, but what is the connection with the world champion?"

"He is the same. One who understands *budo*, real *budo*, sees immediately that this young man certainly has talent, but is far from having grasped the subtle nature of *budo*."

I had just politely learned that I did not know what true *budo* was.

"Budo is rooted in the sense of detail," went on my teacher.

"He has that attention to detail though. Have you not noticed how he quickly reacted to various attempts at being controlled by his opponent?"

"Oh, that? These are just reflexes developed through training. I admire the level he has reached in this area, but it's still pretty basic. Well done, but rudimentary."

"How can you say that watching this video only once? Professionals dissect these scenes, they examine them frame by frame. If that was not good, I'm sure there would be full reviews of this man's weaknesses."

I thought I had managed to corner my teacher, he could not replicate such an argument.

"Maybe because those interested in true *budo* do not waste time with such fighting."

I did not answer, and it's not because I did not want to.

"You will notice that he consistently uses his physical strength," went on the old master, "show me the first technique he does one more time."

The train stopped again, and the lady that I had accidentally hit stood up and bowed to my professor. I bowed out of respect and regret to have rushed it. My mentor excused myself by telling the lady that I was still young and awkward. She smiled away. It was frustrating to be treated like a child. I guess it's part of what a disciple has to endure.

"Will you show me the sequence or not?" Repeated the master.

On the screen we could see the opponent preparing to grab the champion's body. By the time his assailant was preparing to grasp his legs with his arms, the champion put his arms between those of his attacker and opened them by forcing him to spin on himself and fall on his back.

"You may not realize it, but what he did with two arms using the power of his muscles could have been done with two fingers."

"Impossible," I said in a tone that turned all eyes in my direction.

"This is what makes the difference between us. You can not see the small details that make martial arts so interesting."

Answering him would have been useless. I expected a follow-up, but he was silent. The train had stopped and the seat was completely free. I took the opportunity to move a bit while breaking this moment of silence.

"It's still hard to believe," I said, "his posture seems so stable. His opponent seemed as solid as I am now."

As soon as I had finished speaking, he placed his index under my elbow and lifted it. Before I even had time to react, he pushed on my knee, depriving me of any support on my lower back. Trying to get back into position, my body slid to the side and I found myself spread out on the floor. "Excuse him, he does not support *sake*," he said, raising his arm as if taking a sip. He had made me fall to the ground using two fingers. I must say, in my defense, I had kept my backpack on and I was sitting on the edge of the bench. But despite that...

"So, now do you believe that it is possible to control someone this way?"

"I have seen you do something similar before, but you and your opponent were standing and I thought you had taken advantage of a weakness on his part."

"You're right, that's what I exploited."

"I was sitting. There was no flaw in my posture."

"It is nevertheless the case. When you shifted your weight on your buttocks to move, you transferred your weight to get back into place. I used this imbalance to make you fall."

"What loss of balance? I never lost my balance."

"Really? In this case, you must have fallen on your own."

"No, it was you who made me fall. Okay. I know you made me lose balance, but I do not know how."

"That's the small detail that separates the true practitioner from the technique collector. Many people can play music professionally. The general public will not see the difference between two violinists who perform the same partition. However, a virtuoso could hear two pieces that seem identical, but do not have the same personality."

"That, I can understand. So then, why are there not more practitioners of true *budo* out there?"

"Maybe it requires too many sacrifices to get to this level? We have already talked about this, people are often satisfied with the level of quality they have achieved."

"I've found you. Is it likely that there are not enough teachers like you to help everyone?"

"No, it's not that. Good teachers are everywhere. We just need to look. A master can open the door to invite the student, but he can not force him to enter."

Chapter 56
The soul of the *katana*

A few years had passed since I started training under the supervision of my teacher. The fascinating thing about him was that as soon as I thought I had fully covered a topic, he supplied me with new information, thus propelling the technique at higher levels. Of course, I had already experienced the *kata* in question, I knew how to do it, but each time, like an upward spiral, he added new information allowing me to see the sequence from a different angle.

I was in the *dojo* with other students. More than sixty of us were fighting over the plots of free space on the *tatami*. I found this a particularly unpleasant situation, because working with the sword in a confined area proved a feat in itself. As soon as I raised an elbow or moved, I hit one of my training companions. This situation did not seem to bother the old master who himself had the center of the room cleared for him to perform his techniques. That day, I must have been in a bad mood because when he told me that I was not doing what he showed, I retorted that he actually had space to move.

"If I understand correctly, you are unable to adapt yourself," he said, raising his eyebrows to the point that his eyes lost their oblong shape.

"It is impossible to do without space. There are situations where no adjustment is feasible. Try as I might, it comes out all wrong."

The old master smiled. He asked everyone to close the circle around him.

"Move closer, I have too much space," he said, looking at me.

Compressed as he was, he could not perform the technique as he had previously done. He ended up with three times less space than I had. He told some students to clear some space so his opponent could attack with a sword. The moment the *bokken* fell on his head, he just turned his body slightly, raising the weapon in his hand. This gesture was enough to redirect the blade of the attacker. He had done the same technique, but had changed his way of moving to achieve the same result. For the counter-attack, he placed his left palm on his opponent's hand in order to control it and he twisted his blade vertically keeping it very close to him. He ended by pressing the tip of the sword to the throat of his attacker. He had just achieve the impossible. He turned to me and remained silent while holding the tip of his sword against his assailant.

"I think I still have things to learn," I said.

"I think so. Your error was not to be unable to do the technique. It was to have abandoned even before analyzing everything in depth."

My teacher had not held my bad behavior against me. He forgave easily, sometimes too easily. I was ashamed of myself and he knew it. He let it go.

"You may not have noticed, but I used my sword as a shield, or should I say as an obstacle for my opponent. I did not put my sword in front of me, I hid behind it."

"Is it the same when you block *shuriken* with a *katana*?" Asked one of the students.

"It is exactly the same. Most people will tend to quickly position the weapon in front of them, but when the projectile arrives, our reflexes are defensive. It is more natural to hide than to try to put objects in front of you."

"Yes, but you were talking about using the sword as a shield. We place it in front of us to protect ourselves from attacks."

Saying this, I thought of historical films where the Romans and the Spartans used shields when fighting. As usual, the old man gave me the impression of having read my mind.

"It may seem that way in movies, but in reality, your body will move when taking a shield out this way. It will try to hide behind it as the same time as it is positioned. Place yourself in *seigan* no *kamae* with your sword," he instructed.

I put my right leg in front, my *bokken* pointing towards his eyes. My strong posture enabled me to move effectively in all directions. He took the same position. Then he slowly moved aside. Instinctively, I adjusted myself to his posture in order to grant him the least possible openings.

"Well, what did you just do?" He asked.

I realized that with each step, I placed the sword in front of me and changed my position, concealing myself behind the makeshift shield.

"You are right, I hid behind my *bokken*."

"Yes, and if you pay a little more attention, you will notice that your sword positions itself to protect you. A sword has its own life. If you feed it well, it becomes alive."

He was nearing esotericism there, but actually, my weapon did seem to try to protect me.

"Of course," the old man went on, "It is your subconscious that feeds it, but if you trust it, it will move in the most appropriate manner."

For nearly thirty minutes, he made us practice different ways to use our sword as a shield. The fact that we were packed like sardines not even brush my mind. I adapted somehow with the little space allotted to us. I thought that on a battlefield, bumping our comrades in arms had to be commonplace. The master taught us to let the handle of the sword move in our hand, so as to change the attack angle of the weapon's edge.

"Do not try to turn the sword, we must let it move itself."

I was not a beginner in these *katana* manipulation exercises, but it was the first time I had succeeded so well. It seemed that the sword was positioning itself, it knew what it had to do. This maneuver was often used to place the blade below the wrists of the attacker the moment he attacked with a downward swing.

"We must not show the enemy that we are placing our blade that way. We should not telegraph our intention," explained the old man.

Whenever the master performed this type of strategy, there was no indication what angle the edge of the sword would be in until the last moment. It was too late for the attacker the moment he realized what had happened. The class ended with the projection of *ki*. The master stood in *seigan*, blade pointing to my eyes. I raised my sword high, ready to drop it on his head, once an opening allowed me.

"OK, we'll do the technique twice. After you will explain the differences between the two."

He deliberately left me an opening. My sword fell with force, but at the last second, Master moved slightly to one side, and the tip of his weapon touched my throat. The technique was impeccable. Its movement, its perfect angle and good timing had led me to defeat. I got back in position for the second attack. I moved slowly, following his movements. I felt like a tiger waiting for its prey to get within range. Suddenly, an opening presented itself. At the time my sword rushed down, a freezing cold sensation ran down my spine. I felt my legs soften, and my arms having their strength drained. I had become the prey.

"Can you tell us what you felt during those two situations?" He asked me.

"Both moves were the same, but completely different."

I suspected that my explanation was absurd,

"Technically, you moved in the same way to counter my two attacks, but the second time, I felt that a train was about to run me over. I was as useful as a punching bag."

The teacher let the laughter fade and commented on what had happened.

"The sword is alive. Like any living thing, the more energy it has, the more it affects its surroundings. In the first attack, I merely did a defensive technique according to the manual of the perfect *samurai*. In the second situation, I added what we call *okuden*, what books can not show."

Okuden teaching is the oral transmission of knowledge. These secrets are not written on *densho*, the scrolls that could be read by anyone. My master continued.

"The intellect analyses and sees what is logical. The subconscious mind perceives the emotions, it feels the energy that is emitted during a confrontation. It can be used to influence the mind of an opponent. The sword has its own energy, if we add to it our own, then we become a single weapon with the sword. We fight without intent."

During the remainder of the class, I tried without success to recreate this phenomenon. It was then that the old man walked behind me and whispered in my ear.

"For me it's easy, I am old. I draw the energy from the batteries in my pacemaker."

He laughed at my bewildered face.

Chapter 57
Playing Instructor

Some twenty years had passed since I began teaching martial arts when this conversation took place. This discussion showed me a new side of the teacher's role. That morning, there had to be at least fifty people in the *dojo* with the master. This may seem a lot, but most of the time, twice this number of participants attended his classes. I considered myself privileged to benefit from private meetings and training with him. The teacher stopped and explained that we had to support each other. He drew our attention to the fact that we had to be aware of how we moved. A student who was a beginner raised his hand to ask a question.

"*Sensei*, how can we know that the technique executed by our partner is not good? How can we fix it and help him? It was easy in my old martial art, we all had to move in the same way, but here it's so different. Sometimes I can see that there is something wrong, but I can not put my finger on it."

I understood very well what he meant. What master taught us had nothing to do with automatically executed choreography. We had to adapt to each opponent, with each attack and mood. The old man raised his eyebrows, looking at his interlocutor.

"This is an excellent question. Our art was created for people who must learn to adjust to their technical stature, their physical strength, their gender and their temperament. The first step is to trust your instincts. If you feel that there is something wrong, it's probably because there is. This is already a great step forward. Most practitioners do not even realize when they see unrealistic techniques. They accept such performances without asking any questions. Do you sometimes have the feeling that there is a mistake or weakness in the way your partner executes a technique?"

"Yes, but most of the time I tell myself that it is I who am wrong. I am new in this martial art and I should not have the competence to judge."

"It has nothing to do with rank. A beginner can catch errors where a seasoned black belt will not see anything. If your instinct leads you to suspect that there is a lack in the execution, then there probably is. Anyway, there are always weaknesses in a technique."

The master smiled.

"When I feel that something is wrong, what do I have to check first?" Asked the student.

"A technique is a tool that should enable us to win a confrontation by undergoing the least possible damage. If in the making, there is a risk that the opponent strikes, destabilizes us, and regains the advantage, it is certain that there is a problem. In combat sports, an opponent who suffers strangulation may not sink his fingers into the eyes of his opponent in order to escape. On a battlefield, that's the thing to do. One must be aware of these possibilities when it comes to counter-attacks in real situations. We have to wonder if the technique used is realistic and safe."

I interrupted to tell a little story that had struck me.

"I remember seeing in a martial art magazine a teacher showing knife defense moves. He used a hook kick to the attacker's forearm. The technique would be good if we did not take into account the possibility of the opponent being faster or the ground being slippery. By reacting in this manner, he tolerated the blade passing one or two centimeters from his femoral artery. If it were cut, being a vital artery, after thirty seconds the defender would lose consciousness, and in around ninety seconds' time he would die from blood loss. We have to be realistic when adopting a strategy."

The master nodded in approval, then he continued.

"Also, if you are injured to the leg, you can forget the option of running away. In addition to common sense, what should you pay attention to?"

Nobody dared to comment. The old man did not stretch the suspense any longer.

"Distance, we must learn to check if our distance is logical. Imagine someone avoiding being sliced by a sword by jumping back one meter. Is the technique still good? Perhaps, if his intention is to flee. But if there is a wall behind or there are other opponents, the distance he took is too great. It is best to let the tip of the *katana* pass as close as possible to us. The thickness of a sheet of paper is ideal."

"Why should we stay so close?" Asked the same student.

"Because if you are too far, you can not regain control of the weapon. You must be able to move forward quickly."

"It that not exposing ourselves too much?"

"In a fight, there is always a risk," said the old man, "although the blade seems dangerously close, if it does not touch us, there is nothing to fear. The claws of a tiger are not dangerous if we do not find ourselves in their path."

I understood very well what he meant. We do not instantly stop a sword that has gained momentum to cut. If we are close enough, we are a step ahead of the attacker to prevent him from using his weapon. There are a multitude of techniques to control someone by the wrists. The master continued.

"Knowing how to manage distances is essential for a good fighter. Be careful not to attack in a robotic way, in always the same manner.

We must learn to judge distances even in the heart of the storm. No matter the weapon the enemy uses, it is important to gauge its reach."

I recalled attacking with a sword and my teacher had just slightly leaned his head back to let the blade swing pass. I believe that a piece of paper would not have found enough room to fit in this small area. He went on with another point to be checked.

"Not moving well generates a large source of errors. It is not uncommon to see people moving relying on their lower backs which are tilted backwards. It becomes impossible to move smoothly in all directions like this. If you do not position your leg at the right place, you lose stability. We must always ensure that our structure is solid. It must be strong while being mobile."

What he explained reminded me that I had a lot of difficulty losing bad habits that I had developed doing different martial arts. In one of them, all the movements were done in a jerky manner. As fluid movements were not a requirement, I had learned to move sequentially, as if the action would freeze between photos. The master raised another important element.

"When the distance is good and everything seems to flow naturally, we must ensure that the angles are adequate. For example, when cutting with a sword, stepping back at a forty-five degree angle allows us to be out of reach of the enemy's blade for a short time while being close enough to take control of the attacker. We must also take into account the angle of the body in relation to the opponent. If someone grabs you by the collar and you remain in front of him, it will be the strongest of the two who will physically dominate the other, but if you position yourself in the right way, you will largely offset the difference in strength."

He motioned one of the students in the group to seize him by the collar. The old man grabbed him in the same way. He chose someone of impressive stature. He must have easily weighed a hundred kilos. The master asked him to push him back. The fellow leaned forward to ensure better traction, then he began to push. The master slightly broke his opponent's structure while keeping him in front. The giant's face turned red as he increased in intensity, whereas the old master remained relaxed. He thanked the man for his efforts.

"What I have done with our friend is simple. Without him realizing it, I changed the angle of my arms, which required him to constantly change the direction of his thrust. At no time have I given him a chance to stabilize himself. With proper use of angles, I could resist his strength."

I must admit that it was particularly impressive to see this man, who easily exceeded him by one head, not being able to push the frail person who stood before him.

"Oh yes, I forgot," added the master, "in a real situation, nothing will go as planned. You probably will make mistakes and that's quite normal. Being good does not mean successfully accomplishing a codified technique. Being good is to regain control of the situation before it escapes you. A mistake is when we can not do anything to win a fight. If we can adapt, it becomes a strength. If you can not predict what you will do, you will not indicate what your next move will be, as you do not know yourself. This means that if you are teaching someone and he messes up, do not scold him, instead show him the right way to go and tell him how he can learn from his mistakes. Then, correct him, teach him the proper way to react."

Master cast a glance at the ceiling, looking for elements that might have escaped him. Then he shook his head a few times before moving on.

"Another important thing, we must remain attentive when acting as a partner to someone. Whoever performs the technique is not the only one learning. When one acts as *uke* during training, he should note what he feels, but also observe his partner's technique and tell him if there are flaws."

Now, every time I correct one of my students, if I do not find what's wrong, I think back to that class, and when I really can not see what's wrong, I offer myself as a training partner. It's amazing what you can see from the inside.

Chapter 58
Rewarding meetings

In public places, especially in trains, I often happened to discuss with Japanese people I did not know. For some, it was an opportunity to practice the few English words they had learned, while for others, it was only the curiosity they had about the *gaikokujin* they saw from time to time. Although most of these exchanges were uneventful, they had the merit of forcing me to practice my Japanese. Discussions on my country's climate or the current temperature, a bit of politics and economy, that summarized the subjects of the conversations. Despite this, I sometimes happened to come across different people. Several of these meetings were true pleasures. One evening, leaving my master, when I was about to take the last train, a man in his late sixties looked at me insistently. I smiled and nodded. He returned my greeting. He hesitated a little, advancing slowly, then with a firm step, he walked towards me. He exuded a powerful energy that I had not often encountered in my life. Aside from my master and a few other senior teachers, it's not everyday that we cross such people.

"You are here to do martial arts, aren't you?" He asked.

"Yes, but I won't ask you how you know that," I replied, laughing.

Most Westerners who were in this small city were there to meet my teacher. I talked to this man during my whole return trip. He had done kendo for years. It was certainly his years of sword training that gave him this energy I felt. He was sandan in this art. I suspected that, despite the fact that he was only third-degree black belt, his skill level was higher. He explained several interesting technical points, but the most exciting topic was probably the difference that existed between the practitioners of his time and those of today. He told me how the training was done when he was younger.

"Today, it is mainly the competition results that count. Practitioners have no idea what they lose training in this light. But what can you do? Looks are more important than content now."

"I'm lucky," I said, "in our art, there is no competition. The only challenge we have is to improve ourselves constantly. If you knew how many times I found myself worthless."

In the purest of Japanese traditions that is politeness, the man told me that I was not like that, on the contrary he suspected that I was rather skilled. It is in the nature of most Japanese to try to compliment you by saying it is not true that you are clumsy or incompetent.

"Today I'm doing pretty well, but I had to work hard to get to where I am."

"This is what is lacking in most people nowadays. Making the necessary efforts. In my day, we did not have our say. If my teacher decided that we had to spend weeks on the same routine, we did. It would have never crossed our minds to question this approach. It was like this: Shut up and train."

"Young people today no longer have the patience. Not just in Japan, it is an international thing," I said.

When this conversation took place, I was already in my fifties, therefore I thought I had the right to speak of the young like so. My companion went on.

"We certainly did not like it, but we considered ourselves fortunate to have access to this teaching. At the time, it was difficult to find a good teacher. Moreover, as my family was poor, my parents could not pay for these lessons. I had managed to convince the *sensei* to let me attend classes in exchange for housework. What I did not know by offering this arrangement was that the good man had six or seven students to do the cleaning. He did not need me, but he still agreed to take me under his wing. I think he said that one more or less person didn't matter."

"If we used your story in a movie, it would seem exaggerated. Reality is stranger than fiction. You were lucky that he accepted you."

"Yes. I was so afraid that he would reject me from the *dojo* that I never dared argue one of his orders. I have seen many students give up, people who came from wealthy backgrounds. We were doing so many repetitions, it was discouraging to many. One day, something extraordinary happened."

The train had just left one more stations that got me closer to my stop. I was afraid of not having enough time to talk to my liking with this man. He continued his story.

"I think he imposed these exercises on us to achieve this result. One day, I had the sensation that I was leaving my body. Fatigued, during repetitions, I had come to observe my body from the outside. No opponent could catch me from behind, I saw everything. I had the feeling of floating above myself. At the time, I thought I had just hallucinated. I was horribly tired and in pain."

I did not know what to say or think.

"My master has told me that one can attain enlightenment through meditation, but also through the use of the body. I guess that's what happened to you," I tried to make sense of this story.

The man looked at me and smiled. It was not the kind of conversation he must have had with everyone. Most people would have thought that he was deranged, but I believed him. I did not know him, but I knew instinctively that I could trust him.

"After that happened, I explained to my *sensei* what had happened," he said, "he just smiled and nodded. He knew what I was talking about."

"Were you ever able to do it again?" I asked.

The man looked at me without saying a word. We must have looked like conspirators, some people seemed to be listening to our conversation.

"Yes, a few times," he said quietly, "and each time, I was able to achieve the same state faster than before."

"But how? What can be done to achieve this?"

I felt like a *kohai* with his *sempai*. I felt like we had the complicity of an elder who had the responsibility of guiding his young disciple. This transmission of knowledge is done at different levels. I found it incredible that this man trusted me so.

"To this day, I don't know how we can achieve this," he said, "I always suspected there was something mysterious happening between my teacher and I. It was him that enveloped me with his energy. I know it exists, I experienced it, but I do not know how to get there. I'm just not sure I understood how it worked. I think the repetitions acted as a form of meditation, as if I was constantly reciting a *mantra*. My mind was detached from my body. It was an incredible experience."

The train that was slowing down gradually, arrived at the last station. I was desperate at the thought that this meeting would end.

"Do you often take the train? Maybe we could continue our conversation another time," I said.

"Unfortunately, I am here for work, I am returning home tomorrow, but who knows, maybe one day our paths will cross again."

I saw my teacher a few days later. I told him about my experience with the man.

"Do you realize the gift you received from this man?"

"I do not know why he told me all that, but it led me to want to live such an experience. Have you ever experienced something similar?"

Just as he was about to answer, a group of students entered the *dojo*. One of them, who was obviously not concerned that we were having a conversation, interrupted the master to have their picture taken with him. I looked up when the intruder and my teacher walked to the altar together. The master turned briefly and looked at me smiling. I do not know why, but I was certain he saw my disappointment.

Chapter 59
Hitting harder

The master's teaching methods often differed from those I knew. I realized this fact one day, as I was re-learning how to punch. For years, I had the certitude of hitting harder, of producing a much more powerful impact than the average person. Naturally, under his supervision, it did not take long to find out that I was far from reaching 100% efficiency. And yet...

"Who taught you to hit like that? Did you train to hit inflatable dolls?" He said, laughing.

Later, I learned to appreciate his sense of humor which was sometimes a bit strange. Despite this, at the time I did not appreciate his allusion at all. The number of fights that I had won in competitions was the guarantor of my ability to hit. Moreover, I had done a lot of demonstrations breaking boards and bricks. In short, everything needed to inflate my ego, which I realized only much later.

My knuckles still remembered their joust with an apple tree when he told me about the striking techniques using shockwaves. Today, he had made up his mind to teach me how to use my fists in the right way. From our first meetings, he had told me about the alignment of the bones, and how to position my hand. Instead of placing my palm facing down, he advised me to attack with the fist vertically, as if gripping a ski pole. It made me understand that doing it this way, there was less power degradation. To prove this, he pushed on my horizontal fist while I was trying to resist. Under the pressure, my shoulder moved, which dissipated part of the energy my body generated. By putting my fist vertically, my arm became solid, thus preventing the loss of valuable energy. He called it a *fudoken*, roughly translated as the unwavering fist.

We were in the outside *dojo* near the small cave where I had learned that time is not always what it seems. I was hitting on bamboo that he had me cover with fabric. I did not know if it was to protect my hands or the tree from my strikes. I had often asked myself the question.

"Do not try to hit harder. For now, it is useless."

"I do not understand. If I want to increase my power, I absolutely have to hit harder."

"This is the way that most teachers do it, but I work differently. Rather than trying to make you hit with more intensity, I am using the fact that somewhere deep down, you have the capacity to use 100% of your power. The problem is that with many small mistakes, you project your energy to the left and right. It's like a waterworks system.

If there is a loss of water, the pressure will be lowered because of all these leaks. We will try to plug these energy flows."

He took a break and looked at me carefully.

"I do not know if it's possible to make something new out of the old," he said, observing me from top to bottom, "come on, hit the target so we can see what we can arrange, see if it is repairable..."

I began to assault the poor tree that seemed to support my attacks quite easily. As it bent slightly under my repeated attacks, my joints were not suffering too much upon contact. Somewhere inside of me, I was hoping the trunk would break. That is what happened in the old kung fu movies of my youth, but no, it held on. It even seemed to taunt me. My teacher stopped me.

"You are committing one of the most common mistakes. Your front knee is not placed correctly. You need to point it in the same direction as your toes. If this is not properly aligned, your energy will be scattered. Your bone structure alignment is as scattered as your concentration."

I began to hit while paying attention to my knee. It was not easy. No one had ever made this remark to me before. I had years of bad habits to correct. The comments of the old man sounded something like: No, no, almost, maybe, yes, but, no, almost... It was demoralizing. After my joints began to inform me that they would soon abdicate, I finally managed to get several consecutive goods.

"Well, one problem solved," he said, "for now..."

These last words were not encouraging, but I knew that I could not give up. He accepted me as a disciple, it could only be a test. I had to persevere.

"Good. Let the poor vegetation regain some strength."

I do not know if he was talking about me or the tree. I did not linger on the question.

"You will now pretend to hit something, we will see what else we can repair."

He had me attack by stepping forward. After each assault, I got back to my original position in order to start again. After ten executions where he examined me carefully, he nodded repeatedly.

"That's what I feared. Your hips and arms are not coordinated at all."

"Of course I am coordinated. How else could I..."

The way he was looking at me, I guessed it was better that I shut up.

"When your fist reaches its target," he explained, "your pelvis is already stabilized. You punch using the upper half of your body."

I was not able to correct this bad habit of mine. To achieve this, he made me practice a technique he called the *kata* of the earth. A small routine which consisted of projecting fingers grouped forward using the sway of the body with one step. It sounded simple, but I realized immediately that this technique harbored considerable detail. Later, he taught me the remaining four *kata* of this series on the elements.

"In addition to developing your synchronization, your fingers grouped together will help you to correct your elbow which tends to move away from your body, breaking your alignment," he said.

By performing this routine, I realized pretty quickly what he meant by my lack of coordination. This exercise made me feel my body in a rather unique way. I spent almost an hour working on this movement.

"I think we can take a break," he told me, "I'm a bit tired."

He sat down on a stone that the sun had warmed.

"When hitting or you fighting a battle, remember to be *sanshin*," he explained.

The best translation that came to mind was the three hearts. I could not see what he was referring to, I let him continue.

"It is necessary, at the time of impact, that our body, intellect, and our emotions work in the same direction. If you hit someone and your mind tells you that it's not the right thing to do, there will be a loss of energy. This is also what happens if your feelings contradict what your will wants to do. And if the body is injured, if you are not in top shape, there will be a loss of energy."

All this was perfectly logical. I had never thought of connecting these three aspects of our personality in a fight. Yet they depend on each other. He continued his lesson.

"To be able to reach your maximum, first there is duty: to believe in the legitimacy of what we do. This is where the soldier draws his energy. The justification to attack or fight. If one feels guilty defending themselves or when facing an opponent, they can not be completely effective."

"I understand. If you attack me, I am entitled to defend myself, but if I provoke you for no reason, it may be different. Unfortunately, there are many thugs who do not have this sense of morality."

"That's right, but if they attack you, you give yourself the right to use all means necessary to protect your life. It may go as far as plucking an eye out or even killing if necessary. You have a duty to survive for you and your family."

I had never stopped at the idea of having to poke out the eye of an opponent to survive.

"Then comes the desire," he said. "The will to live, the love of life and the need for survival. Your emotions should lead you to victory. Without them, a soldier is only a puppet who is running towards his own demise. Fear, rage, feelings of injustice are all elements that keep the flame of the fighter burning."

"I see, but it can also be frustration, distress. These emotions can lead to defeat."

"That's why it's important to learn to manage them. And finally, we get to power, the ability to respond to an attack and use the full potential of the body. A sick, disabled, or fatigued body can not offer its maximum potential. It must be constantly maintained so that it is healthy."

"I know. Sleeping, eating, healthy lifestyle," I said.

The master looked at me without saying anything. I swallowed my saliva. At that time, I was not yet used to his look, his words, and all the emotions he could project. Fortunately for me, the silence was kept short.

"When you have all these three aspects combined, concentrated power in a single point. It's a little like the strength of a laser."

I understood his example, focusing all the energy in a single moment, a single point, allowed us to obtain greater power. With what he had taught me, I realized that most people dispersed their energy trying to hit hard. A misaligned knee, an imperfect angle and that was enough to fail to put an opponent down.

"The more difficult thing still remains," he said.

I was worried. What else could there be to correct?

"Once you master all that, you have to trust you can win. You must believe in yourself."

Chapter 60
Kage no me

Many of the lessons the old master had given me brushed the esoteric more than the logical laws of physics. However, despite the cryptic appearance of certain techniques, the expected result was usually waiting for you. Sometimes it was fast and on other occasions, it could take years before I could see the effectiveness of these medieval principles. I wanted him to instruct me and I was ready to endure and do anything to have the privilege to receive, if only a small part of his knowledge.

Almost every two years, a recurring theme was addressed, *kage no me*, something that could be translated as shadow eyes. I probably put in more than ten years of training before I could effectively use this teaching. Regarding this aspect of my training, I can say that Master didn't go easy on me. Today, I understand why he acted this way. When he first told me about this, we were in one of the outside *dojo*. A comfortable afternoon when the sun of March not hit us too hard.

"Has it already happened for you to have a strange feeling that made you turn around and find out that someone was looking at you intensely?" Asked the master.

"Yes, very often. I have already discussed this subject with friends and I think that everyone occasionally experiences something similar. I remember once in particular, I was sitting in a movie theater and I had the feeling that someone was watching me. Looking back, I saw a friend of mine looking at me, he was not sure it was me or not. I had sensed him."

"This is what we will work on today. You will not master this now, it will take a few years to do so, but we must start somewhere."

In my little brain and the oversized ego that I had at the time, I thought he would be surprised how quickly I could learn. I was convinced that this would count in months rather than years. I was very naive at that time. It is with a confident look that I watched the master explain what it was.

"To survive dangerous missions, warriors were to develop a sense that we all possess at different levels. I'll introduce you to what is called *kage no me*, the shadow eyes. This expression seems simple and can have several meanings. In your opinion, what do you think it means?"

"I think it symbolizes hidden in a place we can not see. It is the camouflaged person that we can not see easily."

"Not bad, but it's more complex than that. It is also the eyes of our own shadow that scrutinizes our backs and protects us."

I immediately imagined those cartoons where a dark shadow with bright eyes is watching our every action. The old man was not distracted by my childish smile.

"Everything is energy, everything is connected. If you look at someone, you send him energy or at least what might be called the power of intention. With proper training, you can sense the energy that penetrates your soul."

"In competition, I have already blocked kicks without even seeing them."

The master did not seem all that impressed by my words.

"You may win as many championships as you like, if your shadow is unable to detect what is in your back, you will not be able to avoid someone who tries to stab you between your shoulder blades."

I suddenly thought that besides the word shadow, one of the possible translations of kage was back, or behind. Protecting your back was an important military rule for survival. I decided not to put more emphasis on my sporting prowess. I was eager to start this training. What mystical technique would master use to elevate me to the level of the feudal warrior?

"We'll begin with a simple little exercise," said the master, "you'll walk until you reach the entrance of the cave and you will notice the times I point my finger at you. You will raise your arm to signal that you have felt me. In the end, we will count the number of times I have actually pointed at you. I will not tell you right away whether or not you guessed right. I will remain hidden so you will not see me. Give me a two minute head start so I can hide. You understand what you have to do, right?"

"Of course. I have to raise my hand every time you point a finger at me. It's pretty simple, it should be easy to do."

"You seem very sure of yourself, it's good to have confidence in your abilities. Be careful not to overestimate yourself though."

I took advantage of the time I gave him to stretch my back a little. I thought that by relaxing my back muscles, I could better perceive this energy. It was a very difficult exercise and I told myself that a one hundred percent success rate would be impossible. Seventy-five percent seemed a good quota. Then, on reflection, I thought that fifty percent would be my goal. I strongly closed my fists as if it would help me feel better. I was about five kilometers away from the goal. I took the path leading to the cave. The trail passed through the small clearing we usually trained in, a strange sensation in my neck made me think I was getting my first attack. I raised my arm without hesitation. It was going to be much easier than I had imagined. I had to be good at this kind of thing. He had asked me not to look at him hide, but I could not help but cast a glance in his direction. A little further, I saw a branch move slightly. I thought that a one hundred percent result was not so unrealistic after all.

At another point I was able to guess his presence, a large raven blacker than my shadow flew away a few seconds before I raised my hand. I had probably overestimated my teacher. I always thought he could move without disturbing the nature around him. The flight of a bird was sufficient to indicate the guards of a castle that an intruder was in the vicinity.

A little further, a cold chill ran through my spine. I was certain that it could only mean one thing, he was lurking there behind me. With my ears on guard, I heard a branch crack. A slight, sharp sound that could escape someone untrained. I raised my arm to indicate I had spotted him. I was a bit disappointed with his performance, but thinking about it, there was the age factor. My teacher was no longer young. Without a doubt he had lost much of his agility. I think that at his age, I probably would not be as fit as him. I lowered my arm and then I continued to advance towards the cave.

The more I progressed, the more I was proud of myself. I was sure he would be happy with my performance. On several occasions, I would detect his presence. I perceived energy in various ways. Usually, my back gave me valuable information that indicated that he was watching me. The sensations varied from cold to mild tingling feelings and through heat waves that went to the base of my neck.

At that point, I had raised my arm eleven times. Eleven attempted attacks that would have failed because I had seen with ease. It was possible that I had missed some of them, but I was more than happy with my performance. After taking the last curve in the path, I finally arrived at the foot of the small rock wall where was nestled the entrance of the cave. Master was sitting there with his back against a rock. He was snoring. He probably had to move quickly in order to position himself and better ambush me. I felt bad for him, the poor man must have been so tired.

"How did you manage to fall asleep so quickly?" I asked in attempt to be polite.

"That was a good nap. An hour like this and I'm ready for the rest of the day. So how many times did you feel that I pointed my finger at you?"

"I counted eleven, but there were probably a few more. I lack experience, but I think if anyone had wanted to plant a knife between my shoulder blades, it would have been difficult."

The old man looked at me and nodded. I thought he had to be proud of me. I anticipated his congratulations impatiently.

"To be honest, I was too tired to train with you," said the old master, "I came here directly to take a nap while waiting for you."

Chapter 61

Aging

Some days, Master seemed ten years younger, and sometimes his body betrayed him. That morning, I had gone to pay him a visit without having informed him the day before. When I entered his house, he had his head bent over ancient parchments. For a moment I regretted having come to disturb him. I felt that he had aged several years in an instant. He must have sensed my discomfort.

"Come in, a break will do me good."

He rose from his desk and stretched his limbs.

"My old bones can no longer bear to sit that long," he continued, "I'm not looking forward to growing old."

Coming from someone who had passed the eighty year-old mark, these words made me smile.

"I think you are doing quite well for a man of your age. In my country, it is uncommon for retirees to be as lively as you. People stop most activities. I always have the feeling that they are at resting while you constantly give me the impression of lacking time. I think you work too much."

"In my head, I'm not there yet. Stopping work or doing what you love is to die a little. I have a secret to stay fit; I have never confessed to my body how old it was," said the master, laughing.

"I'm not sure being able to successfully accomplish half of what you are doing when I reach your age. I admire how you can do so much."

"The recipe is not to complain. Of course, a healthy lifestyle helps a little. The biggest part of the secret though, lies here," said the old man pointing his finger at his temple.

He moved to the small kitchen and filled a kettle of water. Then he took a bag of green tea powder.

"Are there things you regret having or not having done?" I asked.

"No, I think I had a privileged life. Most people endure their lives. I was able to run my own during all these decades. Of course, I have not always done what I would have liked, but overall, I can't complain."

"Would you not like to go back fifty years?"

"If it is to the detriment of the knowledge I have now learned, the answer is no. What I have is worth more than a few years of tear and wear."

"Yes, but you know, you can not take this knowledge with you."

"You do not believe in reincarnation?"

I had not thought of that part of the equation. The master did not give me time to cogitate further.

"Anyway, my assets will not be completely lost. You can transmit them to others. It's your job and that of all those to whom I have taught to pass it down."

"Yes, of course, but I'm far from having all your knowledge."

"I taught you everything that is needed to find it all. The rest is only a matter of understanding, playing around, and common sense. It comes with age."

I was silent for a long moment, then said what was on my mind.

"If I had not met you, my martial ability would have atrophied over the years. Thanks to you, I was able to compensate speed with better timing, and I started to manage the control of time. Like it or not, from thirty-five or forty years of age, speed decreases. Then I also learned not to be a prisoner of technique, but to use the feeling and connection I have with my opponents. Finally, instead of pushing my body to the limits where the damage becomes irreversible, I swapped it all for precision and control of energy. No one else could have taught me those things, and the best part is that you continue to acquire new knowledge and improve. In most martial arts, people over fifty years know many techniques, but they don't stand much chance against the caliber of young people in their twenties, but in your case..."

I was looking for my words without finding exactly what I meant. It was he who completed my sentence.

"My martial power is far superior to the one I had before my fifties."

"Yes, that's it. I think that confronting young twenty-somethings would not scare you."

"Perhaps, we do not know, we will never know. I do not feel the need to prove anything. I'm too old to want to play the strongest."

The more I talked with him, the more I had the sensation that his wrinkles faded. I had already noticed this change in appearance with him. Sometimes he entered the *dojo* giving the impression of walking with difficulty. Once on the mat, he was no longer the same man. I asked him how he could do that.

"It's easy when we do what we love. Also, if what we do is appreciated, this becomes an incomparable source of energy. How many elderly people are not taken seriously or are treated like children? Many of them have amazing expertise. Many of them have lived extraordinary things. Most people have prejudice towards them. There are stupid people in all age groups. We must learn to see past the wrinkles. How do you think you will be perceived when you reach my age?"

I had never asked myself the question. Of course like everyone else, I was already moping about the idea of getting older, of losing my precious independence.

"I do not know. I guess it depends on what I have accomplished in my life."

"For most people, getting older means becoming invisible," said the master, "the aura of beauty fades with the years. The presence of arrogance and confidence will impress others less and less. The slowing of the body will create frustration and hatred in those standing behind to climb stairs or simply enter a bus."

"What you are saying is horrible. I do not want to grow old."

"This is why you must stay creative. We must live every moment intensely and not simply wait for a ticket to the other world."

I suddenly had an epiphany. I came to understand how, or should I say, why the master continued to evolve, to learn and teach us new techniques. This aging body was not his. It was only a vehicle he was using to move around in. He was as bubbly as he must have been fifty years ago. His mind remained active.

"You are very wise. It's one of the advantages of old age."

"What advantage, what are you talking about?" He asked, staring at me intensely.

"About wisdom, we become wiser with the years."

"I know children who have much more wisdom than many older people I have met. The years do not make us wiser. If we do not have this seed since childhood, we will not become wiser."

"Then why are there so many changes that come with age?"

"That is not wisdom, it is simply tolerance. Most people develop more tolerance over the years."

"In this case, how can I be sure that I will be a wise old man one day?"

The master took a sip of tea and closed his eyes for a moment.

"It's simple. Just be aware of the present moment and appreciate it, no matter what it offers."

Chapter 62
Extreme fatigue

It was really hot that day. The high humidity made me feel like I had run a marathon. Even the birds who were normally so abundant around the *dojo* remained hidden in some secret places, away from the stifling temperature. Training in these conditions felt like masochism, or should I say that this demonstrated the demanding nature of my teacher. Over fifteen years had passed since I had become his disciple. Over the years, I had learned to refuse no lesson he offered me. Every experience in his company was a gem of knowledge. The more contact I had with other martial artists, the more I realized the gap was widening between us.

Master had told me to wait for him at the entrance of the park nearby. The simple walk there had drained much of my energy. As I sat down at the foot of a tree, I thought back to a conversation I had with him, years ago. It was another very hot that summer. Not too hot nor as humid as that time, but the temperature was harsh enough for me to complain.

"What are you doing?" Asked my teacher, "you're on vacation or what?"

"You don't think it's a little too hot to train so intensely?"

"No," he simply said, pointing to the bamboo rod which I used as a *bo*.

I picked up the piece of wood and began working my striking technique on a rock that represented my opponent. My speed was very much lacking. It did not take long for my mentor to comment.

"Tell me, do you act like that out of fatigue or laziness? If it's fatigue, what could you have done to find yourself in such a sorry state?"

His penetrating gaze disarmed me. I had already had to face it, but this time it really made me uncomfortable.

"It...it is not laziness, it is the heat and humidity. It's stuffy, I feel that it deprives me of all my energy."

"You mean you're easily influenced?"

"I feel like I'm breathing hot water. I'm not sure I even have enough oxygen to train."

"Then you just have to use less. Stop wasting it."

How could he say that? I did not see how I could waste oxygen.

"Your body is currently controlling your mind. You must do the opposite. Imagine yourself on a battlefield, well wrapped up in your armor. Just before you got there, you had to walk for hours under the scorching sun. The humidity made you lose more water than you could swallow. Without warning, the enemy attacks you. Outnumbered, your troops must engage like demons."

"I think the fight is lost in advance."

"Luckily not everybody is as feeble as you," he said, advancing his head toward me, eyes wide open.

"How could these men fight in such conditions? They are already dead before they can even cross swords."

"Luckily they do not think like you. Yes, they are tired, yes they lost a lot of energy, but the most precious thing is still remains."

"I suppose you mean their lives."

"It's more than that. They have will. They are not there for fun, they are there to protect their families, their villages, their master."

I was a little worried that those words were aimed at me.

"I have will. What I lack is energy."

"You think that these men on the battlefield were well-rested, that they had energy?"

He spoke of this confrontation in past tense. I came to understand that he was referring to a fight that had already occurred.

"I guess if our life is in danger, it is easier to find the strength to continue."

"No. Many people allow themselves to die rather than make an effort, when they feel extreme fatigue. It is the simplest path to take. Overruling this state is not within the reach of all."

"How do you train for this? I do not understand."

"Has it ever happened to you to postpone a job, or a task because you felt a little tired?"

I hesitated to confess this procrastination that I maintained so well.

"Of course! Like everyone else, it has happened to me."

"Was fatigue an excuse to hide a certain laziness?"

Looking at me as he did, I had the impression of being compressed in a narrow bubble.

"Yes. I must admit, I have at times been a bit lazy."

"Today your training is slow, badly executed, if not pathetic. Is it because of laziness or fatigue?"

I jumped on the loophole he offered.

"It is because of fatigue."

"Alright then, what is fatigue?" He asked me.

"It is when the body refuses to obey," I said, proud of my response.

"False, it is a message to inform us that our energy reserves are declining. If the indicator light in your car warns you that gasoline is running low, is your car going to stop before it completely runs out?"

At first, I found the example a bit far-fetched, but thinking about it, I think he may have been right.

"No, it will roll to the last drop."

"The same applies to the body. It sends you signals to inform you. Once the message received, you can go a long way before being forced to abdicate."

"What if I have a heat stroke, it can be dangerous."

"That's right, but there is a big gap between the moment your body tells you that it is tired, and when you can no longer continue."

I thought about some football games I had with friends. Although we were exhausted, we could deploy a lot of energy. The fun of the game motivated us.

"For most people it is laziness that will take over when their life is not in danger. It's so much easier to do nothing when the circumstances are a little more difficult. Okay, it's hot. Yes, it is humid, but it's an opportunity to learn how to tap into your energy reserve that you can't miss."

I let out a long sigh and then walked back to the rock that acted as my target.

"Okay! I'll see what power I can dig up in some hidden corners."

"Do not try to draw or even think about your energy and fatigue. Just keep existing in the present moment. Work with one idea in mind: to achieve the best training you've ever done."

Painfully, I began practicing dodges with the stick. Each movement was difficult, my every step reminded me of the overwhelming heat that assaulted me.

"Stop feeling sorry for yourself. Live each moment rather than suffer it."

Whenever fatigue returned to my thoughts, I was making a greater effort to feel the velocity of my strikes, to feel my movements and focus on my target. Gradually, I gained speed. I had the feeling that my *bo* no longer weighed anything. My movements were becoming more fluid. I began to feel pleasure training. I jumped into the air and slammed the bamboo end on a rock, then I broke my fall by rolling to finish by stabbing the end of the stick on a tree. I do not know how long I trained like this, but I felt that I could go on for hours. I pivoted on myself to do a dodge an imaginary attack and retaliated banging on the rock. My stick broke under the force of the impact. I remained speechless watching the bursts of bamboo on each side of the stone.

"Very well, I think that's enough for today," said my master.

"I feel like I could go on for several more minutes," I said, proud to have learned how to tap into my energy reserves.

"Speak for yourself," he said, "I'm hot, I'm going back before I get a heat stroke."

Chapter 63
Learning curves

A long time had passed since it last happened to me. I think it was the year before the last one I was with him. For a few days, I felt that I had been stagnating. I was learning, sure, I had never ceased to discover new things since I had become his disciple. However, for several months, I seemed unable to assimilate anything. I had already experienced these walls that made me question myself and everything I knew, but this time was different. I stared at my *tantanmen* bowl without eating a bite. I was playing with a few noodles when Master started questioning me.

"Alright, what's bothering you?" He asked in a paternal tone.

"Nothing, really."

"Seeing as you haven't touched your favorite food, I find that hard to believe."

"Actually, it is I who am a little weird."

"I knew that already. Aside from the obvious, what's wrong?"

"I have the impression of not being able to learn anymore. Yes, I can assimilate techniques and reproduce them, but for some time, I have had difficulty understanding what lies behind them. It seems like the new principles you are teaching are too advanced for me. Maybe I've reached the peak of my incompetence."

"Oh, that's it? I was afraid you might have had bad news."

"You're speaking as if it was not serious. It really worries me, it even keeps me up all night."

"I noticed you looked a little beat up. What makes you think that you can not evolve?"

"I can no longer understand what you're teaching me. I'm not stupid, far from it, I even think I'm pretty smart. Yet it strangely seems like nothing can enter my mind."

"You find it abnormal?"

"There have been times when I stagnated, but I knew it would pass a few weeks or months later. This is different, I have the feeling that I will never see the light at the end of the tunnel."

"I think you're worried for nothing. At the training stage you're in, I expected it to happen."

"You knew it would happen?"

"Yes. The only surprise is that I expected it to occur much later."

"That's what I thought, I reached my peak of incompetence too fast. I must not be as bright as I thought."

"No, quite the opposite If it happened earlier, it is only because you were able to quickly understand what I taught."

I did not know if he said this to please me or if it was true, but it had the merit of cheering me up.

"I might have been good, but now I feel completely overwhelmed. Why did you think this would occur? You think that what is happening to me is normal?"

"Life is made up of cycles. If we were evenly tempered and our emotions constantly remained the same, we would be robots. Some periods pass in a few days time and some stretch over weeks and sometimes months. When you start something, either for martial arts or anything else, there is a learning curve. The musician must study his notes. He must practice in order to master the instrument he wishes to tame."

I liked when he used analogies like that. It added some perspective to his explanations.

"You play your instrument, you're constantly improving. Then certain chords, or some difficult pieces give you the impression that your fingers will never manage to move at the required speed. You move on to something else, to an easier partition, then one day you realize that what you found impossible is now feasible. You did not give up, you just stopped being obsessed with the obstacle that stopped you."

He paused to swallow a piece of *gyoza*. I took advantage of this moment to swallow some noodles in my bowl.

"Now you master your instrument very well. You stand out from your companions who play the same instrument. You decide to push your studies a little further. You manage to be accepted into a reputable music school. The teachers all have impressive resumes. You have to work hard, but you feel like you progress rapidly. During your holiday vacation, you run into your old musician friends, and you really see the gap that has opened up between you. You try to help, you give them advice, but some of them seem not to appreciate it, they are perhaps a little jealous. You do not insist, for you are aware of this reality."

I had experienced that feeling many times with former training partners. They grudgingly welcomed the new material I had to offer. The old man continued.

"You are now a virtuoso. You are of the caliber to play in the most prestigious orchestras. Your teachers have told you that on the technical level, you had gained all that you could. You can interpret any piece from the greatest composers. The mastery of your instrument is perfect. You have reached this level," he said, staring at me intensely.

I should have rejoiced at this. Being told that I was among the most competent should have made me happy. Coming from a master like him, I could not doubt these words. However, I was demoralized. Did this mean that I had reached the maximum I could hope for?

"Does that mean that I can not improve anymore?"

"A technician would tell you that you have learned all that you could. I say that you are now at the beginning of your journey."

I found his words rather contradictory. I mastered the technical aspect, but I was a beginner.

"Competent musicians able to reproduce any work are found in every orchestra," said the old man, "but few of them stand out because they are merely plagiarizing other works. They do it with all their heart, but it is not enough. Why can two musicians play the same work with the same notes, but one of them stands out more? Because he gives life to his music. He manages to convey emotions that his colleagues will never reproduce. This is where we can distinguish a master from a good performer."

The parallel he had done with the music made me think of Vanessa Mae, who played famous violin pieces, but the sound of her instrument managed to produce was different. You could feel her soul vibrate through the strings.

"I see, but how can we learn this? Are there teachers who can lead us to this point?"

"When the student is ready, the teacher will appear on his path. Why do you think I'm here?"

I was stupid not to have raised the fact that he was there. I was afraid of having insulted him, but he did not seem in the least bothered by my clumsiness.

"Your mind has absorbed all that is needed to execute any type of movement. Your skills are no longer doubted. Now we must learn to work with your soul. It is necessary for your body to manage to use this energy that will make you a virtuoso. You have the feeling that something is there before you, that all you have to do is reach out and grab it, but it moves away when you approach it."

"Yes, that's about right."

"At this point, many people give up. They switch instruments to feel like they are continuing to evolve."

I thought back to a few friends who were good martial artists, who have changed martial arts styles a few times. They had acquired new knowledge but their skill levels remained the same, and in many cases, they regressed in skill.

"I understand what you mean. I have friends who have lived this. But how can we take this step? There are no points of reference, no guides which we can rely on."

"Why do you think I'm here? It is the role of the master to accompany the disciple on this path."

"These things can be taught?"

"No, at this level, even if we continue to learn, we can not receive new knowledge. We can only be guided."

I had long noticed that my teacher was improving year by year. From my first years with him, I thought it was impossible for him to get better, as he was so far ahead of anyone else, but I was wrong. Sometimes he came up with new principles, new skills. Nobody was teaching him, but he continued to learn.

"The most laborious thing for you to do is to stop doubting yourself. You will also have to stop doing techniques in the hope that others will admire you. The hardest part of all this is to have faith. To have confidence in yourself. You shouldn't believe you are good, but you need to know that what you're doing is the right way to do it. At this point, it is a new mindset that you have to acquire. Many people take this route, but few have the wisdom to comply."

He was frightening me. Where should I start?

"Usually, people who are invited to follow this path have talent. Talent and a strong ego. It is not uncommon to see these people who consider themselves sufficiently prepared distance themselves from their master, believing themselves equal to him."

"What happens when they stray?"

"I can not explain why, but during a short period of time, they are like a flame that glows brightly in the dark. Then, after some time, the intensity decreases. The more the disciple drifts away from the master, the more the fire diminishes. If they have built a strong enough empire, they can continue living on this momentum. But gradually, their followers will find that they are no longer progressing, that they are not getting what it takes to reach a higher level."

I thought of some teachers who were popular for some time and then disappeared. An ephemeral glory. I told myself that I was not like that. One of my qualities was loyalty. As long as respect and trust was there, I would stay.

"Where do we begin?"

I suddenly realized I was motivated again, eager to get to work. I anticipated all the strange exercises he could make me do to find my way. As he did not respond quickly enough, I repeated my request.

"So, where do we start?"

"We begin by completing our meal, savoring it as if it were our last."

Chapter 64
A Pure Heart

That day, my teacher asked me if I would accompany him to one of his friend's house who was celebrating his seventy years. I hesitated to accept but rejecting the invitation would be rude. I imagined myself sitting at the end of a small table, listening to a group of elderly people recount the memories of their youth. As they probably spoke in older Japanese, there would be a high chance that I would get lost in their conversations.

We walked more than half an hour from the train station. My master must have come here often, because despite the fact that these streets were a maze, he seemed to find his way easily. I would have been unable to return to the station by myself.

"Why not take a taxi? We would be less hot," I suggested.

"I like to walk in these narrow streets. There are so many memories that hide along this route."

The image of a conversation between seniors came back to mind. It's with a sigh that I continued following him.

"You'll see, he is very friendly. He is a philosopher. He is the person I know whose knowledge about human psychology is the vastest."

The strong July sun was beating on our heads. I was happy whenever a tree left to itself was large enough to protect us in its shadow. The alley led us to the foot of a small hill with abundant vegetation. A path offered us a passage to the top. A tunnel of trees offered us some freshness. The path led to an old house that sat on top of the hill. Misaligned tiles reflected the age of the structure. Sitting on the porch, an old man raised his head when he saw us coming.

"*Ohisashiburi desu* ne!" He called.

"For far too long, I'm afraid," replied my master.

After having bowed to each other many times, he introduced me to his friend, Suzuki-san. Without saying a word, the latter examined me from head to toe. I had the strange feeling of finding myself before a customs officer who did not like my face. Then, after seconds that seemed like an eternity, he finally spoke to me.

"You have no idea how lucky you are, my friend. I am curious to know why he has accepted you as a disciple. I was sure he would never take on another one again."

I did not know why, but I was intimidated by this man. Despite his tiny size, he exuded the energy of a giant. Looking at me, his eyes did not blink once. I felt he could read me like an open book. A smaller lady came from behind the house. She took off her work gloves and placed a pair of shears on the corner of the porch. My master bowed to greet her and gently pulled and pressed her against him. I saw his friend smile watching them. Then for several minutes, a conversation between the three accomplices took place. As I had feared, I lost a lot of what was said. My master reached into his shoulder bag he had brought and pulled out a small package he gave to Suzuki-san who bowed repeatedly to thank him. The man unwrapped the present. A large pipe of about one foot long sat there. It seemed sculpted from a single piece of metal decorated with a thin wooden neck. After observing it, the man handed it to me.

"It's heavy, you could almost use it as a weapon."

The two men laughed. Suzuki-san looked at my teacher and said that he understood his choice a little better now.

"The *samurai* sometimes used this as a weapon," said Suzuki-san, "in some castles, bearing a sword was forbidden. The enclosure was supposed to ensure the safety of its occupants, but the threat could come from people close to them as well as the outside world. In the hands of someone skilled, these pipes would become effective weapons."

Indeed, its rigidity meant that we could use it to control someone as well as for hitting. The weight of the metal end of the pipe would be sufficient to break a skull while the other end could easily pass through a rib cage. The object was balanced so as to obtain maximum velocity to strike with the heavy end. It shouldn't have been a surprise to me, but the ingenuity of the *samurai* never ceased to amaze me. The lady returned with a tray of iced tea.

As I had feared, the two men recalled some memories of another era. At some point, my master was laughing so much that I saw tears flowing from his eyes. Seeing him that way, I was almost afraid that his heart would not take it. Then one sentence caught my attention.

"That's because he did not have a pure heart," said my master, resuming his laughter.

After allowing them to calm down a bit, I finally spoke.

"You just mentioned *kokoro*, the heart. You said he did not have a pure heart. In Japanese martial literature as in what you have taught me, the notion of a pure heart comes back very often. To a Westerner like me, it's a little hard to understand. Like everyone else, I nod when you talk, and I have a vague idea of what it is, but I think I'm missing something. What it's like to have a pure heart? It is certainly not in the Christian sense of the word."

"It's a very good question," Suzuki-san answered for the master, "in the Judaeo-Christian culture, to be a pure being is not committing what you call a sin, but in Japanese culture, it is a little different. We do not have a civilization based on guilt."

"Having a pure heart comes from the present moment," went on my teacher.

"I do not understand," I said, "I think I am even more confused."

"As you know," explained Suzuki-san, "*kokoro* means the heart, but also the spirit, and sometimes the soul. This is where we play between knowledge and belief, between will and power and even between a sense of duty and pleasure."

All this is trying to make me understand better?- I thought. My master took over.

"To have a pure heart is to act in the way which is best or necessary. If you fight someone, it must be for a noble cause. To defend your country, because it is your duty. If you do it for fun, you will not be acting with a pure heart."

"In your culture," went on his friend, "an angel has a pure heart and a demon is unclean. In ours, a demon who must fight can do it with the spirit of a pure heart. It is not judged by what it is, but by its actions. It is not condemned in advance because it is a demon. If you act and your conscience is not at peace, that you do not feel totally in your right to fight, your heart is not pure. Your mind is not free, only a pure heart can enjoy total freedom."

"As I understand it, having a pure heart simply means being in our right to defend ourself."

The two men looked at each other and smiled. I had the feeling of being a child in front of them.

"It's more than that," said the master, "having a pure heart testifies that we do something with a noble spirit. When I give a class and I ask people to do a demonstration, many of them do it in the hope of impressing me or to be admired."

"We do not do a technique for others, we must do it for ourself," said his friend.

The master nodded. Suzuki-san went on.

"If you face an opponent and you only think of victory, there are chances that you will not see everything he could do to you. You become blinded by your own will to win."

"For example, you are facing ten warriors and you are mad. Your anger blinds you, but you decide to fight them all the same. Your power will surely fail you," said the master, "your heart is not pure, it is as chaotic as if you swam in a muddy pond in the heart of the night."

"Your opponent raises a sword," Suzuki-san went on, "seeing him, you know in advance what attack he can perform. Unfortunately for you, he knows nothing about the sword fighting and attacks you in a totally different way. You will be betrayed by what you believed. His inexperience makes him unpredictable."

"If, however, he was an excellent swordsman." master said, "when his *katana* crashes down, he will not doubt that you are a good warrior, and he will act accordingly. His knowledge has betrayed you. You relied to what he should do, not what he could do. Your heart was not here and now, it was already elsewhere. Being pure of heart is achieved in the slot of the present moment."

"The pure heart is detached," Suzuki-san said, "it does not act for fun, it does what needs to be done in the ultimate goal of finding happiness."

Listening to the old man talk like so, I thought he must surely have an impressive martial background. He too, had to be a master. Indeed, he seemed to know the human spirit very well.

"You must have done martial arts for a long time," I told him.

"No, I've never done any, but I rubbed shoulders with many high-level masters."

"I do not understand. What kind of work were you doing if you did not teach martial arts?"

"Me? I was a janitor at the village's municipal *dojo*."

Chapter 65
Unpretentious

In the *dojo*, there was a fairly good turnover of students throughout the year. While some faces were familiar to me, others were totally unknown. December had already begun when I saw the master acting strangely with one of them for the first time. The evasion technique that seemed simple at first was perhaps not as easy as it seemed. Our partner gripped our wrists from behind, making it seem like we had handcuffs on. We just had to turn our palms outward and push while sliding ourselves under one of the arms of the attacker to end up at his side. When the master passed the student, I heard the tall blond man make a suggestion.

"I think the technique would work better like that," he said, advancing his hands forward while raising his palms upward, "in my old martial art this is how we used to do it."

The master listened to the young man in his mid-twenties.

"If I understand correctly, this is the first time you are practicing *budo*," he said, eyes wide open.

"Absolutely not, I have a lot of experience in..."

The master turned his back without paying attention him. The student seemed frustrated to be treated this way.

"I thought he was more competent than that," he said.

In one moment, I felt my blood pressure rise to levels it had rarely reached. I exhaled heavily to regain control.

"Maybe it's you who are not competent," I said.

"What? Look how easily I'm getting out of this position with my technique. It is much more effective. Grab me, you'll see."

As I felt my hands being pulled, I walked forward quickly, lightly kneeing him in the tail bone. The shock was small, but sufficient to bend his legs, making him sit before me. I finished with a controlled blow to the head.

"This is why we position ourselves near the opponent, stepping back. We must not remain in front of him like you did. I was nice with you, now imagine if I had hit you hard."

"My way is still effective. It does not mean that in the streets, someone would think of hitting me like you did. My teacher is excellent and would never teach anything that could end up being dangerous for us."

Despite the fact I had demonstrated his vulnerability, he wouldn't listen. Glancing at the master, I saw him smile. He was enjoying seeing me trying to reason that student.

"In a real fight, you have to leave the least possible openings," I said, "hoping your aggressor won't knee you is like gambling. In *bugei*, there is no room for chance."

I returned to train with my partner. On several occasions, the tall blond student modified the master's teaching to make it fit his mold. Every time, I saw flaws in his approach. At one point, I could not help but intervene again. Doing his nonsense was one thing, correcting other students was another. We were doing a technique against two opponents. The objective was to use one of the perpetrator's arms to interfere with the other attacker. Each time, the tall blond guy left the hand of the second attacker near his face. Of course, they weren't able to punch, but they did not need that to be able to attack him.

"Are you here to train or to show that you are good?" I said in a slightly arrogant tone.

"Why don't you mind your own business? Go play in your corner," he replied.

"I can do the technique with you. I just want to make you aware of the opening you are leaving."

He looked at me with a smirk.

"There is no opening, but if it makes you happy to learn something..."

The first opponent grabbed his collar as we had to do. I then attacked like the technique taught us to do. He captured my first arm and redirected it under the first attacker's armpit, then he grabbed my other hand when I tried to hit him, leaving my fist inches away from this face.

"You see, you're done. It's been a pleasure teaching you."

"Me too. Look if you can..."

I moved my hand and pushed the tip of a finger in the corner of his eye, then rubbed while pressing slightly. The master had used this defense on numerous occasions. I knew I could use it without hurting him. He jumped back, cursing.

"What's with these wild techniques? This isn't *budo*."

"No, it's *bugei*," said a voice behind me.

"Most people would not dare aim for the eyes on the street. This isn't legal," said the blond.

"This is how it's done in our martial art," I said, "the goal is not beauty, but efficiency. We must take the necessary means to survive and if we must attack the eyes, we do so without hesitation. Does your martial art teach you to survive or simply shows you how to do flashy moves?"

I found it strange to speak like that. I was not sure why I was talking about flashiness, it came out on its own.

"You are a group of narrow-minded fanatics, I'm leaving this *dojo*. I won't learn anything intelligent here."

I was prepared to reason with him when the master put his hand on my shoulder.

"Leave him, he is not ready. Perhaps he will one day return."

The class continued without a hitch. A more pleasant atmosphere now occupied the *dojo*. After he left, I realized that many students did not appreciate the erroneous corrections he distributed generously. When all had left, I joined the master to discuss what had happened.

"I hope we will not have people like him too often. There are people who never understand anything. I have rarely seen someone so full of himself."

"We should not blame him, it's not his fault."

"If it's not his fault, then whose is it?"

"His teacher's," said the master.

"He is not the one who made him so pretentious."

"He had the responsibility to bring him back on the right path."

I had forgotten how the teacher-student relationship was powerful in the minds of the Japanese. If your dependent does not behave in the right way, you are partly responsible.

"Yes maybe, but it is also a matter of judgment. He didn't want to hear anything when I showed him the flaws in his techniques. He did not even realize he had lost the fight even after getting poked in the eye. He did not see the logic, it seemed like he refused the fact that his knowledge could have weaknesses."

"His ego was just too big. It can deflate, you know. Do you remember?"

He was referring to my little person, the detestable temperament I displayed in my early days with him.

"Why did you tolerate him though? Why did you let him correct the other students if all he did was wrong?"

"I could tell you it's because it would have been a waste of time, but to be honest, there was another reason."

I was curious to know. I thought it was because he did not want to disturb the others. Giving such a show is never healthy in a *dojo*.

"I did not intervene because I was testing you. I wanted to see if you could easily see the faults of what he showed."

I did not know what to say. Should I take this as a compliment? I did not insist on the subject.

"Why was he taught techniques with so many weaknesses?" I asked.

"Many martial arts were created for a spiritual purpose. Popping one eye does not quite fit in this spirit. Most people do not do martial arts to end up on a battlefield. They do it as a hobby and this mode of teaching is more than enough for them. Think of all the harsh things I made you endure for you to be able to see these weaknesses in an opponent's technique."

"He was still pretentious. Even if he has not learned the right things, it does not give him the right to disrespect you."

"Oh, so you feel he disrespected me?"

"I don't just think about it, I know it."

"What part of me should have been insulted by his behavior?"

I found the question rather strange.

"Well... Your pride. Being corrected this way by a young pretentious man like him..."

"I would feel frustrated if I had something to prove, but I know what I'm worth and believe me, his behavior affected me in no way whatsoever."

At the time, I did not understand how he could tolerate such actions. Today I have come to accept this kind of situation. For years, in similar contexts, I reacted aggressively, until I realized that what was at stake was not my martial ability, but my ego.

Chapter 66
The other's stare

At times, the teaching offered by the master leaned on the esoteric more than how martial arts are conceived in the West. That day, I realized for the first time that art, in all its forms, was a channel connected to martial arts. The painter, sculptor, musician, everything was connected. I accompanied the master to a painting exhibition that was held near Shibuya station. We made a small detour, passing by the statue of the most famous dog, Hachiko.

"You like looking at him, don't you?" I asked.

"Yes, but it works both ways, I'm letting him look at me," the old man replied.

This odd reply should have raised many questions in my mind. I do not know why, but at the time, I was too stunned by this phrase to revive the subject. When I finally felt ready to ask him what he meant, the master pulled me by the arm.

"Come, it's here. I look forward to seeing this exhibition. I've waited two weeks for this."

"I do not understand why you are so excited about this. There are no works by famous artists displayed. I feel that you will be disappointed."

"On the contrary. Famous artists, as you say, do not offer anything new or unpredictable. Here, we can expect anything. Be it good or bad. In addition, it will be a good opportunity for you to understand how everything around you is watching you. An opportunity not to be missed."

It was the first time I had heard of this principle. I did not try to deepen the subject, knowing he would show me the path to follow soon enough. The room was filled with tables of all sizes. There was something for everyone. There were scenes of old country homes where tiled roofs intertwined with those of straw. Beautiful mountainous sceneries regularly came up. Between these more traditional works overlapped paintings where I would have been incapable of describing what the author wanted to express.

We were stopped in front of one of them, I hesitated to call it a work of art, a painting which at first sight meant nothing, if not a superposition of several layers of paint that ultimately gave the impression of being a huge stain.

"Do not try to see or guess anything. Just let yourself be absorbed by the image, let yourself be penetrated by it. It is the picture that wants to talk to you, give it the chance to express itself without judging it."

The author had created it using calligraphy brushes. Staring at it intensely, a shape seemed to take form. At the time, I was unable to say what attracted me by it. This painting, or I should say, this makimono had something mysterious, captivating.

"What is it supposed to represent?" I asked the master.

"Do not try to see what is on the paper. Let the painting watch you. Feel observed, imagine how it perceives you."

"But this is just paper and ink. It can't perceive anything."

"It is not just paper and ink. The author has injected energy that makes the work alive. Do not analyze it, let yourself be penetrated by its eyes."

For once, I did not call into doubt the master on something so... esoteric. Little by little, in spurs of short moments, I had the impression of being watched. Naturally, I thought that this was only a figment of my imagination. These feelings were fed by the master's suggestions. Then something strange suddenly happened. From the shapeless chaos arose a human form. Small, bright eyes stood out. A shape sitting and holding something in his hands. Then, I thought I could see an elongated object in his right hand, something that looked like a sword. I was not certain, but I felt like his body was surrounded by flames.

"What do you see?" Asked the master.

I described what I thought I could make out, though I was not sure of anything. He nodded, smiling.

"What you see is a representation of *Fudo Myo*, one of the five protectors of Buddha. He converts anger into acts of salvation. It is said that his spirit is immutable."

"What does it symbolize?"

"For now, it does not matter. What matters is the fact that you were able to discern what the intellect does not want to see."

"If you had told me that I should try to see, I would have managed either way."

"The aim is that you try to learn to perceive hidden things by yourself. Be it a painting, a martial art or a musical piece, you have to accept that they observe you. They have a vision of the universe, you have to let yourself soak into it. A painting is not only something to admire, it also teaches you."

"I do not understand the connection with martial arts. Is there any?"

"In a fight, the technique is there, dormant. It spies on you, wishing with all its might for you to understand it. When you looked at the painting, you analyzed it with your intellect. Everything came from you. You only saw things from the surface. Yet *Fudo Myo* was there, hidden in the confusion of your mental. He was trying to get your attention. In a confrontation, it is the same thing. The technique you must use is there, watching you in the hope that you will perceive it. You just have to be open to the idea of letting it observe you."

"It's a strange thing to say that one is observed by a painting or technique."

"I know, but there are many things that are beyond our understanding. We should not see this as magic. It is only a forgotten skill that we possess. You must understand that it goes a little further than simply being looked at by a drawing."

I was anxious at the thought of what I was about to hear. I knew he had not brought me here just to contemplate art. If it had only been to see these paintings, he would not have bothered to invite me.

"It's part of the process of connecting to the world around us. Ki is everywhere, in different forms. We must discover how to use it, feel it. Matter has energy."

"It is not by chance that the authors of Star Wars speak of the force. It is based on *ki*."

"Yes, they had a good knowledge of ancient martial arts," he said.

"Are there other ways to learn to use this energy, to connect with it in this way?"

"There is never only one way, but for now, do what I have taught you with these pictures and you will see a fairly rapid progression in the way you perceive your surroundings."

I walked up to a canvas where the center was occupied by a big blue spot. I stayed there several minutes to let the painting look at me.

"I think you're wasting your time," said the master, "like men, some works are sometimes meaningless."

Chapter 67
Kihon to the rescue

That morning, I was taking a walk with the master around the American Market of Ueno station.

"Do you come here often?" I asked.

"As rarely as I can," he replied.

"So what are we doing here? You told me you wanted to hang out, get some sun. Between these buildings, we do not see much of it."

The rainy season had been wrapping us in its dreary atmosphere for almost two weeks. A sunny day like this was like a balm.

"I like to come here for a walk once every five years. It allows me to see that the human race is not evolving too quickly."

I needed much more than that from the old master to surprise me. I gladly entered his game.

"Why do you say that?"

"Because these merchants always offer the same things."

The area included various types of similar shops. You could find all the necessary goods to introduce yourself to golf, to change your wardrobe or to purchase a new handbag. Naturally, there were a large number of perfume shops which stood next to shops that sold all kinds of knives or police equipment. That's not counting the exotic fish stalls so dear to the Japanese.

"There are no shops where you can buy items related to traditional culture," I said, "It's unfortunate."

"No, there's nothing kihon here," he said.

He had used an expression that could be translated by fundamental. In martial arts, it was assumed that the kihon were the basic techniques, the essential foundations of the art that we practice.

"I do not quite understand what you mean by kihon? Do you mean traditional clothing shops or something else?"

"No, I mean basic things. There is nothing here that can teach us how to live. Everything is superficial, useless for a spiritual journey or to help anyone change in any way whatsoever."

"I'm getting more confused. Why use the word kihon? I see nothing here that can resemble a martial technique."

"What is kihon?" He asked me.

"They are the basic techniques. The word itself means fundamental. The kihon is to martial arts what ranges are to musicians. It is by repeating that one can hope to become a virtuoso."

"That's right," the old man replied, "what do you see here that could help anyone become a virtuoso in a useful area other than sale?"

"Nothing, but this place is essential for Ueno's economy. This area must generate incredible income. Look at the number of tourists here."

"You're probably right, but kihon does not teach us just one thing. Like an onion, it has several layers of skin."

To explain his point of view, he referred to a simple technique that I knew well. When an attacker is trying to reach us with a punch, we only have to retreat in an angle to absorb the energy of the fist like a wave, we then rush back at him by responding with a hit with the edge the hand.

"In this technique, we can change our angle of attack, and steal space from the opponent to destabilize him. Different targets give different results. When the fist comes, if we back up far enough, we attract the aggressor in our bubble, we make him fall into the empty space in order to control him. This simple technique is an instructor who teaches a multitude of ways to approach a problem. It allows us to develop our empathy and know what the person in front of us is feeling. Receiving the punch could be adjusted by blocking outside the arm rather than inside, and you can counter the same way. But here, people only exist on one level. Whether it be buying or selling, this area will bring nothing to anyone except another acquisition."

I found the master extremely down-to-earth. I made an attempt to improve the image he had of this place.

"Perhaps you're right on the evolution aspect, but these people must work in order to feed their families. The cost of living is so high that to pay rent, you have to..."

He did not give me time to finish.

"I agree with you on that. However we can do all that while learning. Most people, and this is valid for the entire planet, are doing what they have to robotically, even in a way that is blasé."

"They work hard, accumulate many hours to make ends meet. How else could they do this?" I asked.

"By being aware they are alive."

I did not expect this kind of response.

"I do not understand. What do you mean?"

"To be alive is to reconnect with others, with our surroundings. Thus one can hope to evolve, flourish."

The master stopped and peered around before focusing his gaze on a very precise place.

"Look carefully around us. How are these people? Describe what you see."

I took care to better examine the people composing the crowd that moved in all directions.

"I see that some are in a hurry, others are shouting to attract customers. I also see young people who are laughing and having fun, but they go back to being serious quickly enough. I see tourist couples who hold hands without saying a word."

"Do you see any trace of change in them when you look at them?"

I was lost. How could I find transformations in so little time?

"Well, no. It is normal, it takes time to change."

The old man looked at me, smiling. At that moment, I knew I would learn something. What could it be in such a place?

"Look at the elderly lady selling flowers on the street corner, over there. Observe the people before and after they enter her boutique."

Most people who crossed the saleswoman seemed to change attitude when walking pass her. Shoulders raised, laughter rang out, the way people walked changed upon her contact.

"How is this possible?"

I was amazed by what I observed. Then I realized that the old master had brought me here to see her. He seemed to know her well.

"She is a friend of yours, right?"

"No, I do not know her, but she has been here for decades and the result is always the same, her magic works every time. Whenever I lose faith in humanity, I come here to give myself some hope. She has mastered kihon."

"What does she tell them to get such reactions?"

"She reads people's hearts," he said, "come, let's pass her shop."

Just ahead, a businessman with a stern face was walking in our direction. Back straight, shoulders proudly raised, this man had all the characteristics of someone who knew how to be obeyed. The saleswoman looked at him smiling and called out:

"How would your wife feel if you brought her a flower today? Here, you can keep it."

The man was completely destabilized. He paused, looked thoughtful for a moment, then smiled.

"Happy," he simply replied.

The End

Lexicon

Abunai: It's dangerous, be careful
Bo: long wooden stick measuring a little less than two meters
Bokken: wooden training sword
Budo: Martial arts
Budoka: someone who practices martial arts, especially Budo
Bugei: school whose goal is survival
Bushido: moral code of conduct of the *samurai*
Chiba: Prefecture in Japan
Daikon: kind of big Japanese radish often used in cooking
Densho: parchment in which the school's techniques were described
Deshi: disciple
Do: means the way (example: kendo, the way of the sword)
Dohai: two students of the same level
Dojo: training location
Doshite: litterally means "why?"
Emakimono: painting done on a parchment on the wall
Fudoken: fudo which is an immutable divinity, and ken means a fist
Fudo Myo: protective deity in Buddhism
Gaikokujin: alien, foreign national
Giri: a sense of duty
Gyoza: kind of big Japanese ravioli
Hachiko: famous dog whose statue was erected in Shibuya for his loyalty
Haiku: poem composed traditional 5-7-5 syllables
Hakama: pants worn by *samurai*
Hara: the center of the body, the balance point
Hara-Kiri: dishonor ritual suicide, which consisted of opening up one's belly with a knife
Hasso no kamae: sword position where the blade is held vertically
Henka: variation of a codified technique
Henso jutsu: ninja art of disguise and depersonalization
Hiragana: one of the Japanese phonetic alphabet
Ishiki: consciousness
Jedi: character from "Star Wars"
Judo: combat sport based on locks and projections
Judoka: person practicing *judo*
Kage no me: the shadow eyes, Kage (shadow) and me (eyes)
Kakemono: scroll for calligraphy, which hangs on the wall
Kamae: fighting stance based on emotions
Kami: spirit or deity in the *Shinto* religion
Karateka: person who practices karate

Kata: structured technique to transfer knowledge
Katakana: phonetic alphabet used for foreign words
Katana: sword of the *samurai*
Ki: energy
Kiai: energy projection by sound or by the mind
Kiai Jutsu: the art of projecting energy
Kimono: traditional Japanese clothing
Kisssaten: teahouse
Koan: short phrase whose purpose is to get us to think without our logic
Kohai: student, disciple who is trained by a *sempai*
Kokoro: heart, but also everything related to spirituality
Koppo ken: hit made with the knuckle of the folded thumb
Kuatsu: medical techniques used in ancient martial arts
Kyojutsu: distorting the perceptions of the adversary, false reality
Kyusho: pressure points
Mantra: word that is repeated to achieve a meditative state
Mika: from *Mikazuki* (crescent moon)
Miyamoto Musashi: Greatest Samurai of all time in Japan
Muto dori: unarmed technique against sword
Ninja: warrior specialized in infiltration and espionage
Ohisashiburi desu: Long time no see
Okuden: what is transmitted by word of mouth, usually secret
Oni: Demon
Ryu: Traditional Japanese martial art schools
Sake: rice wine
Saiminjutsu: techniques of hypnosis and self-hypnosis used by *ninjas*
Samurai: Traditional Japanese warrior
San: after a name, meaning sir, madam, miss
Sanshin: three hearts, name of a series of exercises that are performed alone
Salaryman: office worker wearing and tie and often a small briefcase
Satori: enlightenment, universal knowledge
Seigan: position where the arm or the weapon is pointed at the eyes of the opponent
Sempai: person who has more seniority, who guides the *kohai*
Sensei: instructor, teacher
Seppuku: samurai ritual suicide (*hara-kiri*)
Shinto: religion based on nature spirits
Shitsurei shimasu: excuse me
Shizen: natural, nature
Shuriken: Ninja throwing star
Sobaya: Soba noodle restaurant
Sumimasen: excuse me

Tachi: sword with blade more curved than the *katana*. Ancestor of the *katana*
Tai Chi: Chinese traditional martial art
Taihenjutsu: the art of moving and dodging attacks
Taijutsu: how to move with the body
Tai Sabaki: defensive move
Tantanmen: Chinese spicy soup with noodles, vegetables, and pork
Tatami: woven straw mat that covers the floor of the *dojos*
Tsuki: Stab attack with a sword. Also meaning moon
Tsunami: giant wave usually triggered by an earthquake
Tsuyu: the rainy season
Uchi komi: Judo position with one arm grabbing the collar, and the other grabbing the sleeve
Uke: a person who serves as training partner
Ukemi: break-fall
Yamabushi: mountain monks formerly warrior ascetics
Yen: name of Japanese currency

Special Thanks

Writing a book is something relatively easy to realize. Ending up with a quality product is a whole other adventure. Are the phrases well-structured? Can the reading be done fluidly? Is everything clear to the reader? Is every situation described in the novel realistic and coherent? Can the texts bring something new to the reader? That's not even mentioning the typos found throughout so many novels.

To reach such results, authors need to surround themselves with a strong team. People who won't hesitate to criticize severely when necessary. People who are there to express what the author truly means, but also are there for the work itself. It is all those people who I wish to thank.

First, Francine Tremblay, my spouse, who took the time to read the texts and underline the illogicalities as well as everything that may have brought the readers to confusion. Every page read by her ended up with an incredible number of corrections. Thank you to a good friend of mine, Marie-Jeanne Gagné, who has participated greatly in the corrections process and comforted me in the idea that this book would also be appreciated by someone who doesn't practice martial arts. Thank you to my friend Éric Pronovost and his spouse Isabelle, who broke down the texts in order to clarify the nuances of the French version. Thank you to my friend Alex who spent many hours translating this work into English. Finally, my loyal friend Frédéric Simard, who designed the layout and had a final look at the texts, a huge thank you for his patience and generosity.

A book like this would not exist without all the precious interactions I had with all the martial artists that have crossed my path. Especially Hatsumi *sensei*, and all the Japanese shihan who surround him, including the deceased Oguri *sensei*. More than 40 years of martial arts training were necessary to accomplish this work. And it is just the beginning...

Legal Deposit – Bibliothèque et Archives nationales du Québec, 2016
Legal Deposit – Library and Archives Canada, 2016

www.ingramcontent.com/pod-product-compliance
Lightning Source LLC
Chambersburg PA
CBHW070731160426
43192CB00009B/1390